BEYOND
THE CONCEPT OF
RUSSIAN HISTORY

Edited by Jeremy Smith

Suomen Historiallinen Seura
Finnish Historical Society
Societas Historica Finlandiae

Studia Historica 62

Edited By Jeremy Smith

Beyond The Limits: The Concept Of Space In Russian History And Culture

SHS/Helsinki 1999

Cover picture: Erik Bulatov: Red Horizon (1972)
Private Collection, Paris

ISSN 0081-6493
ISBN 951-710-113-9

Contents

Jeremy Smith
Introduction 7

Sergei Medvedev
*A General Theory of Russian Space: A Gay Science and
a Rigorous Science* 15

Elena Hellberg-Hirn
Ambivalent Space: Expressions of Russian Identity 49

Christer Pursiainen
Space, Time, and the Russian Idea 71

Paul Fryer
*Heaven, Hell, or ... Something in Between? Contrasting
Russian Images of Siberia* 95

Katerina Gerasimova
The Soviet Communal Apartment 107

Anna Rotkirch
*Traveling Maidens and Men with Parallel Lives – Journeys as
Private Space during Late Socialism* 131

Pentti Stranius
*Space in Russian (Soviet) Cinema: The Aesthetics of Censorship
and the Case of 'The Mirror'* 151

Timo Vihavainen
*From Globalism in Confinement to Egocentrism Unbound:
the Spheres of the Russian Intelligentsia* 167

Arto Luukkanen
Sacred and Secular Space Intertwined...A Case Study: The Bilateral Ecumenical Negotiations between the Evangelical Church of Finland and the Russian Orthodox Church – Space for 'Useful Idiots' and Sincere Kebisty 179

Chris J. Chulos
'A Place Without Taverns': Space in the Peasant Afterlife 191

Jarmo Eronen
Distance and Logistics as Problems – Their Soviet Solutions 201

Robert Argenbright
Space of Survival: The Soviet Evacuation of Industry and Population in 1941 207

Jeremy Smith
Delimiting National Space: The Ethnographical Principle in the Administrative Division of the RSFSR and USSR, 1918–1925 241

Richard Stites
Crowded on the Edge of Vastness: Observations on Russian Space and Place 259

Introduction

Jeremy Smith

Russia is big. Very big indeed. Stretching half way around the northern hemisphere, from the Polish border in the west to the Bering sea in the east, at the height of Soviet power, the USSR occupied 22,402,200 square kilometres – one sixth of the world's total land surface, and more that twice the size of the next biggest countries, Canada and China. Even after the break-up of the USSR, the Russian Federation remains by some way the largest country in the world. Nor is this the end of the story. Unlike China or Canada, Russia's length is far greater than its width – the distance from Kaliningrad to the Bering Strait exceeds 9,000 kilometres. At no time in history has any other state had to deal with anything like such vast distances.

The central role of the extent of Russia's physical space has long been apparent to historians. Nicholas Riasanovsky's classic history of Russia opens with the following quotation from the 19th century Russian historian Mikhail P. Pogodin:

> Russia! what a marvellous phenomenon on the world scene! Russia – a distance of ten thousand versts in length on a straight line from the virtually central European river, across all of Asia and the Eastern Ocean, down to the remote American lands! A distance of five thousand versts in width from Persia, one of the southern Asiatic states, to the end of the inhabited world – to the North Pole. What state can equal it? Its half? How many states can match its twentieth, its fiftieth part?... Russia – a state which contains all types of soil, from the warmest to the coldest, from the burning environs of Erivan to icy Lapland; which abounds in all the products required for the needs, comforts, and pleasures of life, in accordance with its present state of development – a whole world, self-sufficient, independent, absolute.[1]

---

1 Nicholas V. Riasanovsky, *A History of Russia* (5th edition, Oxford, 1993), p.3.

More recently, for Geoffrey Hosking Russia's size and the subsequent tasks of maintaining the state and patrolling her borders is at the centre of his explanation for the inability of Russia to develop as a classical nation state.[2] Undoubtedly, the extent and variety of Russia's physical space is one of the key factors determining the course of Russia's, and subsequently the world's, history. In the first place, there is the process of expansion itself. From the beginnings of the rise of Muscovy up until the late 19th century, Russian armies, settlers and administration have found themselves drawn, as it were, into one void after another left first by the withdrawing Mongols and subsequently by the relative weakness of lesser powers. Over large expanses of territory, the path was laid by individual adventurers, most vividly represented by the Cossack commander Ermak's expedition into Siberia in 1582-84, while much of the conquest of Central Asia is now ascribed to the personal ambition of individual generals rather than to any grand design on the part of the Tsarist state. Nevertheless, the role of the state in expansion should not be underestimated. As well as providing support to and following up the private expeditionaries, the state waged major wars of conquest at various periods of history, most notably under Ivan the Terrible, Peter the Great and Catherine the Great.

A number of explanations have been advanced for Russia's frighteningly rapid and seemingly unending advance over four centuries. The idea that Russia, like other modern states, was simply advancing towards natural frontiers which were not reached until the late nineteenth century is supported by the fact that, with perhaps the exceptions of Peter and Catherine, Russia's rulers showed relatively little interest in expanding their influence into Europe or in taking on more developed, if smaller and weaker, states. Almost all of Russia's expansion has been to the East and to the South. According to this explanation, once the Urals had been crossed, the absence of any major natural barriers or strong powers meant the advance of Russia's settlers and armies was inevitable to the point that it came up against the Pacific Ocean, the Pamir, Altai and Sayan mountain ranges and the great powers of Japan, China, and the British and Ottoman Empires.

The need for land to accommodate a growing rural population and to reward veteran troops is another factor cited for Russian growth. Other economic explanations include the lack of sufficient sea ports to

---

2 Geoffrey Hosking, *Russia: People and Empire 1552-1917* (London, 1997).

become an effective competitor in international trade, which in turn led to a quest for raw materials which was to succeed in making the Russian economic space virtually self-sufficient. But whatever the original motivation for Russian expansion, the process itself has led to a Russian fascination with her physical space which has undoubtedly developed its own internal dynamic. From the desire of individual peasant households to increase their landholdings to the conquering ambitions of generals and the aggressive expansionism of a series of Russia's rulers, the desire to expand and control physical space has become an integral part of Russia's character. Many commentators have noted Russia's ambition to ultimately expand her influence well beyond her own borders, whether it be over her Slavic brethren as advocated by the 19th century Pan-Slavists, or to the whole of Christendom as expressed in the notion of Moscow as the Third Rome, or ultimately the establishment of a single global communist system as willed by Lenin and Trotsky, and in the end partly realised in its Stalinist distortion as soviet influence spread across large parts of the globe.

However different and ultimately incompatible these different programmes were, evidence for a general Russian urge to subdue physical space is found in the ultimate spatial programme undertaken by the Soviet state in the post-war period – the conquest of Outer Space. It is perhaps no coincidence that the soviets invested such vast resources into the exploration of Outer Space and that for many years the exploits of Iurii Gagarin and other cosmonauts served as the ultimate symbols of the superiority of the communist system and inspired more admiration and unity from the soviet population than perhaps any other factor. In spite of the complete impoverishment of the Russian economy in the 1980s and 1990s it is only now, as the century draws to a close, that Russia has been forced to accept it can no longer afford to run its own space programme and has conceded hegemony in Outer Space to the United States with the decision to abandon the *Mir* space station.

Russia's physical size and nature has left its mark in many ways; Russia's human and material resources have underscored the Great Power status of both the Russian Empire and the USSR to a far greater extent than has been the case with other modern great powers. Indeed the abundance of resources has affected Russia's participation on the world stage in contradictory ways: on the one hand, her strength and wealth has fostered a kind of duty to be involved in international affairs and made Russia a frequent target of foreign aggression, while on the other hand the ability of Russia to rely on her own internal resources has made it largely unnecessary to compete directly with other leading powers in terms of trade or conquest. In economic terms, this potential self-sufficiency has had both its advantages and disadvantages. Certainly the lack of dependence on the outside world has been of great benefit in times of international crisis or isolation, most notably the period of the Cold War. On the other hand the lack of international competition has undoubtedly retarded the social modernisation and technical progress in most spheres. One exception has been the military sphere, particularly in the three decades or so after the Second World War, where direct competition with the West has forced Russia into the forefront of technology. But even in warfare, Russia's sheer size has been the major determining factor in the major wars of the last two centuries. True, Russia's military ability has been severely hampered by the extent of her borders and the long lines of communication (a factor exaggerated by a poorly developed transport infrastructure). But in the wars of 1812 and 1941–45 the exploitation (some would say skilful, some would say lucky) of Russia's vast natural space has proved crucial to the eventual outcome, while many historians also ascribe the Bolsheviks' victory in the Civil War of 1918–1920 to their control of the large central space of Russia, in contrast to the forces of the Whites which were strung out around a large outer periphery and unable to maintain communications with each other.

The nature of Russia's physical space is, inevitably given its size, enormously varied. The climatic conditions range from the arctic north to the deserts of Central Asia, while almost every conceivable geographical and geological condition can be found somewhere across the Russian expanse. A huge variety of nationalities, cultures and religions are embraced by Russia. The size of Russia itself poses a number of administrative, transport and developmental problems which successive regimes have been forced to address. Finally, the Russian physical space has a particularly lop-sided character: most of the population, the main administrative, diplomatic and commercial centres are concentrated in the western, European part of the space, while the vast expanses of Siberia are sparsely populated, largely uncultivated and dotted with pockets of valuable mineral resources. This peculiar east-west divide, not to mention the altogether different character again of the Caucasus and Central Asia to the south, is one of the most important spatial features in Russian history and culture.

But while Russia's physical space is the dominant factor in any discussion of Space in Russian History and Culture, the spatial dimension works at a number of different levels. The definition of the word Space is itself fluid, with a number of possible translations available in the Russian language, and the whole concept has been the subject of widespread philosophical and empirical discussion at least from the time of the ancient Greeks. Russia's physical space has frequently been used as an analogy for the Russian 'spirit' or 'soul' – and undoubtedly physical space has left a major mark on the character of Russian political systems as well as the individual way of life. The way in which Russia's space has directly influenced particular aspects of the Russian character is one of the major themes of this volume.

Rather less obvious is the connection between the peculiarities of Russian physical Space and the particularly Russian conceptions of 'private' and 'public Space. Whereas in modern western societies these spheres are so clearly demarcated as to resemble, at least conceptually, physical space, in Russia the distinctions are much more blurred. At the local level, the tradition of the Russian peasant commune, and within it of living arrangements whereby large extended families shared accommodation with their live-stock, allowed little possibility of a private life away from members of ones family or from other members of the commune. At the broader level, the efforts of both tsars and communists to exert control over the vast physical space involved the accompanying regulation of what might otherwise be deemed as properly belonging to the purely private Space - sex, religion, ethnicity, art. An almost paranoid suspicion of the population coupled with a genuine need for the collection and dissemination of information and ideology if any sort of cohesion was to prevail in such a heterogeneous land strengthened the authoritarian tendencies of successive regimes. The lack of any organised Civil Society, in the western tradition the principal intermediary between the public and private Space, was both a result of and reinforced this tendency to abolish the private/public distinction.

At a number of different levels, then, the concept of Space is a subject which is of great fascination and importance both to Russians themselves and to those who have sought to understand Russia. And yet, the study of Space as a category in its own right is in its infancy as far as the academic world is concerned. The break-up of the USSR has added relevance to this topic, not least because it poses new questions as to the character of Russian space. As Russia seeks to redefine its place in the global Space, the literature on the role of notions of Space in Russian History and Culture will no doubt continue to grow.

* * *

This volume seeks to make a modest contribution to the discussion of the concept of Space in Russian History and Culture. It stems from an international seminar on Space in Russian History and Culture organised by the Department of Russian and East European Studies of the Renvall Institute at the University of Helsinki in June 1998. The papers of this seminar form the basis for this volume, together with a number of specially written chapters and two previously published articles. In order to provide the widest possible scope of discussion, no definition of Space was laid down, and each contributor has been allowed a free hand to develop their own ideas on the relevance of the concept of Space. As a result, while most of the themes mentioned above are at least touched on, this volume does not claim to provide a comprehensive picture of the many possible applications of the concept. Instead, it aims to provide an introduction to the discussion of Space, as well as to present the results of the latest research which may be of interest to specialists on particular areas and the general reader alike. The result has, for me, been highly satisfying. A multidisciplinary approach, deploying a depth of expertise in a number of areas has resulted in a rich variety of contributions producing a surprisingly coherent volume.

Russia's physical space naturally preoccupies a number of the chapters, but at almost every level, from the Russian conception of heavenly Space and the role of Russian Space on the global scene down to the organisation of space in the communal apartment and the workplace. On the dichotomy, or lack of it, between public and private space, studies on religion, sex, cinema and intellectual life are presented, while the connections between physical and social space and the Russian character are explored in greater detail.

The opening three chapters emphasise the relevance of the concept of Space to the Russians themselves. Sergei Medvedev, in outlining a general theory of Russian Space, presents an original interpretation of the relevance of spatial, vertical and horizontal concepts to Russian political traditions, and draws on psychoanalysis, semiotics and anthropology to explain how physical Space may have left its indelible imprint on the Russian character. Elena Hellberg-Hirn focuses on the use of space in traditional Russian symbols as well as in the physical manifestations of distance and speed. Christer Pursiainen examines the way in which different Russian intellectual traditions – including Slavophiles, *zapadniki*, and Eurasianists – have made use of the concept of space to define Russia's proper place in the world.

A number of the chapters deal with more specific aspects of physical space. One of the most intriguing, and largest, spaces on the Russian map – Siberia – is the subject of Paul Fryer's chapter. Fryer relates popular images of Siberia to those of Heaven and Hell, a theme taken up by Chris Chulos in his chapter on peasant perceptions of the afterlife, which he shows to be based on earthly spatial imagery. Jarmo Eronen discusses the economic problems posed by the vast distances involved in Russia's space, and describes the Soviet approach to solving them. Jeremy Smith deals with one of the aspects of creating a regional administrative structure for the USSR, the nationality factor. Robert Argenbright provides a detailed study of one of the most extraordinary episodes in history of the management of Space – the evacuation of industry and people from the western USSR to the Urals in the face of the German advance of 1941. Two chapters look at the organisation of Space on the level of day-to-day living: Richard Stites' description of the apparent misuse of space in Russian offices and public places will strike a chord with anyone familiar with Russia – but behind the chaos Stites is able to uncover a surprising logic. Katja Gerasimova looks at a phenomenon which perhaps shaped daily life in Soviet cities more than any other factor – the communal apartment, an institution which was in part expedient, but also fitted certain ideological notions and ultimately served to increase the state's ability to watch over and control its citizens by denying them a private space.

This lack of privacy led many to seek escape from the stifling communal environment. The sexual adventures of many Soviet men and women on holidays on the South Coast and on *komandirovki* (business trips) in pursuit of a Space of privacy forms the subject of Anna Rotkirch's chapter. The chapters of Gerasimova and Rotkirch introduce the distinction between private and public Space, a distinction which disappeared in many aspects of Soviet life. Arto Luukkanen shows how the belonging of religion to the public Space controlled by the state was exploited by the regime to great effect by taking advantage of the inability of western churches, public and politicians to see religion as belonging to any sphere other than the private. By contrast Pentti Stranius illustrates how the regime's attempts to circumscribe the Space in which artists were able to operate were not always successful, at least in the case of cinema, where directors were frequently able to carve out a greater space to manoeuvre and express their ideas and criticisms than has generally been supposed. Nevertheless, the space in which intellectuals could operate for most of the soviet period was severely limited, and Timo

Vihavainen examines the effect of the opening up of that space under Gorbachev's *perestroika* on Russian intellectuals.

Can any general conclusions be drawn from this diverse collection of appraisals of the significance of Space in Russian History and Culture? Perhaps the most constant theme is the very ambivalence and contradiction of the concept of Space: Russia's massive space is an advantage and a disadvantage, it is good and evil, heaven and hell, vast and crowded; vertical competes with horizontal, national with supra-national, the general with the particular, the temporal with the spiritual; private space is denied by the state, so it has to be created by individuals, while spatial restrictions both limit and inspire intellectual life. To describe Russia as a land riddled with contradictions is nothing new. By using the concept of Space to explain these contradictions, Russia will perhaps become something less of a mystery.

* * *

I would like to express my deep thanks to all those who have contributed to this volume, and especially for their patience through the time it took me to complete the editing. I would also like to thank all those others who participated in the original Helsinki seminar, and whose comments and observations have undoubtedly improved the quality of this book. I would also like to express our gratitude to the editors of *Alternatives: Social Transformation and Humane Governance* and of *Sotsiologicheskii zhurnal* for permission to reproduce the articles by Sergei Medvedev and Katerina Gerasimova respectively, and to Jakub Lopatko for translating Gerasi-mova's article. The views expressed in each chapter are the authors' own, while any mistakes that have crept in through the editing process are entirely my own.

A General Theory of Russian Space: A Gay Science and a Rigorous Science[1]

Sergei Medvedev

Living in a brave new world of jumbo jets, the Internet and McDonalds, we are tempted to believe that geography can be overruled by technology, that space can be conquered by means of communication. However, there is an exception lying flat and square across Eurasia and occupying about one seventh of the world map. This is Russia where space reigns supreme, defying modern communications, technologies and beliefs, and defining the political institutions, economic activity, and mentality of its population.

Space is generally considered to be a major Russian asset, but isn't it also a major pain in the neck? True, it shapes a "mysterious Russian soul", with its breadth and depth, its abysses, and "the ideal of Madonna living side by side with the ideal of Sodom" like ebony and ivory on a piano keyboard, as testified by Dostoyevsky. True, Russia's coat of arms is a double-headed eagle, borrowed from Byzantium (or mutating after Chernobyl?), with one head looking east, and another one west. And yet again, it is true that Russia, with its vastness, "cannot be embraced by mind",[2] as observed by Fedor Tyutchev, and

---

1   Originally published in *Alternatives* 22 (1997), pp. 523–553.
2   The whole quatrain cited by Russophiles all over the world is:
     Russia cannot be embraced by mind
     Or measured by common measure
     It is a thing in its own right
     One can only believe in Russia.
     A century later, poet Dmitry Alexandrovich Prigov somewhat demystified the national symbol:
     Papua-New-Guinea cannot be embraced by mind
     Or measured by a common measure
     It is a thing in its own right
     One can only believe in Papua-New-Guinea.

repeated by many for over a century as an ultimate justification for everything that happens in that country.

But it is the same space that has prevented Russia from developing civil institutions, civic society and the rule of law (Rechtsstaat) – in fact from developing the entire concept of civility, from civitas as a specific Western way of development by urbanization. In Russia, there has been little need to settle down and work on a plot of land. Endless space is forgiving and undemanding, irresponsible and undiscriminating; its human embodiment is a weak-willed and dreamy Iliya Iliych Oblomov from Ivan Goncharov's classical novel, a Russian archetype. If we accept the old German differentiation between culture and civilization, space is about culture, not civilization. Russia has good literature and bad roads. For Russia, space is like a suitcase without a handle: it's not too easy to carry, but it would be a shame to throw it away.

RUSSIAN SPACE AS A BURDEN

Russia's territory is not just quantitatively vast, it is qualitatively infinite, amorphous and contradictory. As pointed out by geographers Leonid Smirnyagin and Vladimir Kagansky,[3] Russia's immensity involves such equivocal properties as:

1. Savage nature. Russia is located in the north-eastern corner of the Eurasian landmass. Three quarters of its territory lies in the tundra or taiga, always in the grip of the permafrost. Barely a fifth of the territory is suitable for ploughing, and even here, a half of this area lies in the so-called zone of "risky agriculture". Nearly all of the surrounding seas freeze over and most of the frontiers are unpopulated: these run across mountains or through dense forests. Rather like the Tsar-bell which never rang, or the Tsar-cannon which was never fired, Russia possesses the longest roads which lead nowhere, the greatest number of seas on which no one sails, and the longest frontiers on which no one lives and hardly anyone crosses.

- - - - -
3   A.Yu Livshits, A.V.Novikov and L.V. Smirnyagin, 'Regional'naya strategiya dlia Rossii', *Region: ekonomika i sotsiologiya*, 1994, no.3, pp.32ff Vladimir Kagansky, "Sovetskoye prostranstvo: konstruktsiya i destruktsiya", in Sergei Chernyshov (ed.) *Inoe. Khrestomatiya novogo rossiiskogo samosoznaniya*, Vol. 1: *Rossiya kak predmet*, (Moscow, 1995), p.125.

2. Boundless space. Amorphous Russian space tends to spread, since there are no natural limits and barriers, and no single mother-region (Eurasia can hardly be regarded as a single region). At the same time, while natural confines were lacking, the space was bound together by external isolation and/or internal repression; one can speak of a integration by coercion.

3. "A Great Polyperiphery": Russian space is a conglomeration of peripheries. It includes peripheries of the European culture, Mediterranean and Near Eastern Christian culture, Near- and Middle Eastern Islamic culture, Buddhist-Mongolian culture, Chinese culture, etc. The same applies to ethnic and language groups represented in the Russian space and having their historical centers outside it. Even Russian nature is in a sense "peripheral": the landscape of the East European plain has been mostly formed during the ice age by glaciers from Scandinavia, and weather in most of Russia is defined by Atlantic cyclones and Pacific monsoons.

At the same time, the Russian space is a young one. Elements of different and sometimes contrasting peripheries have not yet melted together into a cohesive cultural landscape, but have been rather arbitrarily combined by the state. Russian space is like a suspension that has not yet settled.[4]

4. Low population density (which involves difficulties in implementing reciprocal action, and the costs of overcoming huge distances), and, furthermore, contrasts in population distribution. Three-quarters of the population are concentrated in the European part of the country which itself comprises only one quarter of the total territory. In the other three quarters, there lives only one quarter of the population. Much the biggest proportion of the abundant resources for which Russia is known are situated far from the main industrial centers, and mainly in the far north.

On top of that, all capitals of the Russian space have been historically situated either on the western border, or close to it (Novgorod, Kiev, Moscow, St. Petersburg); Moscow is 20 times closer to the western border than to the eastern one. Centers and nuclei of the Russian space are essentially eccentric, almost on the frontier; the country looks like a hollow shell, it does not have a "middle".

5. The "one-dimensional factor". The developed part of the country is squeezed down towards the southern frontier and stretches west to

---

4   Kagansky, "Sovetskoye prostranstvo: konstruktsiya i destruktsiya", p.125.

east in a 10,000-km-long strip. Beyond the Urals, it barely has any thickness, and is situated within reach of the Transsiberian Railtrack. As in the case of the contrasts in population density, this simply adds to the problem of huge distances.

6. Geographical contradictions. Here, contrasting qualities combine. The monotonous low-lying settled belt is cut across by great Siberian rivers and mountain ranges (such as the Urals); this makes for greater difficulties in communications. A patchwork of nationalities (150, as proudly claimed by Soviet propaganda) used to live under the overwhelming dominance of one of them, "the most prominent".[5] A rigid monocentric culture (in the USSR, over 60 percent of all economic links went via Moscow) coexists with traditional autonomous, distant regions. Finally, there is a disproportion in the level and nature of economic development: from pre- to post-industrial.

7. A culture lacking a spatial sense. This may sound ironic in a nation living under the spell of space, but there is a weakness in Russian culture of a distinct reaction to space, i.e. a relatively vague sense of distance, border and places. In this sense, Russia is not a Utopian, but rather an atopic culture. In part, this is linked to the particularities of natural conditions – distances are too great and natural boundaries are not delineated. This characteristic reconciles Russians to the centralized government, and they have become accustomed to defining their geographical surroundings according to administrative/territorial divisions, rather than by historical/cultural regions, as do the majority of the world's nations. (Therefore, the prevailing global trend is regionalism, the emergence of historical and cultural regions, while the FSU tries to cope with regionalization – disintegration along administrative lines). All of these factors have helped the Russians to widen the area of their settlement but have at the same time prevented them from mastering it.

In fact, this is the basic dilemma faced by any extensive culture: the more you expand, the less you control. A heterogeneous, diversified, paradoxical space has been, and remains, a major challenge for the authorities. For Authority in general. It is not just center against periphery; it's order against anarchy, it's cosmos against chaos, it's

---

5   Russian supremacy was proclaimed in a famous toast pronounced by Stalin to "the most prominent of all nations of the Soviet Union", to "the leading Russian people" at a dinner celebrating victory over Germany in May 1945; *Bolshevik*, no 10, 1945, pp. 1–2.

structure against entropy. According to the second law of thermodynamics, entropy prevails. Titans defeat Olympic Gods, Valhalla perishes in flames, a ship made of nails of the dead sails on.

In the Russian language, the opposition between power and space is conveyed by grammatical gender. Spatial phenomena are essentially feminine; quite often the word matushka (affectionate for "mother") is used: zemlya-matushka (land-mother), Rossiya-matushka (Russia-mother), Volga-matushka (the Volga is in a way synonymous to the length and breadth of Russia), etc. This feminine line culminates (with Freudian overtones) in Alexander Blok's exclamation "O Rus' moya, zhena moya!" ("O my Russia, o my wife!").

The attributes and locations of power, on the contrary, are never given feminine names and epithets.[6] There's an instructive difference between rodina ("motherland", which is also a common Slavic root for "family") and otchizna, or otechestvo ("fatherland"). Rodina expresses more of a natural, organic, family-type belonging, while otechestvo has overtones of citizenship and state affiliation of a person. The incarnations of power and space into figures of mother and father, husband and wife can also be seen in the Russian rite of coronation (venchaniye na tsarstvo, "marriage to a tsardom") which since Ivan IV literally repeats the wedding ceremony, with the Tsar symbolizing the husband, and Russia being the wife. Russian Orthodoxy, too, is very much a cult of the Mother of God, Bogoroditsa. James Billington has observed the indigenous, intimate character of the veneration of the Holy Virgin that developed in Russia's hinterland,[7] while the feast of the Protection of the Virgin (Pokrov) is perhaps the most "Russian" of local religious holidays.

Summing up this feminine discourse, Nikolai Berdiaev wrote somewhat disdainfully on the "always womanish" in the Russian soul ("O vechno-babiem v russkoi dushe"),[8] stressing the same irrational, undiscriminating elements in the national consciousness. According to Hellberg-Hirn,

---

6 The only exception is "Moscow, the mother of Russian cities"; but this is a common idiom used almost in all nation-states: cf. Czech "Praha, matka mest", etc.
7 James H Billington, *The Icon and the Axe. An Interpretive History of Russian Culture* (New York, 1967), p.19.
8 Originally, "baba" is a name for a married, esp. older, peasant woman, and in many cases this word has a humiliating meaning, and is different from the neutral "zhenshina", woman. Nikolai Berdiayev, "O vechno-babiem v russkoi dushe", in *Sud'ba Rossii*, (Moscow, 1990), pp. 36–40.

[T]he adherents of the female myth of Russian nationhood persist in seeing the essence of Russia in submissive and suffering passivity, as if she were an eternal baba always 'awaiting her bridegroom', a hero who will redeem and deliver her, be it the Varangian Prince, the Byzantine priest, Western Enlightenment, German socialism or the European market[9]

In Goscilo's reading, this passive quality matches the open landscape of the steppe, its black, fertile soil, which like the dark continent awaiting discovery and 'civilization' (or colonization), was imagined as "the female body ever ready to be tamed and impregnated".[10] Interesting to note that the same argument was used by the Germans in their Drang nach Osten ideology: the manliness of the Aryan race had to subdue the soft womanish nature of the Slavs (Slaves).

However, Russia as a wife has always been obstinate, unwilling to submit to foreign invaders and home rulers alike. Napoleon's army dies in the snows. Bold reformers become corrupted bureaucrats. The space is vast, amorphous and frightening, so the power has to seek compromise with it. In fact, most of Russian history is about the standoff, interplay and compromise between power and space. Their relationship is a permanent Taming of the Shrew, and much too often, Love's Labour is Lost.

In its present shape, the interplay between authority and territory goes back to the mid-16th century, the reign of Ivan IV, and his conquest of the Tatar capital of Kazan. It was at this historical point that the original Rus' extended beyond its confines, began to expand eastwards beyond the River Volga and the Urals, and became Russia. It was at this period that the Moscow Prince became the Tsar, the Metropolitan of Moscow became the Patriarch, and that the country actually started turning into an empire (although the term "Russian Empire" was codified almost two centuries later, under Peter the Great). Finally, it was at this point that an uneasy relationship between the state authority and a vast, heterogeneous and ungovernable space emerged as a key contradiction in Russian history.

9   Elena Hellberg-Hirn, *Soil and Soul: The Symbolic World of Russianness* (Aldershot, 1998), p.126.
10 H. Goscilo, "The Gendered Trinity of Russian Cultural Rhetoric Today – Or the Glyph of the H(i)eroine", in Nancy Condee (ed.) *Soviet Hieroglyphics. Visual Culture in Late Twentieth-Century Russia*, (Bloomington & London, 1995) p. 69. Boris Groys interprets Kazimir Malevich's Black Square as one of the key symbols of Russia in world art: "the darkness of some cosmic pra-vagina" Utopia i obmen (Moscow, 1993) p. 247; (cf. Malevich, Essays on Art, Copenhagen 1968).

The central role of space calls for a special field of Russian studies – A General Theory of Russian Space (all capitals, please). GTRS is comprehensive and interdisciplinary: its thorough student has to look into politics, economics, folklore, architecture, law, etc.; the number of approaches is as indefinite and infinite as the space itself. Following is a brief outline of this aspiring discipline, an attempt to define some levels of interpretation.

THE ART OF SPACE GOVERNANCE

Statecraft in Russia can be seen as authority's permanent quest for compromise with territory, with inexplicable, desirable and unattainable Russia. Any political action has a spatial meaning. But politics is not the only field of power-space relationship; the intercourse between authority and territory takes place simultaneously at several levels, including:

Firstly, the economic level, at which the power, obliged by long borders to defend, numerous neighbors to combat (until the 18th century, Russia had had to wage two wars annually on the average), and a vast territory to develop and sustain, had to withdraw a large portion of production for these needs, i.e. for the purpose of controlling the space. Driven by the empire's increasing military power, the state acted as a main customer of agricultural and industrial output. It was through the Treasury (Kazna) acting as a main buyer that the state, in fact, directly controlled production without any necessity whatsoever of worrying about the circulation sphere. The national economic model has thus put forward the figure of the producer to the detriment of the merchant, and relations of distribution (basically distribution in kind) to the detriment of exchange. Over the centuries, the Russian state has therefore emerged as a key economic agent, sort of a manager of the nation's capital, and since 1917, also the legal proprietor of all this capital (on behalf of the "people").[11]

---

11 For an original analysis of Russia's national economic model from spatial perspective, see Vladimir Chervyakov, "The Russian National Economic Elite in the Political Arena", in Klaus Segbers and Stephan de Spiegeleire (eds.) *Post-Soviet Puzzles: Mapping the Political Economy of the Former Soviet Union, Vol. I: Against the Background of the Former Soviet Union* (Baden-Baden,1995), pp. 205–282.

Today, the situation remains essentially unchanged: the Treasury (the federal budget) still has the responsibility of upholding distant territories and decaying industries. The space claims its heavy toll, and the hypertrophied role of the state prevents effective liberalization and privatization, providing for corporatism, corruption, and the emergence of an authoritarian state capitalism in Russia. The spatial factor, exogenous from the viewpoint of canonical economic theory, once again proves to be decisive.

Secondly, there is the territorial level, at which the power tries to master space by setting up a system of multi-functional institutional districts: gubernias in Russia and oblasts in the USSR. The case of the Soviet "administrative-territorial division" (ATD) is particularly evident. ATD was created to control the Soviet space with all its "contents", to organize the operation of state institutions as well as people's everyday life. The whole spectrum of state activities (law enforcement, military draft, ideology, education, health care, housing, day-to-day management of local industry and agriculture, etc.) were carried out entirely on the regional level, and almost never went beyond it. All state functions were concentrated in the regions, which became focal points, vital centers, and, as a matter of fact, principal institutions of the state.[12]

Indeed, this cramming together of all forms of social life within the confines of oblasts and republics of the USSR has led to the ossification of administrative/territorial divisions, and the transformation of regional borders into "Chinese walls". These borders can easily be made out even from outer space, on a good day: that's where a network of roads opens up and the specialization of agriculture changes; moreover, almost all borders are overgrown by thick forest.[13]

However, this logic of administrative subordination contradicted the natural logic of territorial relations; the former suppressed the latter. Instead of an organic regional system, which would respect all geographical, historical, ethnic, and demographic differences and in which local communities could be interacting in a natural manner, it

. . . . .

12 For the analysis of the administrative/territorial structure, and concepts of "the bourgeois revolution of regions", "the society of regions", and phenomenology of the Soviet space, see Kagansky, "Sovetskoye prostranstvo..."; Vladimir Kagansky, "Russian Regions and Territories", in Segbers and de Spiegeleire (eds)   Post-Soviet Puzzles, pp. 49–56; Sergei Medvedev, "Post-Soviet Developments: A Regional Interpretation. A Methodological Review", in idem.
13 Livshits, Novikov and Smirnyagin, 'Regional'naya strategiya dlya Rossii', p.35.

set up an artificial system of ATD in which any territorial or ethnic differences and natural interaction of localities were disregarded, and regions simply became functional units, agents of the universal state/ society. Instead of promoting unity by nature, it imposed unity by order that turned out to be superficial and non-resistant to future transformations of the Soviet system. In this sense, the centralization, imposed on the Soviet territory, contained seeds of disunity, and today's regionalization of Russia is a "revenge of the territory".[14]

At the administrative level, the economic and territorial forms of the authority-space relationship combine to develop a specific Russian phenomenon of the "administrative market". The dual alienating/ distributing relationship between the Center and the periphery, coupled with the hierarchical subordination of territories (ATD) resulted in a situation where any two adjoining levels of the administrative and territorial hierarchy were in a state of permanent bargaining (especially in Soviet times). It was this bargaining that essentially pertained to the proportions between the industrial, alimentary and raw material goods alienated from a lower level and distributed by a higher one that constituted the administrative market, another unique national form of coexistence between authority and territory.[15]

In the meantime, apart from territorial governance, economics and administration, assimilation of space was also taking place in psychological, symbolic and cultural forms on which I would like to concentrate in detail. In particular, there are three interpretations of the authority-territory relationship:

1) the semiotic interpretation meaning that the authority has been assimilating the territory in symbolic form, by producing and

---

14 Kagansky, 'Sovetskoye prostranstvo...', p.92
15 The concept of "the administrative market" in the USSR, together with the notion of "administrative currency", was developed by Vitaly Naishul and Simon Kordonsky. See Vitaly Naishul', "Vysshaya i poslednyaya stadiya sotsializma", in *Pogruzheniye v tryasinu*, (Moscow, 1991); Vitaly Naishul', "Liberalizm i ekonomicheskiye reformy", *Mirovaya ekonomika i mezhdunarodniye otnosheniya*, 1992, no.8 (August) pp.35-54.; Simon Kordonsky, "Nekotorye sotsiologicheskiye aspekty izucheniya khozyaistvennykh otnoshenii", in *Teoreticheskiye problemy sovershenstvovaniya khozyaistvennogo mekhanizma*, (Moscow, 1986); Simon Kordonsky, "Paradoksy realnogo sotsializma", *Voprosy filosofii*, 1991, no.3 (March), pp.75–94; Simon Kordonsky, "The Structure of Economic Space in Post-Perestroika Society and the Transformation of the Administrative Market", in Segbers and Speigeleire (eds.), *Post-Soviet Puzzles*, vol. I.

circulating signs of power and control;[16]

2) the psychoanalytical interpretation, in which the national discourse interprets space as the subconsciousness;

3) the approach of cultural anthropology examining two specific Russian forms of spatial behavior: people's desire to spread across the territory, and government's attempts to settle and attach people to the land.

THE SEMIOTIC INTERPRETATION

There is some anecdotal evidence that in 1925 an Extraordinary Large Scale Cartography Commission was created under the auspices of the Council of Peoples' Deputies. The commission was assigned to prepare a special edition of the map of the Soviet Union for the tenth anniversary of the October Revolution. At first, it was suggested to use the one-mile scale map of the tsarist General Staff but in the course of their work the cartographers, full of revolutionary zeal, decided to use a larger scale: the first state of workers and peasants deserved to have the most precise map in the world. However, the completion dates were put off because the task appeared to be extremely difficult.

In the 1930s thousands of cartographers were involved in the work of the commission which was supervised by the all-mighty NKVD, the Peoples' Commissariat of the Interior, in an atmosphere of top secrecy. Unknown cartographers were constantly enlarging the scale of the map. The work went on even during World War II, when the commission was evacuated into the town of Kamyshlov in the Urals. At the final stage of work all the printing capacities of the country were involved and the map was completed in late 1949 to be

. . . . .
16 For the application of the simulationist paradigm to the analysis of Soviet/ Russian space, see Boris Groys, *Utopia i obmen*, (Moscow,1993); Mikhail Ryklin, "Metamorphoses of Speech Vision", in *Between Spring and Summer. Soviet Conceptual Art in the Era of Late Communism* (Cambridge-London, 1990), pp. 135–145; Mikhail Ryklin, "La conscience dans la culture du discours", in *Les Temps Modernes*, 1992, Automne; Mikhail Ryklin, *Terrorologiki*, (Tartu-Moscow, 1992); Sergei Medvedev, "USSR: Deconstruction of the Text. At the Occasion of the 77th Anniversary of Soviet Discourse", in Segbers and De Speigeleire (eds.), *Post-Soviet Puzzles*, vol. I, pp. 83–120.

presented on Joseph Stalin's seventieth birthday. It was a 1:1 scale map in light-pink. It was unrolled at night on 21 December 1949 by Internal Ministry soldiers.

The further story of the map becomes vague and has to be unraveled from numerous and often speculative sources. Some suggest that due to certain natural cayses and the negligence of the keepers, the map gradually deteriorated and that today only fading fragments of it can be seen in distant parts of the state (in the Sayan mountains and in the Kyzyl-Kum desert, in particular). Others believe, on the contrary, that the map, which was made of Stalitex® (light, firm plastic) has survived but that it was the country that deteriorated and began to decay. The gigantic map exists and underneath it, the remnants of the state keep decaying like the body of a fossilized creature.

Regardless of whether it happened or not, the story is quite typical. There is something sad in it, like a song of a coachman, something endless, like the road in the steppe. One thing in this story is irrefutable: Russia is doomed to text, to the power of signs, symbols, maps. Orientation of the national cultural tradition to the word turns the words into something spellbinding. "Potemkin villages"[17] were examples of a specific Russian text, a system of signs without referents. Another example is "great Russian literature" which used to perform most of the social and political functions, substituting for the institutions which did not exist.

The Russian Empire was the consequence and a hostage of its geography, but not in the geopolitical sense. The boundless, insuperable and heterogeneous space lent itself not to practical (highly impractical, in fact) but rather to symbolic assimilation. The growth of Russia was not an act of economical, strategic or metaphysical necessity – it was a spatial and symbolic act, a semiotic act.

In this context the crisis of representation has been embedded into the semiotics of the Russian Empire. A taste of cardboard has remained from the "Potemkin villages" as if from the scenery of Vladimir Nabokov's Invitation to an Execution. Signs like "Russia" and "empire" hardly represented any feasible political, economic and

. . . . .
17 "Villages" of false wooden façades constructed along the roads by Grigory Potemkin, a favorite of the Russian Empress Catherine II, in order to make her believe, as she travelled in the Ukraine, that the countryside was rich and flourishing.

ethnic reality at all; instead, they simulated it, serving as functions of other signs, as words that had to be written down in the blank spaces on the map. Russia has always been a playground for non-referential semiotics, symbolic exchange and simulation.

These principles have been elevated to a norm during the Soviet period. The new authority, unable to practically control the space in accordance with ideology, translated its revolutionary ambitions into a symbolic sphere, deploying a self-sufficient Soviet discourse. Everything external to this discourse was driven out of life. In retrospect, the Soviet power could have written on its banners the maxim of Jacques Derrida: "There exists nothing beyond text" – because everything actually became text. The USSR as a form of social, state, economic and cultural organization became a space of total textuality. This was a total text, total aesthetic, total art of mature Stalinism. Within the USSR, the inherent geographic determinism of Russia turns out to be semiotic determinism, a terror of signs.

There is an old GULag joke: a guard talking to one of the prisoners of the labor camps asks him what he was sentenced for. The answer is: "For nothing". –"You are lying to me, you swine", replies the guard, – "For nothing they give you ten years here, but you've got fifteen!" In this anecdote, reality (not just reality of crime, but reality as such) does not exist; "great terror" arises from symbolic exchange, from total semiotics of Russian space.

Through the Khrushchev, Brezhnev and Gorbachev eras, the semiotic relationship of the power and the space remained essentially unchanged. Any attempt at "normalization" (late 50s, late 80s) reveals a frightening emptiness, the absence of reference behind the text, the absence of reality beneath the gigantic map. Signs compensate for the absence of things. At the VDNKh[18] exhibition in Moscow, the "Poultry farming" pavilion featured model farms surrounded by a pastoral landscape and called something like "Project of Poultry Farm No. 6 in the Kholmogory district of Kostroma oblast". In the same stand, the hypothetical products of the farm were shown–rows of tins labeled something like "Cock-rooster in wine", or "Duck liver mousse". Nobody had ever seen such delicacies on sale (not even under the counter, or in the closed Party retail establishments), these were mere ideas of food consumed by means of words.

18 "The All-Union Exhibition of Achievements of People's Economy".

Gorbachev's perestroika was also a semiotic maneuver aimed at avoiding reality (the exhaustion of natural resources and the challenge of the outside world). This was an attempt to save the very principle of symbolic exchange by introducing new (market, western and other alien) designators. Perestroika was the replacement of decay by non-corporeal transformation, of explosion by implosion, of external blow by internal shock.

The birth of new semiotics in Russia and in other post-Soviet states has expanded the resources of the symbolic exchange. New designators pretending to have a national, organic character (nation, territory, religion, Fatherland, heritage, historical justice, liberation of personality, return into the civilized world, etc.) are as far from reality, as their Soviet pseudo-international predecessors. In this sense the Soviet discourse preserved itself at the expense of introducing post-Soviet (mainly Russian) designators. From the semiotic point of view both the USSR and "post-Soviet Russia" are two sides of one coin, a binary opposition which provides for the existence of a semiotic field.

As always in Russian history, the authority in Moscow performs a strategy of simulation. To support its image (or to simply justify its name), power has to simulate some controlled space which it is possible to calculate, forecast or subdue to the laws of referentiality and causality. This kind of simulacrum has been called Russian politics. The generative model of this hyper-reality is Moscow – the focal point in space, a special semiotic system, a political matrix. The very high density and combination of signs and texts within an area of several square kilometers (mainly within the Garden Ring encircling the center of Moscow) generates a field of pseudo-events aimed at simulating Russian politics. Designators like statehood, Great Power, national interests, etc. are of specific Moscow origin and have their value in Moscow's symbolic exchange. The only concern of authority is to produce symbols and effects of power[19] and to broadcast them into the humble space of Russia. Juggling with signs like "legislative, executive and judicial" does not in any way differ from the 19th-century ideological triad of "Orthodoxy-autocracy-nationality"[20] or

---

19 See Jean Baudrillard, *In the Shadow of the Silent Majorities – Or the End of the Social and Other Essays* (New York, 1983), p.10; Jean Baudrillard, *Selected Writings* (Stanford, 1988), pp.179–80.
20 This formula was proposed in the 1840s by Russian Minister of education Count Sergei Uvarov as an official ideology of the ruling regime.

later Soviet "mind-dignity-conscience"[21] and "Lenin! Party! Komsomol!" chanted by thousands at youth congresses. Whether Orthodox, Communist or democratic, words are the usual – the ultimate – the only Russian reality.

THE PSYCHOANALYTICAL INTERPRETATION

Russia and Freud is a matter of some considerable interest, above all in light of the fact that Freudianism has been almost stubbornly disregarded by the Russian philosophical and humanitarian tradition. The ideological repression in Soviet academia only in part accounts for this remarkable neglect; the reason may lie in the deeper layers of the Russian culture and its fundamental difference from the western discursive practices. [22]

The main difference here is that if a patient in the West refuses to submit to psychoanalysis, this is mainly because he is reluctant to admit that his conscious and rational self is determined by the subconsciousness. On the contrary, Russia has never claimed to be all too rational; she did not really need psychoanalysis since her subconsciousness had been already exposed and implicitly recognized as the most important element of her national identity. Russia's self-consciousness is about the subconsciousness, although this national self-reflexion has been formulated in non-Freudian indigenous terms.[23]

Indeed, most Russian philosophers have observed a certain irrationality and amorphousness of the national character. This line of argument started with Pyotr Chaadayev and his Philosophical Letters (1836) in which he asserted that Russia "did not belong to any of the great families of humankind", "stood out of time", that Russians did not have "fascinating memories, or gracious images in memory" [i.e., that memory was repressed, "erased" – S.M.], did not have "anything

- - - - -
21 A ritual triple epithet applied to the Communist party and inscribed on Party membership cards.
22 A. Pyatigorskii, "O psikhoanalize iz sovremennoi Rossii", in *Rossija/Russia*, 1977, pp. 29–50.
23 Groys, *Utopia i obmen*, p.245

individual, on which thought could rely" – in fact, did not have tradition, morality, culture, duty, justice, etc.[24]

According to Boris Groys, Chaadaev construed Russia as "an absolute Other, absolutely external to thinking, as the space of the subconscious".[25] This leads Groys to conclude that

> Russia is not the domain of subjectness, is not a subject, or consciousness. The space of Russia is the space of losing space, of losing spatial certainty, individuality. The time of Russia is the time of losing time, losing history, memory, 'consciousness'. Russia lives in post-history (...), but it also lives in pre-history, before the Creation. Russia does not 'create' anything, because creativity is only possible in the chronotope of the individual, or collective, conscious experience; all creations of other nations dissolve within her, losing their certainty, and enter into random combinations: Russia as a dream, as the space and time of a dream, but also a field of Lacanian psychoanalysis, based on free combination of the signifiers, as the practice of Surrealist 'automatic writing', etc.[26]

This description refers to the Russian psyche, but also to Russian space: boundless, insuperable, lacking subjective creativity. As mentioned above, this self-perception of Russia is often represented in figures of femininity and motherhood. Russia-the-endless-steppe, Russia-the-caring-Mother, Russia-the-loving-wife, Russia-the-big-family are all just various guises of the same unpronounced subconsciousness. These definitions are summarized in the famous Orthodox term *sobornost'*, literally meaning "conciliarity", and implying a bunch of meanings – from communality to spirituality and irrationality.[27] Looking at sobornost' from the perspectives of Schopenhauer and Nietzsche, Marx and Heidegger, structuralism, race theory, deconstructivism, etc., we see that sobornost' is the Russian name for the libido, Eros, language, Wille zu Macht, for class

. . . . .
24 Pyotr Chaadayev, *Statyi i pis'ma*, (Moscow, 1987 [1836]), p.36. After the publication of this letter, Chaadaev was pronounced insane by the Czar, and placed in a madhouse.
25 Groys, *Utopia i obmen*, p.248.
26 Idem, p.246.
27 In this bunch (Italian fascio), the prevailing meaning is communality. The bundling nature of *sobornost'* begs for a comparison with Italian fascism. At least, they both are rooted in communal, Gemeinschaft-type habits in Russia and Southern Italy.

consciousness, archetype, simulacrum – indeed, the Russian name for the subconscious.[28]

However, there is a meaningful difference. Whereas in mainstream Western narratives the words "unconscious" and "subconscious" tend to sound ambiguous (i.e. "out of control"), in Russia figures of the subconsciousness are traditionally interpreted in a positive manner. Apart from the Orthodox *sobornost'*, other positive readings of the subconsciousness include:

narodnost' (nationality) from Count Uvarov's triple formula of official ideology of the1840s: "Orthodoxy, autocracy, nationality", as well as all later guises of the "Russian idea" stressing the irrational and communal belonging of Russians rather than citizenship of a state;

– the Bolsheviks' *classovost'* (class consciousness), and

– later Soviet *partiinost'* (adherence to the Party principles);

– Leo Tolstoy's idealization of the "unconscious life" of the Russian peasant;

– Vladimir Soloviev's Sofia, and his reading of Nietzsche's Übermensch as a step to the "God-Man" (Bogochelovek) Christ;

– Lenin's vitalism ("being determines consciousness"), and his practical Nietzscheanism;

– Mikhail Bakhtin's theory of the carnival,[29] created in parallel to, and in a way conceptualizing, the irrationality of Stalin's "Great Terror", and finally,

– anonymity of the Soviet political anecdote,[30] and similar anonymity of the Soviet verbal practice of denunciation (*donos*, or *anonimka*[31]).

In a sense, Russia is permanently describing and reformulating herself in terms of the subconscious (not in Freudian terms) by inventing various names for the communal, feminine, family-type belonging, trying to avoid a definition of the amorphous, endless, unpronounced and unfathomable space.[32]

. . . . .

28 Groys, *Utopia i obmen*, p.249.
29 Russia in general is in a sense a carnival of European culture, a space of parody and transgression, like Venice in February. In Russia, European culture and institutions are emulated and sometimes parodied, becoming non-referential signs that enter into random combinations, into a perpetual play.
30 Groys, *Utopia i obmen*.
31 Sergei Medvedev, "USSR: Deconstruction of the Text. At the Occasion of the 77th Anniversary of Soviet Discourse", in Segbers and De Speigeleire (eds), *Post-Soviet Puzzles*, vol. I, pp.93–4.
32 Contemporary Russian political and philosophical narratives, especially of the nationalist (*pochvenniki*) and Eurasianist vein, too, stress the subconscious nature of the Russian space, especially in its relationship to the West: according to Sergei

THE ANTHROPOLOGICAL INTERPRETATION

Another form of assimilating the space was the inherent Russian contradiction between the population's desire to spread across the territory, and the efforts of the authorities to fix and settle the people down. Sergei Soloviev describes it in terms of a "habit of spreading out in the population" (privychka k raskhodke v narodonaselenii) and government's desire "to catch and attach". Soloviev vividly depicts the inherent rootlessness of the Russians:

> In this structure of space, there are no firm houses which would be hard to abandon, which would be inhabited by generations (...); there's so little immovable property, that everything can be carried away, and building a new house is easy since materials are cheap... That is why ancient Russians so easily left their homes, their cities and villages: they escaped from Tatars, or from Lithuanians, from heavy taxes, or from a bad *voivode* [local governor] or *podyachy* [local state official]; the Russians didn't mind moving along because everywhere one found the same, everywhere one could smell Russia.[33]

Moreover, according to Vassily Klyuchevsky, spreading and stopovers are not just two trends, but rather periods.[34] In this sense, and with a

. . . . .

Kortunov, "Russia is the memory of the West about the Universal, the memory of the West about itself... Russia is the imperial principle of the Universe, its spiritual hypostasis, the embodiment of its freedom of will". In the same passage, Kortunov, referring to Sergei Kurginian, recourses to a more bodily metaphor of the subconscious, what Bakhtin called the "aesthetics of the bodily bottom" (estetika telesnogo niza): "The West should understand that Russia is a place from which one can see its prospects and its diseases. This is not a dumping site (*pomoika*) of the West, but its rectifier, its intellectual drainage (*smyslovoi drenazh*). Stuffing this drainage with its own waste, the West kills itself" (1997, pp.62-63).
Inadvertently, the Russian pochvennik finds almost the same metaphor as Marcel Duchamp in his acclaimed Fountain: a urinal, le pissior as a symbol of the subconscious and post-Freudian culture, as a drainage of traditional valorized rational culture.

33 Sergei Soloviev, *Istoriya Rossii s drevneishikh vremen,* Vol.VII, (Moscow, 1962), p.46; The idiom "it smells of Russia" (Rusiyu pakhnet) originating in folklore and taken up by Russian literature (cf. Derzhavin's dym otechestva, ["the smoke of fatherland"]), appears to be quite important for a culture lacking a spatial sense. Russia is so immeasurable and plain, there are so few landmarks, that in fact it cannot be properly seen, but rather smelt.

34 Vassily Klyuchevsky, *Sochineniya,* Vol. IV (Moscow, 1956).

considerable degree of approximation, Russian history can roughly be interpreted as a rotation of two-phase cycles of spreading out, or spillover (space and chaos take the upper hand) and fixation, or "hardening" (government temporarily takes over). (See Appendix).

Periods of spreading out (especially late 15th century; late 17th century, with its movement of schismatics (*raskolniki*) into the northwest; 1860s and 70s, following the abolition of serfdom; 1920s; the Khrushchevian late 1950s and 60s, with millions going to the virgin lands of Kazakhstan (*tselina*), or the Komsomol construction sites and joining in the subculture of mass tourism; or the Gorbachevian late 1980s) can be interpreted as socio-spacial phenomena. Moving along becomes an act of free will, and often an act of protest (schismatics). The inherent Russian desire to move along the plain created a special institution of wanderers (*stranniki*), and was reflected in the novels of Andrei Platonov, displaying the specific "strolling spirit" of the 1920s. In this context, one can speak of a specific Russian "democracy in space", like the American Frontier, which effectively contributed to the making of democracy in the United States. In Russia, however, this spread of the population did not contribute to democratic institutions: when people stopped (or were stopped), instead of forming local communities, they were turned into subjects of the State.

The State, for its part, sometimes tended to ride the wave of migration for the purpose of exploring and developing new lands, and even institutionalized it as a state service (cf. the institution of Cossackdom, used to protect the southern and eastern borders of Russia from the Great Steppe, or to explore Siberia and the Far East (expeditions of Yermak Timofeevitch); Prime-minister Peter Stolypin's policy of support to peasants moving to Siberia in the early 20th century; or the 1950s *tselina* movement); but more often than not, the Russian state tended to settle its subjects in controllable units, like landlords' estates, or on controllable administrative (not historical or cultural!) territories, like gubernias in Russia and oblasts in the USSR. There is a striking similarity in the language of ordinances of Tsar Alexei Mikhailovitch, and of the Council Code of 1649 establishing full serfdom; also the decrees of Tsar Peter the Great ordering people to be brought by force for the construction of St. Petersburg and forcing the nobility to move into the new capital;[35] and

---
35 This brings to mind a Soviet anecdote from the 1930s when a Party activist is assigned to organize a kolkhoz in the countryside. Several days later, he sends a telegram: "The kolkhoz is organized. Send in the farmers".

laws of the USSR Supreme Soviet in the 1930s, introducing the passport system, the institute of residence permits from local authorities (*propiska*), and ultimately taking away passports from the peasants, so that leaving the *kolkhoz* became a criminal offense which in fact could entail death.[36]

The inclinations of spread and settlement can be further described as horizontal and vertical, centrifugal and centripetal, spill-over and crystallization, femininity and masculinity (see above), heterarchy and hierarchy of Russian space. In a study undertaken in the 1970s, architect and designer Vladimir Paperny makes an impressive attempt to project this dichotomy of cycles into the history of Soviet architecture, and Soviet culture at large.[37] He calls the culture accompanying the period of spread "Culture One", and that corresponding to the period of settlement – "Culture Two", and argues that the former ruled between 1917 and approximately 1930, and the latter from the early 1930s to 1955. Culture One is a culture ad libitum, a culture of fire and improvisation. The architecture is horizontal, develops the idea of movement (cf. ideas of de-urbanization and movable dwellings in constructivism, or Le Corbusier's houses "on legs" in Moscow), and pays special attention to the plan. Culture Two is about water, hierarchy and etiquette, and strictly adheres to the score (a *battuta*, continuing a musical metaphor).[38] Its architecture is stepped (cf. the final variant of the

. . . . .
   By the same token, here's another anecdotal dialogue from the later Soviet period:
   – Can we build a Swedish model of socialism in the USSR?
   – Of course we can, but where can we find so many Swedes?
   As was the case of St. Petersburg, we see a purely semiotic approach to reality (which Baudrillard calls a "precession of the model"): first comes an abstract institution, a form, and only afterwards the authority fills it with human contents. In fact, the entire Russian space can be interpreted as an ideal form, an intention of the authority – but people have not yet been sent in.
36 In today's Moscow, the institute of propiska is actually being revived by mayor Yuri Luzhkov, while most Muscovites readily welcome this move.
37 Vladimir Paperny, *Kultura Dva* (Moscow, 1996). For the interplay of "horizontal" and "vertical" in Russian architecture, see I.E. Grabar', *Istoriya russkogo iskusstva,* (Moscow, 1912) vol.III: pp.5–199.
38 Culture Two completely codifies people and places, turning the Russian territory into a space of total etiquette. In this sense, the Soviet civilization of the period of Culture Two can be compared to other highly codified cultures like the Jewish or the Chinese which created strict rules for all occasions in life. Thus, we read in the Mishnah that on Saturday night a tailor must not go out with a needle; in the Book of Rituals it is written that a guest must drink the first glass with a serious look and the second one with a respectful and happy face. The same strict etiquette can be found in Soviet practices. During Lenin's lifetime, and later in the

Lenin Mausoleum, which evolved from a temporary wooden structure to a Babylonian zikkurate of granite), hierarchical, vertical, and gives priority to the façade. The ultimate manifestation of Culture Two was to have been the construction of the Palace of the Soviets that was symbolizing space in a single edifice.

Following these arguments, a student of Soviet developments is challenged to trace the interplay of Cultures One and Two in 1986–1996 as a sublimated opposition between the power and the space. Perestroika was essentially a Culture One phenomenon: horizontal, open (glasnost), destroying all hierarchies. Black governmental "Volgas" (Soviet "executive cars") were despised on Moscow streets, and the aspiring Boris Yeltsin was once noticed going to work on a trolleybus. As restrictions were progressively removed, a horizontal civil society started to emerge (in fact, in 1987–1991, the Soviet/ Russian civil society, as well as the free press, had their day, and eventually faded away in post-Soviet Russia). The population enjoyed greater social and territorial mobility, and all barriers to emigration were removed on the Soviet side (tragically, some years later, we have seen the other side of this mobility, with hundreds of thousands of migrants and refugees, escaping from Chernobyl, civil wars, or genocide). The ultimate acts of Culture One were the destruction of the Warsaw Pact, of the Communist Party, of the USSR proper in 1991, of the socialist economy through shock liberalization and privatization in 1992, and finally, of the institution of the soviets in 1993. Gods were dislodged, and the old world of all things Soviet was engulfed in flames.

What is important, is that Culture One of the Gorbachev and early Yeltsin epochs was very much about the emancipation of space, of its

. . . . .
1920s, names of members of the Politburo were listed in alphabetical order, but starting from Stalin's 50th birthday in December 1929, his name appeared first, and then the others followed in alphabetical order – Abdurakhman Avtorkhanov, *Tekhnologia vlasti. Protsess obrazovaniya KPSS. Memuarno-istoricheskiye ocherki*, (Munich, 1959), p.156. In the same manner, lists of literature in Soviet academic works, defying rules of the alphabet, strictly followed the ideological etiquette. First came Marx and Engels, then Lenin, then the incumbent General Secretary of the CPSU and Politburo members, then Russian authors in alphabetic order, and finally names in unwelcome Roman typeface.

In the same way, rules of applause at Party congresses and meetings were codified: junior Politburo members were met by "long applause", middle ranks were greeted by "stormy applause", top people deserved "long stormy applause, everyone stands to their feet", and the General Secretary got "long stormy applause turning into ovation. Everyone raises to their feet. Shouts "Hooray! Long live our leader comrade Stalin/Malenkov/Khrushchev/Brezhnev, etc".

inherent cultural and ethnic diversity which could not be completely abolished during the Soviet period. It was not only the "liberation" of East European states and Soviet republics, it was the comeback of territory as a principle. Ethnic and local groups were encouraged to discover their roots (or rather soil, *pochva*). When Boris Yeltsin was running for the Russian presidency in June 1991, and told Russia's regions to "take as much sovereignty as you want to", he was in fact saying this to the entire Russian space, calling it into existence from years of administrative subordination. Regions followed Yeltsin's advice to the letter, and regionalization became the principal shaping factor of Russian politics in early 1990s.

The comeback of "settling" trends within the authority and of Culture Two by the mid-1990s can also be interpreted in territorial perspective. The destruction of celestial (Moscow) and earthly (regional) hierarchies (and as we know from Civitas Dei, the latter reflects the former) has fragmented the space to the lowest possible denominator. The primordial chaos of space, unleashed by Gorbachevian policies, ruled supreme.[39] In this chaos, emancipated agents of the territory (sectoral, regional, local elites, etc.) have fulfilled their long-term goals: no longer confined by administrative and territorial hierarchy, they increased mobility, and converted their administrative status into property. In the turmoil of 1986-1992, functional and territorial fragments of space found their new owners. Newly acquired property had to be protected against further redistribution. From 1992 onwards, there has been an ever increasing quest for stability in Russia.

Responding to this quest, the authorities once again attempted to control the space. As much too often in Russian history, this meant reconstructing the hierarchy. There is something in the optics of Russian space, and the Russian mentality, that makes the authorities believe that control always means command, and that building a territorial and administrative hierarchy is the only way of dealing with this space. Over centuries, a "strong state" in Russia has always meant a strong vertical,

---

[39] Looking back at the essential lack of ideology behind perestroika, one has to admit that there was perhaps one vague romantic idea in the spirit of the "Prague Spring": to unleash forces of chaos ("natural", or "healthy" forces, in Gorbachev's lexicon), and to put them to the service of a socialist state. However, these forces turned out to be as ungrateful as a Prague Golem. Once invoked to life, they turned against their creator and devoured the state that was supposed to control them.

and alternative ways were hardly given consideration.[40] Perhaps this is objective (the logic of space, "Oriental despotic mentality", etc.). Maybe subjective (narrowly thinking rulers). Who knows. In any case, the logic of hierarchy once again prevailed in Moscow in 1992–1993.

According to the local logic, the hierarchy starts from the top, not vice versa. The territory had to see a strong man in the Kremlin. A display of strength followed in late September and early October 1993, when the parliamentary opposition took to the streets of Moscow, and Yeltsin responded by moving in tanks and bombarding the parliament. The walls of Jericho came tumbling down, and the reaction was almost unanimous relief. A large part of the intelligentsia praised the long-awaited solution in collective letters of support. Within one month of the shelling of the Russian White House, regions that had been reluctant to pay taxes for the last two years, resumed their payments to the federal budget. The wheels of Culture Two started moving.

POST-SOVIET RESTORATION

In the wake of the 1993 showdown, and especially in 1995-97, the space of Russia once again started to look vertically organized. Functionally different chains of control started to proliferate in the Russian space. These are:

1) The financial vertical, symbolized in an unprecedented concentration of capital in Moscow. Nine of the ten biggest banks are

. . . . .

40 E.g., for Stephen Krasner a "strong state" means something completely different: "[T]he power of the state [is] in relation to its own society. This power can be envisaged along a continuum ranging from weak to strong. The weakest kind of state is one which is completely permeated by pressure groups. Central government institutions serve specific interests within the country, rather than the collective aims of the citizenry as a whole... At the other extreme from a state which is completely permeated by political pressure groups is one which is able to remake the society and culture in which it exists; that is, to change economic institutions, values, and the pattern of interaction among private groups" – Stephen D Krasner, *Defending the National Interest. Raw Materials Investments and U.S. Foreign Policy* (Princeton, N.J, 1978) pp.57,60. Placed into this paradigm, Russia has almost always been an essentially weak state, unable "to remake society and culture" by means of total control. (See Stephan De Spiegeleire, "Levels and Units of Analysis", in Segbers and De Speigeleire (eds.), *Post-Soviet Puzzles*, vol.I, pp. 62–65).

to be found in this city. Their credit policies, centralization of transfers, and operations of regional branches recreate the former links of the Soviet economy and provide for the connection of the federal budget with local economies. This time, instead of resources in kind, a vast hierarchical network is circulating financial resources through its veins.

2) The corporative vertical. Russia is currently quickly evolving along the lines of corporative capitalism, not unfamiliar to many Latin American countries. Powerful vertical corporations based on sectoral elites (gas, oil, banks, energy networks, export-oriented military industry, agro-industrial complexes, aerospace, etc.) bind the country by chains of vested interests and lobbying. The best example of territorially ramified and hierarchically organized corporation is the Gazprom concern which became one of the major pressure groups in the country, and is represented by ex-prime minister Victor Chernomyrdin.

3) The criminal and corruption vertical. Criminal structures have always played a large role in Russia and the USSR where communal links (Gemeinschaft) clearly prevailed over societal models (Gesellschaft) among the population. However, unprecedented growth of organized crime in the late 1980s and 1990s resulted in a situation when, for the first time in the Russian history, the entire territory of Russia, from Moscow to tiny villages on the periphery, is covered by criminal networks. Criminal communities have become highly diversified, specialized and professional, with an ever growing share in business and government. The entire space has been divided into spheres of influence, both territorially and functionally, and in fact the strict criminal hierarchy, with grade, rank and subordination of its own, constitutes another vertical component, integrating Russia's political, business and social life.

Chains of corruption leading from the lowest level of authority into the Kremlin, the White House and the State Duma also have an integrative effect. The Soviet hierarchy of statuses has been replaced by a post-Soviet hierarchy of bribery in which any post, from the local tax or traffic police inspector to the president of Russia, and any economic and political decision have an almost legally determined price in hard currency.[41] In this field, the chaos of space is controlled

---

41 Simon Kordonsky, "Nekotorye sotsiologicheskiye aspekty izucheniya khozyaistvennykh otnoshenii", in *Teoreticheskiye problemy sovershenstvovaniya khozyaistvennogo mekhanizma*, (Moscow, 1986), p.160. In Kordonsky's opinion,

by dollar values, and this makes for the stability and predictability of the entire system.

4) The symbolic and ideological vertical, with the new Russian regime claiming to have the highest sanction. By the late 1990s, a new Byzantine "symphony" between the Church and the state has been re-established, somewhat short of creating a Holy Synod, like in imperial Russia. According to the original plan, cancelled at the last minute, the inauguration of re-elected Boris Yeltsin in 1996 should have taken place at the Cathedral Square of the Kremlin, thus resembling the coronation of Russian tsars.

In the meanwhile, Russia is rediscovering her symbols of statehood. The ideology of derzhavnost (aspirations to a strong state), now uniting "democrats", Communists and nationalists, has become a basic legitimization of the new Russian regime. Ideas of "Great Russia" are also projected both externally (opposition to NATO enlargement, etc.) and domestically: above all, this is a message to the Russian territory, reversing Yeltsin's "take as much sovereignty as you want to". One has to remember, that although war in Chechnya had very practical and down-to-earth reasons, its main legitimization was "indivisible federal Russia". A new hierarchy of spaces is born, this time based not on administrative rank, but on resources under local control (e.g., resource-rich Tatarstan and Yakutia-Sakha have special privileges).

6) The cultural and architectural vertical. In architecture, the new hierarchical ambitions of Culture Two are conveyed by the new favorite of the authority, architect Zurab Tsereteli and his multi-million-dollar-worth and multi-hundred-meter-high monuments in Moscow, like the Monument of Victory on Poklonnaya Hill, or the Monument to the 300th Anniversary of the Russian Navy displaying Peter the Great (note the ideological context of both). In the district of Krasnaya Presnya, the Moscow City is being built, with a number of high-rises to accommodate expanding businesses. The private architecture of the new rich, or New Russians, also reaches for the skies: in a display of wealth, they build three-, four-, or even five-floor

. . . . .
"the all-out corruption and bribery which is gradually destroying [and virtually replacing. – S.M.] the multi-level structure of imperial rule is a much lesser evil than another revolution (i.e., the violent change in the social structure and in property relations)." Kordonsky, "The Structure of Economic Space in Post-Perestroika Society and the Transformation of the Administrative Market", in Segbers and De Speigeleire (eds.) *Post-Soviet Puzzles*, Vol. I, pp.157–204.

country homes with elevators. Even more characteristically, their roofs are crowned with towers, spires, etc., making them look like castles in Disneyland. The new hierarchy requires splendor and architectural dominance.

The culture in general now acquires all features of Culture Two. Gone is the polycentrism and multiculturalism of late 80s and early 90s. The inflow of money into Moscow once again makes it a cultural capital. A deplorable example is the marginalization of St. Petersburg in the national cultural context, following the decay of the city's economy. The Russian culture of the mid-90s, tired of both rediscovering avant-garde and playing postmodernist games,[42] develops a feeling of the END typical of Culture Two. Fin de siècle stylistics and bohemian decadence (fueled by a dramatic growth of drug abuse) become trendy. In contrast to repudiating all things Soviet in 1987–1992, the past is now looked at with much warmth. This is not a conceptualist view of soz-art, but rather "this is our past and we don't have to be ashamed of it". In general, the new ideology is indiscriminate about the past: the new Moscow monuments include busts of all Russian tsars, a statue of marshal Georgi Zhukov, sculptures of poets Sergei Yesenin and Vladimir Vysotsky.

During Yeltsin's election campaign in 1996, the Public Russian Television unraveled a high-quality "social advertising" campaign titled "The Russian Project". In short clips featuring favorite Soviet actors, simple life situations were performed, concluded by a simple moral: "This is my city", "Everything will be well", "Mother, don't cry", "Take care of love", etc. (something like Krzysztof Kieslowski's famous "Ten Commandments", but in a smaller format). These intelligent adverts were carefully conveying feelings of stability and continuity (implicitly connected with the figure of Yeltsin), in fact bringing peace and order, a basic hierarchy of values into the hearts and souls of the electorate.

. . . . .

42 Symptomatically, a brief and stormy period of Russian literary postmodernism, nourished by the underground conceptualism of the 1970s and 80s (Ilya Kabakov, Dmitry Alexandrovich Prigov, Vladimir Sorokin et al.), and peaking in the late 1980s and early 1990s, seems to be almost over, giving way to the Culture Two-type "new sentimentalism" among many former conceptualists (e.g. Timur Kibirov).

A TALE OF TWO TEMPLES

One of the ultimate symbols of Culture Two and the current reassembly of Russian space is the reconstruction of the Temple of Christ the Savior in the center of Moscow. Its story is captivating and instructive. In the beginning there was a swamp: a marshy low place some half a mile upstream from the Kremlin on the Moskva river called "Devil's bog" (Chertovo boloto). On this place, it was decided to build a church consecrated to the Russian victory over Napoleon in 1812. The task was accomplished in 1832–1883, on the project of Konstantin Ton, and the Temple of Christ the Savior stood as one of the biggest churches in the Orthodox world. After the revolution of 1917, it became an unwanted symbol, and one of the last ritual acts of Culture One was the destruction of the Temple in 1934, along with hundreds of other churches and historical monuments in Moscow, as part of the "plan for the general reconstruction of the city". The site was cleared for the greatest construction in history: the Palace of the Soviets which was to become the highest building of the world at that moment – eight meters taller than the Empire State Building, crowned with a 100-meter high statue of Lenin. Culture Two had to immortalize itself in a vertical structure symbolizing and subjugating the entire Russian space and built strictly to the hierarchical canon (the Palace was to consist of several tiers, and each was taller than the preceding one).

However, the construction never went beyond the basement level: as different as could be from the granite of Manhattan, a boggy low place would not hold the enormous structure. Other reasons cited were the lack of metal, and fears that Lenin's statue would be almost permanently obscured by clouds. Anyway, these are all practical explanations, but if we apply the highly impractical terms of Culture Two, the Palace was so ideal and sacral that it could not be built in reality. Then, this story can be seen in iconoclastic terms: the Palace was so symbolically intensive that this prevented its material embodiment. Or rather this rendered its construction unnecessary: in a way, the Palace of the Soviets has been built. It still stands in the center of Moscow, rising proudly above the clouds. If you believe in it strongly enough, then you can see it...

With the death of Stalin, the project was abandoned, and the newly-arrived Culture One with its horizontal and egalitarian intentions builds on its place an enormous swimming-pool: a pure triumph of space and entropy, a return to primordial protoplasm, "apotheosis of the elements" (Joseph Brodsky). But history makes a full cycle, and with another advent of Culture Two in the mid-1990s, the swimming pool was destroyed as an impious symbol, and the Temple of Christ the Savior is reconstructed on that very place. The president of Russia, prime minister and the mayor of Moscow supervise all stages of construction. The Second Temple was completed in 1998.[43]

This story seems symbolic, if not archetypal. Above all, it tells a sad truth that Russia is doomed to a vicious circle of change between destruction and construction, Culture One and Culture Two, determined by cycles of expansion and hardening in space. In general, the binary paradigm seems unavoidable in Russia. In his late work Culture and Explosion, Yuri Lotman identifies Russia with a cultural form for which binary structures are typical.[44] A binary way of thinking, imaginary alternatives (but, in fact, the ultimatum nature of the "either ... or" choice) considerably narrow the political and cultural choice for Russia. Furthermore, according to Lotman, binary structures are doomed to settle conflicts by way of catastrophes, their extreme components are pre-programmed for mutual destruction, for the demolition "to the basement". Transition from the "old" to the "new" is perceived in the explosive terms of binarism.[45]

This observation of Lotman adds a further perspective to the problem of Culture One and Culture Two. The change of paradigms often involves ideal deconstruction and physical destruction of the preceding culture: the First Dome of Christ the Savior, the ground level of the Palace of the Soviets, and the swimming pool were all consecutively demolished. However, there's a difference. Culture Two is about the End and Eternity, and at a certain point it begins to care

. . . . .

43 Following the logic of change between Cultures One and Two, and the metaphor of Jewish history, the Second Temple will be demolished as well. On its place, triumphant Chechens will erect a mosque, and Russians will be left with a Wailing Wall by the Moskva River... (Sergei Medvedev, "Svyato mesto pusto..." [The holy place is empty...], *Nezavisimaya gazeta*, 15 January 1997).
44 Yu. M. Lotman, *Kultura i vzryv*, (Moscow,1992), pp.257–60.
45 "The process that we witness can be described as switching from the binary into a ternary system. However, one cannot but notice the peculiarity of the moment: this transition is being understood in binary notions. In practice, two possible ways are being worked out. One of them, which had led Gorbachev to the loss of power, lay in substituting reforms by declarations and plans and leading the country into a dead-end fraught with the most gloomy forecasts. The other one, which expressed itself in various plans like "500 days" or other projects for the fast transformation of the economy, is aimed at "curing like by like", at curing explosion by explosion" – Lotman, pp.264–5.

about preservation. On the contrary, Culture One is about Beginning and the Future, it implies an uncompromising break with the past and a suicidal rush towards the future.

Many periods of Culture One turned out to be destructive and incurred heavy human losses: such were Peter the Great's reforms; the post-revolutionary decade and the Stalinist collectivization of agriculture; the breakup of the USSR, which caused ethnic violence, wars and impoverishment of a large fraction of the population. The utmost symbol of Russia's Culture One are schismatics, raskolniki, with twenty thousand people dying in self-immolation, in eager anticipation of Doomsday (that was at the end of the 17th century alone!). This was a radical Russian utopia, a deadly millenianism, a rush to the future through self-denial.[46] The same spirit can be found in the revolutionary millenianism of the 1910s and 20s, and, in a weaker form, in the mentality of perestroika.

In this sense, modernization in Russia (Peter the Great, Stalin, the period of 1990–1992) almost always takes the form of a catastrophe: it denies the past, the existent material culture, corporeality proper. Andrei Fadin calls the period in the wake of perestroika an attempted variant of a "modernization through a catastrophe",[47] of hitting the bottom to build up the energy of a breakthrough (this line of development has been terminated by post-1993 Yeltsin's "restoration"), a description which perfectly fits the cultural history of Russia.

But why isn't radical modernization possible that would preserve the material culture of the past, like the Meiji modernization in Japan? The answer, once again, is Russian space, its "extensive" nature, as compared with "intensive" space in Japan. The vastness and amorphousness of Russian space, "in which there are no firm houses" (Soloviev), together with the lack of spatial sense among the population in fact mean the lack of practical sense and reason. The space contributes to the irresponsibility of Russia, as reflected in a popular saying "It's easier to knock things down than to build them up" (Lomat' – ne stroit'.) In fact, Russian space possesses a great destructive potential, and Culture One is simply releasing and

---

46 P.N. Miluykov, *Ocherki po istorii russkoi kultury*, (St. Petersburg, 1897), Vol. II, pp.67–9; N.I. Kostomarov, *Ocherk domashnei zhizni i nravov velikorusskogo naroda v XVI i XVII stoletiyakh*, (St. Petersburg, 1860); A.I. Klibanov, *Narodnaya sotsial'naya utopia v Rossii. Period feodalizma*, (Moscow, 1977).
47 Andrei Fadin, 'Modernizatsiya cherez katastrophu? (Ne bolee chem vzglyad)', in Sergei Chernyshov (ed.) Inoe. Khrestomatiya novogo rossiiskogo samosoznaniya (Moscow, 1995), Vol. 1, pp. 321–342.

sublimating it. A perpetual choice between Culture Two and Culture One is a choice between dictatorship and anarchy, binding by force and destroying by force. Between the authoritarianism of power and the ruthless vigor of space, is a snowstorm in the steppe.

IN LIEU OF CONCLUSION

Interpretations of Russian space may vary greatly. Some are post-structuralist and "culturological" discourses (today, most of the latter anyway tend to be post-structuralist) which, following Nietzsche, can be called "gay science" (fröliche Wissenschaft). Some, on the contrary, are more like Husserl's "rigorous science" (strikt Wissenschaft – don't mix with "straight science"). Vladimir Kagansky, for instance, calls his study of regionalisation in Russia a "phenomenology of Russian space" in the spirit of Husserl, and Simon Kordonsky draws complicated matrices of agents of the "administrative market" in the USSR.

But no matter whether "gay" or "rigorous", the General Theory of Russian Space is a post-structuralist and a post-modernist endeavor. It is essentially polystylistic, combining incompatible discourses and bringing together concepts that complement and exclude each other. The number of interpretations is essentially open, and the five outlooks presented above are nothing more than five patches in an imaginary coat of many colors.

What is more important, the General Theory of Russian Space does not know the temptation of authorship, of an outside observer interpreting Russian space. Following the methods of Derrida's deconstruction (which is a variant of Husserl's phenomenological reduction – say hello to a rigorous science), any non-discourse position is impossible, and any observer is included into the discourse of space. Just as a literary critic is part of the analyzed text, a student of Russian space is part of this space: a subject has merged with an object. Being inside, he can observe and interpret, but cannot comprehend or embrace the space proper. It is as endless, inexhaustible and totalitarian as the text itself. At the end of the day, Russian space is text, just plain text. A plain map. The Great Russian plain.

APPENDIX

Russian History in 22 Periods, With an End

Acknowledgment: The author hates any systematic discourse and binary oppositions; however, the temptation of squeezing Russian history into a strict scheme like Mendeleev's periodic table was irresistible. This is not history as a rigorous science, but rather a "glass-bead game" on the themes of Russian history.

Years	Culture One: Horizontal (Spread, spill-over)	Culture Two: Vertical (Hardening, structuring, fixation)
1480s-90s	Nil Sorsky, "non-seekers" (nestyazhateli)	
1500-1520s		Council of 1503: victory of Joseph Volotsky. Conquest of Pskov and Smolensk, growth of the Muscovite State. Ideology of "Moscow the Third Rome". Construction of brick wall around the Kremlin.
1530s-50s	Political turmoil. Infant Ivan IV, Elena Glinskaia, riots and fires in Moscow. Early reign of Ivan: "The Chosen Council", reforms, looking to the West. Russia spreads beyond the Volga: capture of Kazan.	
1560s-90s		Ivan after Kazan and coronation: "Grozny". Conquest of Tver. "Oprichnina". Terror. Construction of St. Basil's, white stone and earthen walls around the Kremlin. 1589 - instalment of Patriarchate.
1600-1613	Instability after Ivan Grozny. Seven boyars, Godunov, Poles and Lithuanians, fire of Moscow 1611; irregular troops of Minin and Pozharsky.	
1613-1650s		Council of 1613, instalment of Romanov dynasty. Increasing stability under Mikhail and Alexei, a powerful hierarchy, Naryshkin baroque.
1650s-70s	1654 - schism of the Church. Raskolniki (schismatics): Fires, self-immolation, Avvakum, Khovanshchina, spread over North-Eastern Russia.	
1680s-1700s	Popular Movements precede the shock of Peter the Great. Reforms of early Peter. Russia spreads in the West and South, fights wars. New cities built (St. Petersburg, Azov, Taganrog).	

1710s-20s		Late Peter. Russia turns into an Empire (1721). Church is part of the new state as a Holy Synod. "The Table of Ranks": codification of civil service. Origins of the Russian bureaucracy. Ordinances to build with stone in St. Petersburg.
1730s	Catherine I, Anna and the rule of Biron. The inflow of westerners.	
1740s-50s		Elisabeth - a new stately hierarchy. High baroque of Rastrelli (Smolny monastery, Winter Palace, Peterhjof Palace), Lomonosov and Barkov.
1760s-70s	Early Catherine II, the "northern Semiramide", correspondence with Voltaire and Diderot, enlightened reforms.	
1780s-90s		Late Catherine, high Russian absolutism, imperial grandeur.
1800-1825	Pavel I (mason and Knight of the Maltese Order), Alexander I, spirit of Enlightenment, plans of reform, Speransky, Napoleonic wars, fire of Moscow in 1812, popular mobilisation, Russia moves into Europe, Cossacks roam in Paris, young officers smell Europe and decide to reform the Russian monarchy: 1825 December uprising.	
Late 1820s-1850s		Coronation of Nikolai I and the trial of the Decembrists (1825-26). "The dark years of reaction". Professionalisation of Russian literature.
1860s-mid-1880s.	Alexander II: reforms. Abolition of serfdom, judicial reform. Egalitarian trends in the educated classes, "People's Will" (narodovoltsy), nihilists, Chernyshevsky. Continued under early Alexander III.	
Mid 1880s-early 1900s.		Alexander III from mid-80s: a turn to conservative ways. Oppression of the revolutionary movement, industrial revolution reaches Russia: peasants move to factories and settle there. Imperial trends of Nikolai II.
Early 1900s	Emergence of egalitarian, deconstructivist, "horizontal" trend in Russian popular movements (workers' socialism, social democracy) and art (avant-garde, futurism). Revolution of 1905.	

1917-1920s	Popular Culture One culminates in revolutions of 1917 and post-revolutionary decade: egalitarianism and communes, abolition of heritage, class, rank, diplomas, school marks; mass migrations due to wars, famine etc.; mass emigration until 1922; avant-garde, futurism, constructivism, de-urbanism in architecture.	
1930s-mid-1950s		The USSR between late 20s and mid-50s: the acme of Stalinism and triumph of Culture Two. Gesamtkunstverk Stalin. Centralized state socialism. Final settlement of the Soviet people in administrative regions and cities (the institute of propiska). Emegence of strict hierarchy of spaces and people. Deification of the leader. Socialist realism, "grand style", Palace of the Soviets and Moscow "skyscrapers".
Late 1950s-early 70s	Khrushchev and early Brezhnev: fighting the past, Stalinism and the cult of the personality. 20th Party Congress. Population starts to move across the territory: prisoners return from GULag, youngsters got to Siberia to develop new territories, build railroads (BAM), or as tourists. Gagarin in space. Looking to the West: 1957 - the Moscow Youth Festival, Khrushchev's desire to "catch up with and overtake America". Massive cheap housing construction.	
Mid-1970s-mid-1980s		Mature Brezhnev: "feudal socialism", "stagnation", new socialist baroque. The era of cermonies and jubilees. Strict rules of social etiquette. In literature and art, epic prevails over lyric. By late 70s, detente gives way to confrontation with the West: Afghanistan, Moscow Olympics, Euromissiles. Attempts of Andropov to further harden the regime: labor discipline, etc. Early Gorbachev's anti-alcohol campaign, though he was to become a man of a different culture.

1986-1991	Gorbachev: "acceleration" and perestroika. Unleashing the forces of space, greater social and teritorial mobility, including unprecedented emigration. Honeymooning with the West: "new thinking", "common European home", Nobel peace prize. Fighting the party hierarchy, preparing the new Union Treaty (the "Novo-Ogarevo process"). Emergence of civil society and a free press, the winds of change. Breakup of the WTO, CPSU, USSR.
1991-1992	Early Yeltsin: continuation of horizontal trends. Fighting communist structures and soviets, letting Russia's regions "take as much sovereignty as they want to". Gaidar's reforms: destruction of the socialist economy. 1993 - abolition of the soviets.
1993-???	October 1993 - a watershed. Post-Soviet restoration. New authoritarianism. New verticals. Derzhavnost'. Great Russia. National interests. War in Chechenya. Presidential elections and "Tsar Boris".New bureaucratic hierarchy. Culture: feeling of fin de siecle. Architectural verticals:new Moscow monuments, houses of the "New Russians". Reconstruction of Church of Christ the Savior: the Second Temple.

The End of History:
"not with a bang.
but a whimper"
(T.S.Eliot)

Studia Historica 62

Ambivalent Space: Expressions of Russian Identity

Elena Hellberg-Hirn

Shiroka strana moia rodnaia...   **49**

While working on a book devoted to Russian national identity, I came to realize the crucial importance of space and territoriality for the understanding of the cultural construct of Russianness and of the re-emerging Russian nationalism. Here, only a few key aspects of Russian spatial symbolism, from the statist territorial to popular and poetic, will be touched upon using as the starting point the most ubiquitous symbols of national self-identification: the double-headed eagle, the troika, and the *matrioshka* doll. I will try to show their direct and metaphorical relations to space, as well as their oblique reference to other, perhaps less conspicuous, but nevertheless persistent symbols of Russia.[1]

Concentrating on such distinctive spatial features as horizontal/vertical orientation and dimensions, bounded/unbounded character, and own/foreign qualifications, I also try to further explore the puzzling ambivalence pertaining to symbolic expressions of space in the Russian mentality. My tentative suggestion will be that this

---

1   In my book, Elena Hellberg-Hirn, *Soil and Soul. The Symbolic World of Russianness* (London, 1998), Russian national symbols (the eagle, the tsar, the Orthodox cross, Mother Russia, etc.) are treated as a consistent set of metaphors, while their origin, history and various connections to the national myth are pursued in greater detail. For a discussion of territoriality, see Torsten Malmberg, *Human Territoriality* (The Hague/Paris/New York, 1988).

ambivalence may be understood partly as a reflection of a still deeper ambivalence inherent in the geopolitical position of Russia straddling Europe and Asia, and partly as a mirror of the unresolved conflicts between the vital values of freedom and security.

INTERPRETING AMBIVALENT SPACES

1. Ever Expanding Frontier, or, Geography as History

The lines of the song quoted in the motto ('Vast is my native land,' which became an unofficial Soviet anthem in the 1930s) capture the Russians' pride in the vastness of their homeland, a cultural theme persistent for centuries. In the song this pride is related to the feelings of freedom (*volia*) experienced by a Soviet citizen looking at the native forests, fields and rivers.[2]

Indeed, a single glance at the globe will suffice: Russia (nowadays The Russian Federation) is an enormous country, a Eurasian great power, however diminished after the demise of the Soviet Union. Images referring to that vast continental territory expanding in all directions – as seen from the capital centre – stand out as extremely appealing to the Russian mind. Small wonder, that among expressions of Russian identity we find a relatively well developed symbolism of space. But, before discussing various symbols of spatiality in the national tradition, let us first consider some important aspects of Russian development, which on the whole has been marked by catastrophic ruptures, schisms and upheavals.[3]

To begin with, there is a striking imbalance in the position of the centre of power due to the initial contraction of Kievan Russia in the 12th century, and the following expansion of Muscovy (later Russian Empire) resulting in the historical vacillations of the capital city first moving to the north-east, from Kiev to Moscow, and then to the north, to St. Petersburg, and finally back again to Moscow. The centre shifted, while the periphery gradually expanded: eastwards into Siberia and the Far East; westwards into the Baltic, Poland, Ukraine; southwards into the Crimea, Caucasus, and Central Asia; until by the

---

2 *Shiroka strana moia rodnaia*, composer Isaak Dunaevskii, words by Vasilii Lebedev-Kumach.
3 See, e.g., Nikolai Berdiaev, *The Russian Idea*, (Boston, 1962).

end of the last century so much territory had been acquired that it became all too difficult to rule from the eccentrically located centre on the westernmost periphery of the Empire.

Thus, the foundation myth for the three successive states (Kievan Russia, Muscovy, and the Russian Empire) which inherited the name *Rus* – originally attributed to the Viking princes and their Scandinavian warrior troops – implies an illusionary stability and continuity in the turbulent development of the national space.

The history of the Russian Empire is the history of a geopolitical expansion which continued for six centuries spreading from the modest medieval Principality of Moscow (with its position exactly in the geographical centre of Europe) and producing shock-waves in all directions towards the ever widening frontier, but primarily to the south-east, to the much desired 'empty' territories of the lower Volga and Siberia opened by the conquest of the khanates of Kazan and Astrakhan by Ivan The Terrible between 1552 and 1556. The empire grew as an onion grows, in layers surrounding the kernel territory. Can it be suggested, tongue in cheek, that there we find the root of the puzzling Russian predilection for onion-shaped church domes?

It is not a joke, however, that a cluster of onion domes with Orthodox crosses pointing to heaven, to her spiritual home, once again has become a favourite symbol of post-Soviet Russia seeking and manifesting celestial protection. And there is a remarkable semantic and etymological affinity (related to an Indo-European root meaning 'to build, construct') between the word *dome* and the word denoting another notion central for Russian identity, namely *dom*, or home: i.e. one's own kernel space, a protected domestic territory surrounded by secure, sometimes thoroughly sealed boundaries.

The Russian concern with boundaries is notorious: every house in a peasant village, every church building with its churchyard, even every grave is usually surrounded by a fence (*zabor*). Many a visitor of Russian urban institutions often located in former grand palaces or modern imitation palaces, the underground included, wonder why the huge and wide gates and doors are always kept locked, while the customers have to squeeze themselves through narrow and inconvenient entrances on the side, passing unfriendly guards demanding a *propusk*, a permit. Is it for better control over the space in question, or due to some residual sacredness of that (eventually secular) power?

Also in the official symbol of Russian statist territoriality, the imperial eagle, the historical relations of space and power are manifested as controlling conquered territories. The national eagle, now in its renovated version of 1991, is a symbolic supervisor of the state's territory. The power pattern of central political and military dominance over the peripheral provinces of the Russian empire is more readily discernible in the old Russian coat of arms, where the central symbol at the heart of the Imperial eagle is surrounded by the emblems of the subjugated provinces. As Geoffrey Hosking has recently argued, in Russia the state has created the nation, and not the other way round, as in many other European nation-states.[4]

A doubly oriented set of symbols, the vertical and the horizontal ones, manifest themselves in the Russian national space. The vertical orientation is specifically connected to the symbols of secular or spiritual power, for instance as Orthodox church domes, belfries, and spires, or the Kremlin towers (earlier decorated with Imperial eagles, exchanged in the 1930s for the Soviet red stars). This vertical symbolism of power is also expressed by Soviet administrative skyscrapers of the 1960s in Moscow, but also by the cosmic pretensions of the late Soviet space programmes (*pokoreniie kosmosa*, lit. 'subjugation of the outer space'). Behold the vertical thrust of the space rocket – and the cosmonauts encapsuled in their space costumes and squeezed into a thoroughly isolated minimal living-shell protecting them against the totally uninhabitable outer space! Remarkably, the latest Russian space team of 1997 brought an icon into the space station *Mir*, their cosmic home, thus turning it into a modern version of the traditional peasant *izba* with its obligatory Orthodox icon in the 'red' (holy) corner.

It has been observed that a rather regular oscillation between vertical and horizontal dominants in Soviet architecture can be seen as one of the distinctive features of the whole Soviet period, since it reflects the pulse of liberal relaxations (horizontal orientation) and conservative tightenings of the state power (vertical orientation).[5]

The horizontal dimension of the national space offers another ambiguity: it may mean a centrifugal expansion away from the centre; or, on the other hand, a centripetal contraction of space into a shell. Geography seen as Russian history is rather revealing in this respect, especially when it comes to the centrifugal extensions of the Russian territory towards the ever-moving open frontier.

4   Geoffrey Hosking, *Russia: People and Empire 1552–1917* (London, 1997), pp.XX–XXV.
5   Vladimir Paperny, *Kultura dva*, (Moscow, 1996).

The Major Imperial coat of arms, 1915.

2. Siberia: Freedom and Prison

Perhaps it is the Siberian/East-Asian expansion that exemplifies this horizontal aspect of national history most clearly. Siberia is also a very good example of the Russian ambivalence towards the frontier space, which can be perceived either as a symbol of freedom, an escape from the dominant power in the centre, or as a forced exile.

Siberia offered new experiences, different ways of life and methods of self-governance, and available free land, or virtually free land, which gave settlers from European Russia the chance to improve their lives. To fugitive peasants (before the Emancipation Law of 1861) Siberia offered a refuge from the slavery of Russian serfdom. To Old

Believers, it meant an escape from religious persecution after the great Schism of the Russian Orthodox Church in 1666.

Eking out a living from land where the sod had to be broken for the first time was also a return to primitive life conditions in wilderness environments; it further meant confronting the not always peaceful natives with whom composite blends of Orthodox culture were created, in the wake of continual penetration of the Russian frontier guarded by the chain of walled settlements. Siberia was conquered both by the sword and by the cross, and neither the Christianizing mission nor colonization were as peaceful as some Russian historians wish to present it.[6]

Siberia provides an example of strong central power over the peripheral territories of the Russian empire. As was mentioned earlier, Russian/Soviet history has been to a large degree the history of colonization, with the ever-retreating frontier of unoccupied land as the magnet for development. Four centuries after the initial conquest of Siberia by Cossack troops, an enthusiasm for the virgin lands of Southern Siberia was still aflame in the 1960s.[7]

Siberia set forth a popular (and populist) patriotic self-image of Russia as an epitome of unlimited freedom, a treasury of possible riches, an El Dorado for the self-made man, the adventurer, the entrepreneur, the explorer, the 'virgin-lander'. But, surprisingly enough, the environmental determinism of the frontier theme is not as explored in Russian tradition as it is in the American one. In spite of obvious similarities, a frontier ingredient has not influenced much of Russian historical or mentality research.[8]

Perhaps this is due to the other, sinister and officially underexposed side of the Siberian enterprise: Siberia as an epitome of captivity. It all started in the 17th century, but the Soviet leaders elaborated diligently on the old patterns of punishment, and by the 1930s Siberia was turned into a GULAG-Archipelago of prisons and camps. From those thoroughly guarded islands of unfreedom there was practically no escape. If, by chance, a convict managed to flee, an almost inevitable death from starvation lurked in the roadless forests and swamps. And there were no signs demarcating any secure space. All space meant terror: Siberia was the territory of terror.

. . . . .
6   See the Russian historian Vasilii Kliuchevskii (1841–1911) on 'peaceful' colonization as the decisive factor of Russian history, and on the civilizing mission of the Russian Imperial expansion: *V.O. Kliuchevskii o russkoi istorii*, (Moscow, 1993), pp.13–16.
7   Petr Vail, Aleksandr Genis, *60-e. Mir sovetskogo cheloveka*, (Moscow, 1996).
8   Frederick Jackson Turner, *The Frontier in American History*, (Tucson, 1986).

The National Eagle of the Russian Federation, 1993. Designed by E. I. Ukhnalev.

This inglorious (and yet largely unwritten) history of Siberia can be traced in the oral tradition; it could be gathered from the road songs of the convicts walking in columns under control of their armed guards to Siberian prison camps or places of exile.[9]

---

9   The oral lore of this subculture has not yet been properly collected and studied. One recent publication, however, *Folklor GULAGa*, (Saint-Petersburg, 1994) touches upon several Siberian topics.

3. Steppe: Freedom and Speed

A different symbolism is suggested by a different kind of Russian road song – and they usually refer to a different kind of space: to the steppes, the open lands of Southern Russia, Ukraine, the Southern Urals. The typical song of a troika coachman (*yamshchik*) is born in the steppe; there, even if the roads were bad or absent, one could have a free view of the landscape, which gave an illusion of freedom.

Also vagabond Gypsies in their rolling wagons were turned by the national poet Alexander Pushkin into a romantic cliché of unfettered life, free love and passionate self-expression in dance and music. Gypsy songs and dances are often mistaken for Russian national music (especially when performed in Russian restaurants), simply because the Russians have so easily adopted them, longing for the limitless passions usually attributed to outsiders and outlaws not restrained by the rules of civilized life.

Russian self-stereotypes promote an idealized image of the national soul as being wide-open: *shirokaja dusha*, full of passionate feelings, generosity, open-mindedness, hospitality, unlimited kindness, and recklessness verging on anarchy in the constant need for a break-out (this usually explains and excuses periodical binges, violence, marital infidelity, careless driving and other violations of social rules and taboos). Such a *dusha* is supposed to have originated in the open landscape of the southern steppe.

Indeed, there were no fences or borders in the steppe, apart from the military fortresses making up the southern frontier into the late 17th century. Ideally, as in folk tradition, the steppe is 'free' because it provided no natural obstacles either to the direction or to the speed of the troika, three horses abreast speedily moving through the open space. The road songs suggest that the troika gave the driver an exhilarating feeling of power, freedom and control: man controlling the horsepower, directing it at his will, but always forward. Space was conceived as an experience of movement; the road absorbed space.

Nikolai Gogol, significantly a Ukrainian-born Russian writer, coined the famous metaphor of Russia as a troika absorbing space at incredible speed; unfortunately, he did not provide us with any answer to his prophetic question (still valid one and a half century later): 'Where are you going, Russia?'

In another memorable passage from the same epic poem in novel form, *The Dead Souls*, Gogol asks: '*I kakoj zhe russkii ne liubit bystroi yezdy?*': 'Can there be a Russian who does not like heedless speed?' In Gogol's view, the Russians are marked with a longing for wide expanses, bold enterprise, total abandon – in short, for the qualities summed up by the adage *shirokaia natura*, or *shirokaia dusha*: the limitless Russian soul, as befitting the unending Russian spaces, 'in the land that is no joke but does everything on the grand scale, unfolding over half of the world', as Gogol put it.[10]

Fast driving – horses, later cars – has been considered by many Russians a distinctive national trait, a stereotype of male Russianness, pertaining to high and low alike. By way of example: the emperor-brothers Alexander I and Nicholas I are said to have spent their lives on the road, and both loved fast driving. Nicholas I is especially remembered as a speedy traveller; he is reported (by Alexander Pushkin, among others) to have driven in December 1833 from Moscow to St. Petersburg in 38 hours, a record for the travel speed of his days. Contemporaries observed that Russian emperors did not usually travel like princes, rather they used to fly like birds, surprising everybody by their incredibly swift transportation between the old and the new capitals of Imperial Russia.

The metaphor of horse-cum-bird makes the high and the low appear seemingly blended. It proved that all Russians were equal in this respect, and that the emperor could behave like a peasant *muzhik*: for them, speed had priority over comfort. Modest night quarters and simple food (a tumbler of vodka and a slice of salted rye bread while changing horses at a distant post station) would reportedly suffice for the Emperor Nicholas I and his constant companion count A.F.Orlov. The Emperor sometimes even used an ordinary postal troika in order to speed up an urgent appearance, thus unexpectedly arriving before the news of his departure.[11]

The Russian empresses also loved speed; in the winter they used to travel reclined or lying in a sable-lined sledge drawn by a span of a dozen or more horses. Thus, upon her arrival in Russia in January 1744, the young German princess Sophie of Anhalt Zerbst (the future Russian Empress Catherine the Great), accompanied by her mother, was welcomed in Riga by a lavishly decorated sledge sent by the Empress Elisabeth; the future bride of the Crown Prince Peter III was brought to St. Petersburg, and then to Moscow where the court was assembled, with incredible speed: the German ladies believed they were flying.[12]

. . . . .
10   Nikolai Gogol, *Mertvye dushi* [1842], (Moscow 1975), pp. 232–233.
11   *Peterburgskiie chteniia 97*, (St. Petersburg, 1997), pp. 626–629.
12   Evgenii Anisimov, *Zhenshchiny na Rossiiskom prestole*, St. Petersburg, 1997), pp. 287-8.

The troika, a rare *lubok* (popular print) version with a female driver. The Lubok. Russian Folk Pictures 17th to 19th Century. Leningrad 1984.

In St.. Petersburg, owning a pair or a troika of speedy horses was the hallmark of high social status. A daily sledge or carriage ride on the embankments of the Neva was enjoyed by the imperial family and the nobility alike, which may of course be due to the feeling of superiority which high speed usually induces and enhances. Is it perhaps so that power tends to be manifested by high speed? Or, the other way round, that high speed might compensate for the absence of power? Perhaps both, because high speed in itself tends to produce a powerful emotion.

On the vertical scale of values, we usually read HIGH positively as dominant, and LOW negatively, as dominated; thus the traditional superiority of HIGH over LOW rests on the grafting of values on the spatial axis, i.e. on the confluent top marking of power and height. Also the combination of the words HIGH and SPEED (*vysokaia skorost*, or *bystrota*) in the notion of rapidity underscores the fusion of the spatial with the axiological.[13]

13 Generally speaking, spatial symbols may refer to:
 1. Types of space: big-small, inner-outer, material and ideal;
 2. Structure of space and its mapping: ring, circle, line, square, cube, symmetry, number;
 3. Spatial operations: narrowing/widening, counting, partition, movement, classification...;

Conspicuously, the national eagle (and not only in Russia) embodies speed, height and power. Legendary eagles appeared on the sites of the future capitals Moscow and St. Petersburg. The power of the eagle refers to the power of control resting on violence, hunting and killing prey on its territory. The 'imperial eyes'[14] of the Russian two-headed eagle watch over the national territory from above.

Also the new Russian Federal eagle controlling the Russian territory falls nicely into the old Imperial tradition which had been somewhat obscured by the red Soviet star, the star originally not being an imperial symbol. However, as the symbol of Soviet power, the red star indicates the topmost (celestial) position of supreme power radiating from the centre. Since the ruby stars on the Kremlin towers have not been dismantled, they are there to remind us that the central power orientation in the Russian space has not yet been abolished.[15]

What we are dealing with here is not, of course, the 'real' space or territory of the Russian (Eurasian) state, with its variety of landscapes, cities, population, natural and mineral riches, and systems of communication; we are concerned only with traditional (simplistic) mind-mapping of space as a marker of national identity, i.e. with spatial metaphors serving as culturally encoded organizers of social experience.

'Space in general is only an activity of the mind', as Georg Simmel puts it. 'Despite this state of affairs, the emphasis on the spatial meanings of things and processes is not unjustified', he continues.[16]

Since a spatial symbol is short for a (visual) metaphor, identifications employing birds, horses, cars, space rockets or other symbolic

. . . . .
4. Space and its counterparts: the heaven and the abyss as anti-spaces;
5. Space and time;
6. Space and aesthetics;
7. Space and axiology: subjective attitudes to space;
8. Space and science;
9. Space and psychotherapy;
10. Space and freedom: new life, new man, new conditions.
In this typology, the notions of power which are important here, security and freedom, would be found under 7 and 10. See V.N. Toporov, *O mifopoeticheskom prostranstve*, (ECIG: Studi Slavi, Università degli Studi di Pisa, Istituto di Lingua e Litteratura russa, Istituto di Filologia Slava, 1994), No 2, pp. 220.
14 Mary Louise Pratt, *Imperial Eyes. Travel Writing and Transculturation*, (London & New York, 1992).
15 On the history of the Soviet red star, see Richard Stites, *Revolutionary Dreams. Utopian Vision and Experimental Life in the Russian Revolution*, (Oxford, 1989), pp. 32–3. Significantly, the red star became the symbol of the Soviet army, i.e. protecting the system and guarding the national space.
16 David Frisby and Mike Featherstone (eds.) *Simmel on Culture. Selected Writings* (London, 1997) p.138.

expressions of unheeded movement and speed, demarcate the high value assigned in national self-consciousness to the control of space. This may provoke new questions: is space controlled by speed? Is space an enemy to be controlled when conquered?

Evidently, armed imperial control over the national territory presupposes the existence of some inside or outside enemy resisting that control. In the case of Russia, as viewed from either a pre-modern, modern, or even from a post-modern (post-Soviet) vantage point, the inside enemy was most certainly not the continental space itself but the conquered and subjugated non-Russians. The insufficiently Russified peoples inhabiting the national space, especially the peripheral territories of the Empire, are now claiming their independence. The danger of the territorial disintegration of Russia has never been as acute as in our post-Soviet days.

The current neo-nationalist discourse promotes as its most urgent goal the saving of the crumbled post-Soviet empire from further disintegration. The importance of inviolable national borders is underscored again and again. But in fact, the national borders were safe only for a relatively short historical time, namely during the Soviet period when the country was sealed behind the gradually rusting Iron Curtain.

Nowadays, the edge of post-colonial disorder is undercutting the established national (read imperial) order, and Russian public opinion gets very tense each time the territorial conflict with Japan about the Kuriles comes around: *Ni piadi!* Not an inch of our territory is to be given away – not to mention sold – to anybody! However, the old imperial borders are being challenged everywhere around the original kernel of ethnic Russia gathered by Moscow in the 14th century.

It is not without interest that we may observe Russian neo-nationalists together with the re-emerging Russian neo-monarchists vigorously engaged in the revival of the Cossack movement, using the Cossacks as symbols of The Russia That we Lost. The Cossacks, inhabiting the frontier areas in the southern Russian steppes, were traditionally both warriors and peasants, exempted by Catherine the Great from serfdom in exchange for their duty to protect Russian borders. Still earlier, Siberia was conquered by Cossack troops on horseback. In the course of time, the image of the Cossacks as related to national space developed a double set of connotations: they were national heroes, the freedom-loving defenders of national borders, and at the same time a symbol of oppression, since they were also officially engaged as special security troops. The Cossacks represent an ambivalent symbolic terrain of violence in which the spatial patterns of national identification are encoded.

From Russian folklore and tradition, later from national literature and art, even from nationalistically oriented cultural historians, numerous examples can be gathered supporting the romantic cultural clichés of geographical determinism.[17]

Generations of Russian school children have learned by heart such poems as *Rus* (Russia) by Ivan Nikitin (1851):

Underneath the tent
Of the heavens blue
I can see the steppes
Stretching green far off.

On their borders loom
High above the clouds
Giant mountain chains,
Gaunt and motionless.

Seaward through the steppes
Mighty rivers flow
And long roadways run
North, west, south and east. [18]

Or take the epic *bylinas* where the hero (*bogatyr*) always rides out into the steppe to fight the pagan intruders and defend the Orthodox Russian Land. This homeland is qualified by the standing epithet *shiroko pole*, open space. In Russian folk songs, these words are constantly rhymed with *privoliie, razdoliie*, and *volia* — three synonymous expressions for freedom which is also understood as *prostor*: space that is wide-open for unheeded movement and unlimited possibilities.

All this is not to deny the reverse side of the national coin: the noted suspiciousness, animosity, impenetrability of borders; in other words, in the national space we find both *prostor* and *zabor*. The disadvantage of the open frontier is, of course, its vulnerability to intrusion; fear of devastating attacks from the outside promoted concern about thoroughly defended borders and solid surrounding boundary lines. And since natural boundaries were largely absent on

---

17 Dmitrii Likhachev, *Reflections on Russia*, (Boulder, 1991).
18 Translation by Dorian Rottenberg in *Three Centuries of Russian Poetry* (Moscow, 1980), pp.256–7.

the Great Russian plane, strong political boundaries became all the more important. Security needs formed themselves spatially; power motifs and violent military means were justified by the Orthodox spiritual superiority and its civilizing mission upon the non-Christian (pagan or Islamic) peripheral population. 'And it is precisely this which produces what is symbolized in the spatial boundary, the supplementation of one's own positive sense of power and justice within one's own sphere by the consciousness that such power and justice do not extend onto the other sphere.'[19]

Historically accumulated tensions both inside and outside the national boundaries, between nomadic and settled groups with their divergent life patterns have made themselves felt in the Russian space for centuries.

4. Convoluted Space: Home and Homeland

Quite obviously, national space is not homogeneous; and we have to count with a hierarchy of spaces in the Russian mindscape. Valorized distinctions such as own/foreign and bounded/unbounded (open/closed) space are superimposed on the basic vertical and horizontal axes of spatial orientation.

Going back to the two Russian capitals, the national ambivalence towards own/foreign and open/closed spaces can be easily demonstrated; this ambivalence was introduced into Russian history and geography by Tsar Peter, himself the best example of a highly ambivalent Russian personality, and a flagrant trespasser of all traditional borders.

Peter the Great grandly exhibits both claustrophobic and agoraphobic traits. Most of all he loved the open sea; most of all he hated the vaults of the Kremlin quarters with their stifling mix of monastery, harem and jail; but he was unable to fall asleep in spacious palace bedrooms, neither in St. Petersburg, nor abroad, preferring a simple boat hold or his small wooden hut where his bed was arranged with closely draped curtains creating a cocoon of security.[20]

. . . . .
19 Georg Simmel in Frisby and Featherstone (eds.), p.143.
20 M.I. Pyliaev, *Staryi Peterburg* [1889], (reprint Moscow, 1990), p.16; Konstantin Waliszewski, *Petr Velikii* [1912], (reprint Moscow, 1989), pp.195, 391. But this, perhaps, tells us more about Peter's psychological state rather than the Russian mentality?

In answer to Russia's 'urge to the sea',[21] Tsar Peter's new capital was deliberately open to western influences and maritime commerce. From the moment of its foundation in 1703 on the then still foreign territory only a couple of weeks earlier wrought from Sweden in one of the battles of the Great Northern War, St. Petersburg grew as an increasingly un-Russian, eccentric capital (in both the literal and the metaphoric meanings of the word), too close to the national border and thus vulnerable to foreign attack.

Since 1712 when the not yet fully constructed naval port of St. Petersburg became the residence of Peter I, the Russian rulers and their family, the court and officials, diplomats included, were constantly travelling between the two capitals. Also the official ritual life was divided: some of the imperial rites of passage such as weddings and coronations were held in Moscow, while birth celebrations and funeral ceremonies took place in St. Petersburg.

The two-century long opposition of open, multicultural, innovative and secular St. Petersburg to the more traditionally oriented Russian Orthodox Moscow proved to be extremely fruitful for the cultural development of Russia, but it created and sustained the political, social and ideological tensions in the conservative Russian monarchy.

Finally, after the two social revolutions of 1917, the capital migrated again in 1918, back to a more protected central position, to Moscow, thus regaining the national power prestige; its old medieval centre was, however, reconstructed and modernized in the 1930s after the open urban layout of the Petersburgian model. But the Kremlin walls protecting the seat of high power were left untouched, and Moscow remained for most Russians a cherished symbol of national identity, the heart of the Homeland.

The idea of HOMELAND may be represented as a set of concentric circles, employing two kinds of centricity. The national capital with its seat of supreme power (the Kremlin) occupies the centre of the highly valorized collective space. This kind of national centricity is complemented (overlayed) by a private identification with the HOME which is also conceived of as a set of concentric areas, ranging out from one's family house, home city, district, landscape, etc., and in the end coinciding with the concentric Homeland. Depending on various contexts, these basic structures converge or, as in emigration, group deportation, or other cases of displacement, diverge.

. . . . .
21 Robert Kerner, *The Urge to the Sea*, (Berkeley, 1942).

Russian *topophilia* (love for the homeland) qualifies the native homespace or the home country as being morally superior to foreign territories. Folklore and classical Russian literature, especially poetry, provide numerous examples of space-related patriotism, tinged by romantic reminiscences from nomadic life patterns. While one's own national space is usually conceived of as free, orderly, right and just by definition, the foreign space (*zamorskiie zemli*) is essentially an Anti-space, an Anti-world, governed by rules both strange and unjust. Contacts with foreigners are therefore dangerous and should be avoided. There is no need to stress that examples of traditionally xenophobic attitudes to foreigners are legion, and not in Russia alone.

For the topic of national identification it is important, however, to see the connection between the individual experience of one's home as the most protected, most familiar, most secure domestic refuge, and the national space of the Homeland which offers (or at least should offer) security and protection to all inhabitants. A recent revealing example can be provided from the rhetoric of the Russian election campaign of 1996, when the then prime-minister Viktor Chernomyrdin launched the slogan *Nash dom Rossiia* (Russia Our Home) to attract voters to his party by soothing their sentiments of insecurity and growing distress caused by the collapse of the Soviet system.

No doubt, HOME means one's own guarded, controllable space inhabited by kindred people. And what can be more controllable socially, and bounded spatially, than the *kommunalka*, a Soviet urban flat shared by several families; or a traditional Russian *izba*, a poor peasant's house with its single heated living room overcrowded by at least three family generations, in winter including even domestic animals...

One of the most cherished popular symbols of Russia, the wooden doll *Matrioshka*, is a play with identity, boundaries, and the contraction or expansion of space. It offers a symbolic home to generations of similar dolls tightly fitted inside the mother's protecting body. The doll may embody a peasant woman, home, family, origin, safety, tradition, Mother Russia - but if you take a look into the multi-layered inside of her container body, you discover a concentric structure which resembles the familiar onion structure. Moreover: the doll's body not only forms an ordered set of borders. All available space therein is stuffed by borders![22]

---

22 The sealed container of an Orthodox Easter egg also persists as a central symbol of the Russian domestic space imbued with religious connotations. Quite often an Easter egg may contain a surprise, or a series of surprises; it opens like the *matrioshka* doll. Eggs and dolls exhibit a number of converging modern variants

And there we are: depending on the context, borders can imply both security and confinement. Thus, the various borders demarcating the Russian space in terms of such categories as OWN/ORDERED/ SECURE/CLOSED, as different and separated from other things marked FOREIGN, stand out as crucial for resolving ambivalences inherent in the process of national identification. Domesticated identical identities, like the ones inhabiting the *matrioshka*'s body, seem to be the most desirable ones for Mother Russia.

WHOSE SYMBOLS?

As a conclusion to this roundabout route, inspecting spatial symbols and trying to offer a coherent interpretation of the Russian national mindscape, we might wonder: why both *prostor* and *zabor*? What does this inherent contradiction mean? But perhaps it will first be necessary to answer another important question: whose symbols are under discussion here? Are they the ones embraced by all Russians? Do they always count?

The answers tend to be contradictory, too: Yes and No. Yes – because virtually every Russian will agree that the national eagle, the troika, and the *matrioshka* are national symbols. And No, because they denote different positions in the social space, different views of 'essential' Russia, different valorizations of her alleged qualities.

Symbols referring to Russian national identity offer a complementary set of denotations for different discourses; each of them is surrounded by a more or less strong 'field of force'. While it is hard to believe that anybody can die for a 'low' popular *matrioshka*, a great many people have offered their lives (and perhaps as many again are prepared to die) for the Russian eagle with its 'high' imperial connotations, or for the red Soviet star still competing for power.

As viewed from the social top, by the ruling elite putting a premium on power and control, the eagle (or the red star, for that

. . . . .
exhibiting such highly valorized national motifs as the last imperial family, Russian saints, famous writers, Soviet political leaders, etc. While the *matrioshka* may not be seen by all Russians as a national symbol, it is definitely seen as such by foreigners. The same applies to 'the Russian bear'. (The bear represents the north Russian forest, a constraining but also protecting landscape as opposed to the open southern steppe. A birch-tree, another natural symbol often attributed to Russia, refers to the climatic zone in-between.)

A modern set of *matrioshka*-dolls representing the last Tsar Nicholas II and his family.

matter) is the national symbol *par préférence* denoting the whole space of the Homeland, nowadays also officially protected by the Orthodox cross.

If considered from below, from the point of view of the common people (*narod*), other central values come to the foreground: freedom and security. The troika can then provide the image of unbounded freedom supporting the male stereotype, the *matrioshka* can denote the bounded female sphere of domestic life and security. The result of the identification process depends on the crucial choice: whose discourse gets symbolically promoted? Which social identity gets confirmed? In what context? On which side of the conventional

Cossack troops under command of the legendary General Platov, a *lubok* picture. The Lubok. Russian Folk Pictures 17th to 19the Century. Leningrad 1984.

border – as an insider or as an outsider – will the identity-seeking individuals place themselves, or be placed by others?

The national symbols discussed here point to unresolved tensions between *prostor* and *zabor*; between open 'natural' space and domesticated territory; between the vertical (power élite) and the horizontal (popular) dimensions of the Russian social space; between the sedentary peasant life-patterns and the mobility of Asian nomads, of Cossacks on horseback, of military troops, or the modern urban population.

By way of example: the horse for a peasant has been (and in some Russian provinces still is) first and foremost a working aid; for the warrior, an aid in battle; for a *yamshchik*, a professional necessity; for a nomad, a condition of life. But travel metaphors, like homelife metaphors, are forged into a national symbolism denoting an allegedly homogeneous social space – which all kinds of Russians, belonging to all sorts of basically heterogeneous and highly ambivalent cultural, ethnic and social positions, are supposed to subscribe to and to share. 'Can there be any Russian who does not like heedless speed?'

As to the motor car as a symbol of speed and freedom, it has not been prominent in national symbolism, evidently due to the fact that until now very few people in Russia could afford a private car. But fast and careless driving symptomatically persists, however, as a self-imposed and self-sustained national trait. A car, preferably of a foreign brand (*inomarka*), nowadays tends to symbolise the so-called New Russians as conspicuous consumers and new 'Others'.

Another remark on the topic of speed, cars, and horse-symbolism: while rulers on national monuments use to be equestrian, demonstrating their power in frozen motion, cars are not used in this respect. One Russian exception is the armoured car (*bronevik*) on the Lenin monument in front of the Finnish Railway station in Leningrad/ St. Petersburg. There Lenin is shown standing on top of the symbolically rendered car. This exception seems to confirm the rule.

A possible explanation would be that a man mounted on a horse or standing on a high postament is fully visible to the viewers, and obtains an increased view of his surroundings, while symbolically coming higher on the vertical scale of power; inside a car he would be concealed, almost domesticated, his view restricted, thus enhancing the horizontal dimension of motion in space rather than the vertical symbolism of power.

CONCLUSIONS

Summing up, we can assume that since identity rests on the presumption of similarity and homogeneity, spatial symbols promoting national identification are there to confirm Sameness on the one side, Otherness on the other, and borders in-between.

The notorious Russian concerns about impenetrable borders seem to reveal collective insecurity and a strong need of protection. Protection of one's own space from intrusion by all kinds of Others: foreigners, non-Russian compatriots, criminals, unfriendly officials... in short, anybody who does not belong.

The insecurity inherent to drawing borders tends to be resolved by manipulation: either by the power discourse forced from above, or by various private discourses negotiating Self and Other in different contexts.

Russian national space as reflected in symbolic expressions of Russian identity has been examined here in its ambivalence, as both inclusive and exclusive. The unlimited, boundless 'natural' territory is perceived as a symbol of freedom; on the other side, the bounded and thoroughly guarded space as providing security, a refuge from the anxieties accumulated in catastrophic developments. Boundary emerges then as the central spatial concept, defining and dividing order from chaos in private and public spaces alike.

The suggested analysis of Russian national symbolism points to a forced and false homogeneity imposed by the national myth concealing the diversity of ethnic and national expression behind the overly uncontroversial images of the Russian Homeland and its imperial identity.

Besides, it is not only that both the 'high' imperial and the 'low', traditionally peasant-oriented national symbols are pre-modern, gender-biased, and thus obsolete; more important, the temporal dimension is symptomatically absent in symbolic representations of the simplistic national mindscape. Time that stands for language, culture, historical processes... But this is hardly unexpected, since national symbols and national myths are invented to promote fast and stable national identities that usually make claims of being eternal, essential, outside history.

Space, Time, and the Russian Idea

Christer Pursiainen

Space and time are two interconnected variables that are often believed to constitute the 'essence' of nature. In the sphere of social life, they are no less important. The meanings given these categories and their interrelationship have nevertheless varied greatly throughout human history. According to Michel Foucault, medieval space was constituted by a complete hierarchy, opposition and intersection of places; it was the space of emplacement. This space was opened up by Galileo. A thing's space was no longer anything other than a point in its movement. Localisation was replaced by extension and in a way time became more important than space. Our era, by contrast, is taken up fundamentally with space. Today, according to Foucault, the site is a substitute for extension. The site is defined by relations of proximity between points or elements, relations that are no longer hierarchical or temporal.[1] Similarly, David Harvey, who calls space and time basic categories of human existence, goes against the universalism of the Enlightenment project – Fordist modernity, its emphasis on change, time and Becoming – with a postmodernist flexible focus on stability, localism, space and Being.[2]

The same categories, and perhaps even the same general trends, apply when we discuss Russian political thought. Nevertheless, even if most of the trends that characterise the subject – such as Marxism, modernisation theory, or national-romantic ideologies – originate

---
1 Michel Foucault, 'Of Other Spaces', a lecture given on March 14, 1976, reprinted, for instance, in *Documenta 10. The Book. POLITICS/POETICS* (Documenta und Museum Fridericianum Veranstaltungs-GmbH, 1997), pp. 262–272.
2 David Harvey, *The Condition of Postmodernity. An Enquiry into the Origins of Cultural Change.* (Oxford, 1990).

from the traditions of Western philosophy and social theory, in their theoretical and practical applications in the Russian context they often take on new characteristics. Nikolai Berdiaev has described the fundamental difference between Russian and Western thinking by saying that the Russian soul corresponds to the Russian landscape, mirroring the same unlimited space, breadth, boundlessness, and shapelessness. In the West, by contrast, everything is marked, shaped and organised into categories; everything, both soul and landscape, is susceptible to order and the development of civilisation.[3]

Yet the space-time interrelationship has perhaps nowhere been such a contested matter than in the discourse on the essence of Russia. The main connecting thread of Russian political thought that runs through the different grand narratives within it has been the definition of the interrelationship between Russia and the West, or rather Russia's difference from the West. In this discourse, which is best described by the contentious term the 'Russian idea', space is not always mere territoriality and time is not always linear. Nevertheless, in one way or another, through these two categories rival ideas and ideologies define themselves and Russia with regard to the West, and more generally to the world and the history of humanity.

UNIVERSALISM VS. PARTICULARISM

The general treatments of the *Russkaia ideia*[4] usually start at least from 'Russia's Byzantine heritage'. After the collapse of Constantinople, Russia, under the leadership of Ivan III, adopted the role of the 'Third Rome', and together with it came a suspicion of the Catholic and later the Protestant West. As we know, a new phase began with Peter. According to Arnold Toynbee, when the Russians made this attempt to master Western manners and technology – as they have done so many times since – they did so in order to save themselves

---

3   See the introduction in Nicolas Berdiaev, *The Origins of Russian Communism* (Chicago, 1972, first printed in Russian in 1937).
4   When tracing the first use of this term, it is usually referred to Vladimir Solovev's lecture given in Paris in 1888 and published in French in the same year. In Russian the lecture in question was first published only in 1909. The text can be found in V.S. Solovev, 'Russkaia ideia', *Sochineniya v 2 tomakh, Tom 2*, (Moscow, 1909/1989), pp. 219–246.

from being forcibly Westernised, though paradoxically in the process they had to Westernise themselves partially.[5]

In this historical development we can see the basic elements that contributed to the birth of two traditional Russian trends of political thought, *zapadnichestvo* and *slavianofil'stvo*. The former concept is derived from the Russian word for the West, 'zapad'. This 'Westernism' does not necessarily, however, suggest an ideological commitment to emulate Western political institutions at any given time, and even less Western-minded foreign policy. Rather it concerns understanding the fate of Russia in the spirit of the Enlightenment, as a part of a more or less linear development that will lead to a conclusive universal end. 'Westernism' comes into the picture in that the point of comparison is in one way or another West European or Western modernization.

According to the spiritual father of *zapadnichestvo* of the first part of the nineteenth century, P.Ia.Chaadaev, Russia had in no way participated in the development of humankind, and she had distorted everything that had been left over from the progress achieved elsewhere. Chaadaev urged Russia to adopt the Western way of thinking and development, to abandon its old culture and traditions.[6] Only after adopting all the knowledge and education of the West could Russia fulfill her mission in the world, he argued. By learning faster than others and avoiding their mistakes Russia's delay could be turned to her advantage, and then the day would come when Russia would stand at the heart of Europe. The logical result of Russia's long isolation would be its rise to the vanguard of countries who could answer the most important questions facing humankind.[7]

Slavianofil'stvo, slavophilism has emphasized the uniqueness of Russia and 'Russianess' in striving for social development within the

---

5 See Toynbee's 'Russia's Byzantine Heritage' in his *Civilisation on Trial* (London, New York, Toronto, 1949 (third edition)), pp. 164–183, here p. 167 especially. See also Dmitri Obolensky, 'Russia's Byzantine Heritage', in Michael Cherniavsky (ed.), *The Structure of Russian History, Interpretive Essays* (New York, 1970), pp.3–28. See also Dimitri Strémooukhoff, 'Moscow the Third Rome: Sources of the Doctrine', in Cherniavsky, *The Structure of Russian History*, op. cit., pp. 108–125.
6 P.Ia. Chaadaev, 'Filosoficheskie pis'ma', in A.F. Zamaleev (ed.), *Rossiia glazami russkogo. Chaadaev, Leontev, Solovev* (St. Petersburg, 1991), pp. 19–138. See especially the first of the 'Philosophical letters', published for the first time in Russian in 1836.
7 This more positive outlook was articulated later, in 1937, in an unfinished essay: P.Ia. Chaadaev, 'Apologiia sumashedshego', reprinted in Boris Trasov, *Chaadaev* (Moscow, 1990), pp. 558–573.

framework of Russia's own cultural traditions. It opposes the *zapadnik* linear and universal philosophy of history by proposing cultures or civilizations as the basic units of world history, instead of a single world-wide civilization. Like Chaadaev, A.S.Khomiakov, the most famous of the early nineteenth century slavophiles, emphasized Russia's difference from the West, but for him this did not appear as backwardness or underdevelopment. The spiritual and social uniqueness, of which Khomiakov speaks, and which for him appears as the life nerve of the Russian people, is the Orthodox faith in God and through this the Russian people's community and conciliation within the Church.[8] In general, most of these early slavophiles were land owners, educated men, humanists and lovers of freedom, whose spiritual roots ran deep in the Russian cultural soil. They were overwhelmed by an illusory image of the Russian people. They considered the peasantry to be the eternal foundation of Russia, the guarantee of the country's everlasting distinctiveness. The peasantry's spirit of community stood in strong contrast to the West's individualism.

THE INTELLECTUAL ROOTS OF THE REVOLUTION

Zapadnichestvo, or Westernism, in its different versions undoubtedly constituted the main trend in Russian nineteenth century political thought. However, the Soviet Union cast its own image of Russia, as a revolutionary nation cut free from its traditions and past ideas. Yet, Marxism's roots in the country's spiritual soil can be traced back most notably to the intellectual development of the *zapadnik* trend of Russian political thought from the mid-nineteenth century onwards.

One of the first to pay attention to these Russian origins of Soviet communism, was Berdiaev.[9] In his view there were two tendencies to

---

8 See A.S. Khomiakov, *Izbrannye sochineniia* (New York, 1955), especially pp. 79–101.
9 Berdiaev, *The Origins of Russian Communism*, op. cit. See also Nikolai Berdiaev, *The Russian Idea*, (Hudson, NY, 1992); S.V. Utechin, *Russian Political Thought. A Concise History* (New York, 1963); Iver B. Neuman, *Russia and the Idea of Europe. A Study in identity and international relations* (London, 1996); Tim McDaniel, *The Agony of the Russian Idea* (Princeton, New Jersey, 1996).

emerge from *zapadnichestvo* fairly early on. The first was a moderate, 'liberal' orientation that focused on the arts and philosophy, and was particularly influenced by German idealism and romanticism. Then there was a more revolutionary tendency that focused on social questions and drew its inspiration originally from the French socialist tradition. However, Hegel's ideas, which had greatly influenced both the slavophiles and *zapadniks*, promoted the exponents of these leftist versions of *zapadnik* thought eventually to seek theoretical starting points for social reforms from Feuerbach and Marx. In general, however, this leftist wing of *zapadnichestvo* became more Russian in character, and offered a more original interpretation of Russia's path of development than the liberal versions.

One can trace several phases in the development of this leftist orientation, and conceptions of space and time play a crucial role in this process. The *nihilism* of the early second half of the nineteenth century was a revolt against the injustices of history, an uprising against a wrong civilization, a demand for an end to history and time, and for the beginning of a new life above and beyond the previous course of history. It was a claim for nakedness, a demand to remove the trappings of culture, for abandoning tradition, a demand for a natural and finally free human being. According to Berdiaev, it was the nihilist generation that was responsible for altering the face of Russian culture, for degrading it and turning it away from the humanities towards the natural sciences, technology and political economy.

The next phase, which sought a social base for change, led the revolutionary intelligentsia to turn its attention to the peasant population. These leftist *narodniks*, like the earlier slavophiles, believed in 'the Russian people'. However, they did not see themselves as an organic part of this entity: the real people were to be found elsewhere. The intelligentsia felt it had no role or purpose in the life of the Russian people, that it was alienated from them, and it therefore felt shamefaced before the people. Sadly, to the disappoint-ment of the *narodniks* the Russian peasantry did not live up to expectations because it was not interested in revolution. So the revolutionary intelligentsia turned to itself, and placed the destiny of Russia on the shoulders of its own heroism. But in so doing the revolt petered out, and became limited to acts of terrorism by small outlaw groups.

Plekhanovian *Marxism* offered a way out of this intellectual and spiritual deadlock. The Marxist idea of an inevitable revolution, an objective and inescapable process, filled the vacuum of pessimism. This orientation presupposed, however, abandoning the agrarian *narodnik* world picture and adopting the idea of a developing proletariat becoming the social basis and power of the revolution. But, as Berdiaev has pointed out, the socialists of pre-capitalist Russia faced a moral dilemma: how to reconcile welcoming capitalism, and the emergence of the proletarian class in capitalist industrialization, with opposing the evil it represented? This was the dilemma that *bolshevism* solved. Lenin emphasized the feasibility of socialist revolution in Russia before society had reached the capitalist phase of development. Instead of a real class of proletariat, as a social basis for revolution, he created an *idea*, an illusion, of the existence of this revolutionary class.

SPACE AND TIME IN SOVIET COMMUNISM

In origin Bolshevism clearly had more to do with time than space; it was more about the future than the present. However, having acquired the status of a state ideology, bolshevism, or Russian communism, had to deal with many unforeseen limitations. It was constrained not only by its Russian intellectual origins but also by the territorial limits of Soviet power. Originally, in Marxism-Leninism the decisive condition for building socialism, and for the survival of Soviet Russia in the first place, was believed to be world revolution, or at least revolutions in some of the largest and most developed capitalist countries. Following the October Revolution, it was therefore estimated that world revolution would start within weeks. A little later the predictions spoke in terms of months, and after many setbacks the time frame was extended to some years. This reality made it necessary for bolshevism to adapt to some extent to the prevailing practices of inter-state relations, such as state-centred territoriality.

Historians of Soviet Russia like E.H.Carr[10] have remarked that of the two goals that coexisted uneasily in the Soviet foreign policy portfolio of the early 1920s – the encouragement of world revolution and the pursuit of national security – the latter was chosen as the polestar of Soviet foreign affairs. Under the theory of socialism in one

---
10 See E.H. Carr, *Socialism in one country 1924–1926. Volume III* (London, 1964), p. 5.

country, first introduced at the end of 1924, Stalin finally turned the focus from world revolution to the internal development of the Soviet Union. The ultimate goal of world revolution was not abandoned, but its former standing as the precondition for the success of the Russian Revolution was reversed: it was now the survival of the Soviet Union that was the precondition for and the basis of world revolution.

In fact, during this process of adapting to reality, the original Marxist idea of dividing the world mainly across class lines had been gradually superseded by a more state-centred, a more territorial and spatial, world picture.[11] Already prior to the October Revolution Lenin had altered the world picture of classic Marxism by adding to it the solidarity of the proletariat of the capitalist countries with the people oppressed by imperialism – by contrast to the view of Marx and Engels who saw the colonial system as accelerating the social development of the colonized countries. In Lenin's thinking after the revolution, but especially in Stalin's world view, states fell into two camps: that of the anti-imperialist struggle, led by the Soviet Union, which acted as a magnet for the workers of the West and the revolutionaries of the East; and the imperialist camp. Instead of Lenin's 'breathing space', Stalin introduced a more long-lasting 'breathing phase' for the inevitable coexistence of two systems.

In a way, this meant that universal time and the history of world revolutionary progress was considerably delayed or slowed down in the minds of the Bolsheviks. This issue, which is often crystallized in the dispute between Trotsky and Stalin, with the former wanting to make the Soviet Union a more aggressive instrument of the universal world revolution, can also be interpreted as the victory of Russian nationalistic and slavophile traditions over the universalistic *zapadnik* tendencies found in Russian communism.

However, this nationalistic victory[12] was only tactical and temporary. Indeed, a closer look at the historical record and the development of

---

11 This section is based on careful reading of first-hand sources on Soviet ideology. I have discussed and documented my interpretation on several occasions, among others in Christer Pursiainen, '*Pacta Sunt Servanda*? The Development of the Sense of Community and the Principle of Obligation in Soviet and Russian Doctrines of International Law', *Journal of Communist Studies and Transition Politics*, Vol.14, No.3, September 1998, pp.84–108. For thorough analyses of the same phenomena, see: V. Kubàlkovà, A.A. Cruickschank, *Marxism-Leninism and Theory of International Relations* (London, Boston and Henley, 1980); Margot Light, *The Soviet Theory of International Relations* (Brighton, 1988).
12 From this viewpoint, see especially Mikhail Agursky, *The Third Rome. National Bolshevism in the USSR* (London, 1987).

Soviet ideology shows, that after the Soviet Union acquired a global status by the end of the 1950s as one of the two superpowers it was once more possible to emphasize increasingly the world revolutionary features of both theory and practice. In stark contrast to most of Stalin's rule, under Khrushchev Soviet theory finally broke away from its introverted gaze and began instead to underscore the obligations that established socialism had to the world revolution. Space struck a balance with time, and enlarging the Soviet sphere of influence became tantamount to universal progress.

At first developments in this direction appeared fairly moderate, and even as a liberalization of the Soviet concept of international relations. Early in the Khrushchev era, the frontier between the two antagonistic camps loosened somewhat, and this made room for the imagined community, the 'zone of peace' concept, according to which the socialist camp and the non-aligned countries – the latter group emerging mainly from the collapse of the colonialist system – formed anti-imperialistic areas where peaceful coexistence acquired tangible forms. However, it was soon easy to trace a gradual increase in 'the international obligations' of the Soviet Union as its capabilities and prerequisites for international influence improved. Yet, the focusing of world revolutionary optimism on less developed countries – thus contradicting crucially Marx' original concept of world revolutionary progress – led gradually to a sea change in the way of thinking, which manifested itself in a clear binary division of foreign policy strategy: détente for the West and revolutionary activism for the Third World.

However, the development of what was called 'new political thinking' in the early years of perestroika led the Soviet Union's official policy and theory step by step away from the notion of international obligations. By the end of 1988, this development had culminated in the idea that international relations should be made non-ideological. In order to legitimize the sudden disappearance of the international dimension of the struggle between capitalism and progress, Gorbachev noted that in going back to the teachings of Marxism-Leninism one should conclude that the class interests of the proletariat and all-human interests were interrelated, and that in the present world situation the former would have to yield to the latter.

At that time, Soviet theorists began to acknowledge that anti-colonial struggles were things of the past and that in the present situation there were no revolutions which would strive to go beyond national liberation. International relations were no longer interpreted in terms of antagonism, but in terms of co-operation, shaped by the priority of universal values and the universal interdependence of the world instead. National interests became international interests, the world was finally whole – albeit not in the way the bolsheviks had imagined.

UNIVERSALISTIC MODERNISATION WITHIN THE RUSSIAN SPACE

Thus, by the end of the perestroika era it seemed clear that practically all the Marxist-Leninist elements had been dropped from the approaches of Gorbachev and his associates. This process has since been completed by other kinds of *zapadniks*. In terms of space and time, we might see it as simply a different kind of universalism, a different kind of Becoming, and another version within the same metatheory that has replaced – as the mainstream mode of contemporary Russian political thought – both the previous dogma of Marxist-Leninist universalism and the Gorbachevian emphasis on the universal values of humanity. Instead of Marxist ideas of a succession of different socio-economic phases – feudalism, capitalism, socialism, communism - the contemporary liberal-conservative *zapadniks* have adopted *modernisation theory*, the mainstream Western post-Second World War idea of modernisation.

Thus, in the contemporary versions of *zapadnik* ideas the great long-term goal is economic and political modernization in its Western form – on the one hand a (post)industrialized and urbanized consumer society, and a democratic constitutional state on the other. According to this essentially linear theory of progress, modernization is the path which Russia must walk to the end before it can move onwards to post-modernity. In fact, while starting from democratic ideals, and in order to put the modernist concept into practice, contemporary mainstream *zapadnichestvo*, although not every version of it, once again turns out to be a rather authoritarian pattern of Russian development.

At the heart of this story[13] there is the sense of a shattering of the illusion created by the optimistic spirit of Soviet communism. It

---
. . . . .
13 The contemporary *zapadnik* narratives, presented in this section, are discussed and documented in detail in Heikki Patomäki and Christer Pursiainen, *Against the State, With(in) the State, or a Transnational Creation: Russian Civil Society in the Making?* UPI Working Papers 4 (1998) (Helsinki: The Finnish Institute of International Affairs).

became clear for post-communist *zapadniks* that Russia, as at the time of Chaadaev, instead of being a worthy example, remains a backward country compared to the West. Although Russia was partially modernized, in particular during the Soviet period, on the whole she had failed to answer to the call of modernization. Russia's problem within this linear conception of history is that its development appears in reality to have been far from linear. Within this discourse Russia's history, alongside the evolutionary development of the West, looks like a repetitive cycle of harm and misfortune, an exhausting circular march of progress that sooner or later always takes totalitarian or authoritarian forms, thus hindering the complete modernization of society. This failure to modernize has kept Russia isolated from the mainstream of world wide historical progress.

Russia's problem culminates in its state-society relations. The axiom of contemporary *zapadnik* discourse is that the development of the institution of civil society in the West explains the successful modernization of its societies, while the failure of Russia, consequently, stems from the fact that the creation of a functioning civil society in Russian conditions never really took place. In Russia the state has traditionally been almost the sole source of the formation of social institutions. There has been no development from below, no 'natural' evolution has ever come about. All institutions have been closely restricted by the state. This lack of natural modernization from below has been compensated by the process of modernization deliberately pioneered by the elite; it has been a purely economic modernization imposed upon, rather than activated by impulses from, society, and it has not reached the sphere of the political system.

At the end of the nineteenth and the beginning of the twentieth centuries, economic modernization improved in a short period of time, but the political system, which was antagonistic to natural modernization, thwarted the bourgeois reformers. So while Russian communism is seen as an upshot of the failure to transfer the European type of modernization to imperial Russia, at the same time it is seen as a novel Russian-style application of modernization. From an economic point of view, as contemporary *zapadniks* often admit, the Soviet period was not purely negative as it managed to get through the phase of modernization that concentrated on industrialization. However, as a whole the Soviet path of development proved to be unbalanced, and was in many ways merely continuing the experience of the previous imperial model. The roots of this structural crisis were out of reach, they lay deep within the individual suppressed by totalitarianism, in the absence of impulses from below in a society governed from above.

Forced modernization was appropriate for the great leap of industrialization, but not for the challenges of late modernity. Thus, modernization in Russia has still been shelved or delayed.

According to contemporary mainstream *zapadnichestvo*, totalitarianism itself, or the other side of the same coin – the absence of civil society, caused the collapse of the communist system. Although some elements of civil society existed even in the Soviet system, the system was able to push civil society to the edge of the public sphere and even beyond; the environment, where articulation of individual and group identities was secured even in the Soviet era, was found on the margins of the public sphere – family, neighbours, and circles of friends. However, it was only during the later phase of perestroika that civil society acquired more institutionalized forms. Nevertheless, in *zapadnik* discourse perestroika is often seen as a failed attempt at political modernization; in fact, by not creating the preconditions for democracy, and starting reform the wrong way round, it was bound to fail. Consequently, instead of democracy, Russia wound up with anarchy.

Thus, even if there was a basis of civil society which made the collapse of totalitarianism possible, in today's Russia there is no civil society in its complete societal form, in a form which would enable democracy. Western style institutions, such as the multiparty system, freedom of speech, the constitution, and the institutions of democratic power, proved to be insufficient for democracy. Totalitarian and authoritarian behavioural patterns still play a crucial role at all levels, and a social climate or civic culture characterized by active citizens bound together by reciprocity and co-operation, trust and tolerance, is missing in Russia. The dilemma is once again created by the fact that the underdevelopment of Russian civil society hinders the creation of a genuine democratic system and thus prevents the process of natural modernization that should receive its impulses from below.

Some protagonists in the *zapadnik* discourse still place their hopes in the activity of the Russian 'middle class'. They believe that this class will either form a union at the level of civil society and put forward a strategy for economic and political modernization, representing the interests of the majority of citizens, or that a far-sighted political leader will appeal to and find support from this group, thus laying the ground for a constitutional state with a genuine civil society. If neither of these alternatives transpire, then eventually everything will start all over again.

However, at this point in the narrative, the *zapadnik* modernization discourse is often taken to its extreme, almost paradoxical, limit.

Belief in a gradual, unforced democratization through an emerging political civil society has been largely abandoned within the contemporary *zapadnik* discourse. Instead, it reckons that the problem – the absence of a proper civil society – should be solved by the process of modernization led by the unified elite under an effective, integrating ideology. This view emphasizes authoritarianism as the best strategy for the transition period. According to this view, in Russian conditions, the elite functions, and should function again as the subject of modernization. The motor of the development of Russia must be a responsible elite, synonymous with the state, which can formulate clear strategies and realize them, while remaining receptive to ideas coming from below. This positive attitude towards authoritarianism is based on a clear distinction between authoritarianism and totalitarianism. In contrast to totalitarianism, authoritarianism upholds the autonomy of individuals and society in non-political spheres of life; whereas totalitarianism penetrates all spheres of life, authoritarianism concentrates on governance of the state and does not interfere in the everyday life of citizens. Authoritarianism is therefore closer to democracy than to totalitarianism, and Russia has to make an optimal choice in favour of the kind of authoritarian model that furthers the emergence of a constitutional state and opposes attempts to turn the clock back. There is an organic interrelationship between economic modernization and the development of civil society, and therefore authoritarianism should take a form, which is characterized by a special attention paid to the creation of the necessary conditions for modernization, such as a functioning civil society.

EURASIAN CULTURE AND GEOPOLITICS

I have mainly described the development of *zapadnik* ideas through the past two centuries. Indeed, it has been the different variations of the basically *zapadnik* ideas, committed to universal and linear progress – be it a conservative, liberal, or communist version – that have constituted the hegemonic trend in Russian political thought. Yet the *slavophile* and *particularist* traditions have been constantly alive too. In its *panslavistic* version, as articulated especially by Nikolai Danilevskii toward the end of the nineteenth century, the slavophile tradition emphasized the competition of rival 'cultural-historical types', and especially the inevitability of the replacement of the old European culture by the power of a younger, more dynamic Russian culture.[14] Many later developments of the Russian idea – especially the teaching of *eurasianism*, a geographically and culturally enlarged, eastward-oriented conception of Russian space, compared to that of Danilevskii – have further developed this particularistic, culture-centric world picture together with its immanent anti-Westernism.

Classical eurasianism[15] as articulated by Trubetskoi, Savitskii, and others formulated its ideology and political programs in the 1920s and 1930s in exile. The debt to the slavophile tradition was acknowledged, but only in terms of praising the world-wide importance of Russia's cultural tradition. The *narodnik* orientation of the slavophiles, their appeal to the peasant culture and people, their organic hostility to the creative bloom and flood of Russian economic forces, was seen as an obstacle to the abolition of the economic primitiveness of Russia. In this sense some aspects of the *zapadnik* orientation's aim to 'catch up with the West' were accepted. At the same time, eurasianism can be seen from the very beginning as entailing a sharp criticism of Western culture and the proclamation of an alternative.

The core idea was that Eurasia (and not the Slavic world) is connected by geographical, psychological, historical, and cultural interdependence. Geographically, it was its own continental entity and formed an especially huge territory that belonged to neither the east nor the west. The Eurasians had their own psychological base, reflected in the synthetic unity in religious basic principles, norms of behavior, arts, and political systems. Characteristic of this psychology was the power of the absolute over the momentous, the priority of belief over pragmatism that gives the spiritual preference over material life, and manifests the superiority of the collectivist lifestyle over individualism. This geographical and psychological sense of community was rooted in history, with sometimes the Huns functioning as the integrating power, at others the Mongols. The Mongols by no means subjugated Eurasia, as the traditional conception of history claimed. On the contrary, in creating a strong and unified system they saved it

14 N.Ia. Danilevskii, *Rossiia i Evropa. Vzgliad na kul'turniaia i politicheskaia otnosheniia Slavianskogo mira k Germano-Romanskomu* (Saint Petersburg, 1888 [1869]).

from the aggressive designs of Western culture, and after the Mongols, the Muscovite state took on the same function in creating its imperium. Thus, Russian history, the argument went, did not begin with Kiev's hegemony, interrupted temporarily by the Mongol period; instead, Russia should be seen as a direct political successor of the Mongols. This common Eurasian geographic affinity together with a shared mentality and common history led finally to a common cultural and spiritual basis, where religion plays a great role. However, among the Eurasian peoples one can find Orthodox believers, Muslims and Buddhists. These religions share pervasive moral-ethical principles, with the Orthodox religion functioning as the prime conductor of a synthesis of parts.

Classical eurasianism was unable to extend its influence to the domestic sphere of Soviet life, but instead petered out in internal disputes before the Second World War. Despite this, eurasianism has entered a renaissance in the 1990s, and this time inside Russia. Its success and the enormous interest in its ideas has been explained by the claim that it filled the vacuum created by the social-genetic processes in Russia, and that it was natural that eurasianist concepts and ideas would come in to their own because of the failure of Western-minded Russian reformers, who were trying to implant mechanisms in Russia that were conceived and developed by and for a different civilization.

Neo-eurasianism[16] can be seen simply as rediscovery of classical eurasianism coupled with its adaptation to new circumstances within post-communist Russia. However, in a way it too grew up inside the Soviet system, though not in the form of the transformation of the whole society, as the leftist eurasianists of the 1920s and 1930s had thought in their optimistic scenarios. A closer look at the ideas of L.N.Gumilev, a Soviet historian and ethnologist who made his contribution mainly during the three last decades of the Soviet Union and was one of the leading figures in the renaissance of eurasianism in Russian political thought, is illustrative especially in understanding the eurasianist concept of the interrelationship of space and time.

15 For a detailed discussion, see Christer Pursiainen, *Eurasianism and Neo-Eurasianism: the Past, Present, and Postmodernity of a Russian Integration Ideology.* UPI Working Papers 5 (1998) (Helsinki: The Finnish Institute of International Affairs).
16 Pursiainen, *Eurasianism and Neo-Eurasianism,* op. cit.

According to Gumilev, the problem of classical eurasianism was that its representatives could not link the humanistic sciences to the natural sciences. If the eurasianist doctrine was a synthesis of history and geography – or geopolitics – then Gumilev saw himself as a proponent of the synthesis of history, geography, and the natural sciences. The goal of Gumilev's theorizing[17] is basically the same as that of any civilization theory: to describe and explain the development of world cultures or civilizations. Gumilev asserts that in understanding history the first parameter is space, the second is time, and the third parameter is constituted by nations or ethnoses. Ethnoses, living in space and time, are the collective actors of the theatre of history. Ethnoses are not born simultaneously but at different times and therefore have different historical destinies and characters, in much the same way that the course of a person's life shapes the character of that individual. Ethnos is not tantamount to society. In ethnoses, history, geography, and biosphere are intermingled; they constitute a phenomenon which is located between the biosphere and sociosphere. The largest unit after humankind is the superethnos, that is, a group of ethnoses which are born fairly simultaneously in the same space, a kind of a mosaic wholeness, and the ethnoses in turn can be divided into subethnoses, small groups which differ from each other in terms of their language, sometimes in terms of religion, and even sometimes in their way of life, but always in terms of their behavioural stereotypes. Just as an atom is composed of molecules, ethnoses are made up of subethnoses, and superethnoses of ethnoses. Thus, unlike in the narratives of the slavophiles or many contemporary civilization theorists, such as Samuel Huntington, in Gumilev's eurasianism neither race, nor religion, but historically constructed behavioural stereotypes are seen as the decisive element in defining the borderlines between cultures.

Gumilev's main point of departure is the notion that ethnoses and superethnoses are not perpetual. All systems of wholeness are temporal; they flourish and they collapse. This course of history Gumilev describes and explains by his ethnogenesis theory. Ethnogenesis is an ongoing process, which results in the birth of new ethnoses and superethnoses. Ethnogenesis needs energy. In the very

. . . . .
17 Gumilev has presented his general theory of ethnogenesis in L.N. Gumilev, *Etnogenez i biosfera Zemli* (Moskva: Taias, 1994). The study was already prepared by the end of 1970s, but its first printed version was published over ten years later.

first phases of the development of ethnoses, in tribes, for instance, all energy can be used in the internal processes of the system. But at some point there will be a surplus of energy. Here Gumilev comes to the concept of 'passionarity' which is the 'x-factor' of his ethnogenetic theory – the variable which explains the development of ethnogenesis. Gumilev's concept originates from the Latin word *passio*, and in one connection he mentions that its English equivalent might be 'drive'. The essence of passionarity is an understanding that the secret of human life is not in living as such, but in living for something. A human being needs ideals, even those which can often be only illusions or even harmful to the individual protagonist. Passionarity on the general level is manifested in the form of systems; it is not individual actors who make momentous feats, rather it is the general tension in ethnoses, the 'passionaric tension' – in sharp contrast to peaceful indifference, or to philistinism – which brings about great feats and changes.

Gumilev explains the appearance of passionarity in the struggle for existence by referring to the mutation in evolution theories, to a sudden mutation in genetic codes. The passionarity of an ethnogenetic process is created by mutation which gives the first push, a new group of people whose enthusiasm and propensity for action are higher than those of others. Gumilev calls these kinds of people 'passionists'. They strive to and are capable of affecting their surroundings, of creating an organism which in turn can create a great energy. In creating a culture passionarity plays the role of a 'motor', and a passionist is not only an executor but an organizer. Over time, the level of passionarity does not remain constant: ethnos and superethnos once created follow law-like phases which can be compared with the phases of human age. The level of passionarity is the explanatory factor of these phases.

When applying the ethnogenesis theory to Russia[18], one must, according to Gumilev, distinguish between the ancient and later history of Russia. Kiev's Russia, *Rus'*, was the end of one ethnogenetic process. In contrast to the passionaric Mongols, the energy of Kiev was fading, which explains the rise of the Mongols. Muscovite Russia then entered a new ethnogenetic process during which a new superethnos was created. The first passionaric push took place

---

18 From this point of view, the best source is L.N. Gumilev, *Ot Rusi do Rossii* (Moscow, 1995). The study was first printed in 1992.

simultaneously in different areas around the year 1200. Until about 1380 there was an *obscure phase of rise*, and after that until about 1500 there was a *clear phase of rise*. During this period the Russian superethnos began to take shape. However, the period between 1500–1800 was the actual phase of the development of the Russian superethnos; it was the *acmatic phase* during which Russia absorbed the Eurasian nations from the Pacific Ocean to the Baltic Sea. In the general ethnogenetic process it represents the vertical apex of passionaric tension, and no longer expresses the striving of the people to create a wholeness, but a reach for self-awareness and self-realization. Its course is cut usually because of its internal logic: when passionaric development within a superethnos is at its highest, internal rivalry becomes widespread and the people physically exhaust each other, among other things through frequent civil wars. The process of ethnogenesis is slowed down, a greater sluggish development in the opposite direction takes place, and a gradual stagnation and disintegration of the superethnos begins in which the level of passionarity gradually decreases. For Russia, this *phase of breaking*, or the *phase of disintegration*, started especially after 1812, and today Russia is near the end of this phase. Russia still has, however, ahead of her the *phase of inertia* – 300 years of golden autumn, a harvest time and a period of reaping ripe fruits, and building a great unique culture.

Gradually, passionarity passes and fades away. There then follows that kind of degenerating phase of ethnogenesis that comes close to what Oswald Spengler called civilization, a phase of moving from a culture embodied by philosophy and spiritual values to soulless materialistic civilization. In Gumilev's terms this is the *dim phase* when the final erosion of a superethnic system becomes irrevocable. When the sum of the system's energy becomes low, the leading position in society is grabbed by sub-passionists, people who's grade of passionarity is especially low. Finally, the *memorial phase* follows. After that new passionaric efforts are possible but they will initiate a new process, the creation of a new and different civilisation, although not necessary limited to the same area.

Now, we should remember that according to Gumilev there exist simultaneously several superethnoses in the world, which, however, are at different stages in their development in relation to each other. The present Eurasian superethnos, which is the result of the ethnogenetic process that started about 800 years ago, is at the same time 500 years younger than the western, Roman-Germanic, or West European superethnos, the contemporary geographical enlargement of which is the United States. The age of Western civilization is approximately 1,300 years, and if we apply this to Gumilev's theory of passionaric tension, the West is quickly approaching the end of the *dim period*, which is characterized by the lazy and egoistic administration of subpassionists, breaking away with ideas, and the hegemony of consumption psychology, and after the subpassionists have extinguished what was stored from the heroic period, this civilization enters into a *memorial phase*.

Referring to perestroika and its foreign policy doctrine, 'new political thinking', which emphasised the common destiny of the world, Gumilev condemns[19] these stances by saying that all talk about the universal history of humanity is absurd, and theory of universal values is naïve, because as long as there are different levels of passionarity in different superethnoses, history will remain ethnically dominated and no hyperethnos can be developed. Therefore, according to Gumilev, the effort to fulfill the transition into the phase of inertia within the frames of Russia's own ethnogenetic process is the only natural and right way. At the same time, it is the last and only possibility, because if a superethnos does not manage to go through this transition, it collapses as a system and its parts will be assimilated into other superethnoses.

The dimensions of the immanent anti-Westernism of contemporary eurasianism are more clearly articulated by A.S. Panarin, in particular, in his more (post)modern and politicized version of this teaching.[20] The West becomes the object of criticism due to its will to westernize, to interrupt the immanent, natural development of other cultures. However, because of the crucial differences in the very points of departure, mechanisms that work well in the West do not work in other cultures within the settings of totally different traditions. Moreover, according to Panarin, Western civilization proclaims political pluralism as an internal value, but does not stand for pluralism outside itself; it implies that the whole world should be Westernized. Yet, at the same time, Panarin says, the West closes the door in the face of most countries; only a chosen minority is allowed

- - - - -

19   See especially L.N. Gumilev, V.Iu.Ermolaev, 'Gore ot illiuzii', in Gumilev, *Ritmy Evrazii: epokhi i tsivilizatsii* (Moscow, 1993), pp. 174–200.
20   See especially A.S. Panarin, *Politologiia. Uchebnik* (Moscow, 1997); Panarin, 'Vtoraia Evropa ili Tretiy Rim' (Paradoksy evropeizma v sovremennoi Rossii), *Voprosy Filosofii* 10/1996, pp. 19-31; Panarin, 'Evraziiskii proekt v mirosistemnom kontekste', *Vostok*, 1995, No. 2, pp. 66–79.

to reach the post-industrial stage of society. Russia is not among them. Panarin admits that although the West accepts and respects multi-culturality in the world at the level of culturological knowledge, in the form of foreign policy expansion, instead, the West appears as an authoritarian structure reacting aggressively every time it collides with non-Western nations that insist on their own national values.

This aggressive nature of the West motivates Panarin's version of the 'Eurasian project'. His Eurasianism departs from the understanding that the fate of the post-industrial epoch depends on the destiny of Russia. According to Panarin, in the event that Russia adopts the status of a Third Rome as Muscovite Russia did after the Mongol period, there will be a chance for the post-industrial epoch to avoid becoming the world-wide industrial ghetto, which is antagonistic to culture and nature. But unless Russia bids farewell to Americanism and stops imitating the West, it is probable that the post-industrial world culture will be a single level culture, on the level of technocracy. The mission of Russia and the emerging Eurasian power will be to protect the multidimensional character of the world, to save it from the threat of Americanism. According to Panarin, civilizing pluralism and a creative dialogue of world cultures is possible only in a multipolar world, where the West has no hegemony.

MISSION BEYOND SPACE

Zapadnik tradition links the destiny of Russia to the development of universal world history. The tradition of slavophilism is particularistic, and is rooted in the Russian past. Panslavist and eurasianist teachings connect culture-centric development with the idea that Russia is a potential opposite to the deteriorating West. The teachings of Vladimir Solovev of the late nineteenth century, which constituted the basis for the this century's Russian religious and idealistic metaphysics, can in turn be described as Christian humanism and a development of slavophilist tradition towards universalism. Solovev had arrived at 'absolute' idealism's adaptation to religious philosophy via Schelling and Hegel. To Solovev, Christianity was not only an individual experience, it was closely connected to universal social progress. The message of Christianity was that it lit the way which humankind was to walk by itself in order to rediscover its freedom as well as its ties between nature, man and God. The historical development in Solovev's philosophy of history comprised three stages: the Church, the Christian state and, finally, a common brotherhood of love. At the end of the path *'bogochelovechestvo'*, Godhumanity or Divinitykind, was dimly visible. The world envisioned by Solovev was a kind of universal non-institutional church, which connects humanity and divinity, creates the kingdom of God on Earth. All this presupposed, according to Solovev, the unification of the Eastern church, that managed to preserve the divine nature of humankind, and the Western world, which embodied the essence of humanity.[21]

Berdiaev, who created his own philosophy at the beginning of this century in Russia and later in exile, based his existential version of the Russian idea above all on Solovev's teaching. From our point of view, the most important of the ideas that Berdiaev adopted from Solovev's philosophy of history was connecting universal social development with the progress of Christianity, and, at the same time, seeing the role of Russia (the East) as crucial in enabling this development. From Dostoevskii, in turn, Berdiaev absorbed the concept of a dualism of the Russian spirit, a meeting of extremes, and through this the possibility of a synthesis of the natural mission of Russia. Russia is basically feminine, while masculinity is characteristic of Western Europe. While femininity, and so passivity, is a part of the Russian nature, masculinity, or activity, is foreign to Russia. It is still needed, though, but is expected to come from outside. This typically Russian exotic mixture of femininity with a longing for masculinity from the West accounts for the fact that in Russia, unlike other countries, bureaucratic statehood arises from anarchy, slavery is born out of freedom, and crude nationalism grows from universal humanity. In his work from the period of the First World War, Berdiaev sees the war as a means to break this vicious circle. The war can, he argues, wake up the true masculinity in Russia, it can show the world Russia's manly face, provide a missing link between the European East and the European West. To fulfill its universal task Russia cannot lean on slavophilist or *zapadnik* ideals alone. Instead, it has to find both sides within itself – east and west, femininity and masculinity.[22]

21 See especially V.S. Solovev, 'Chteniya o bogochelovechestve', in Solovev, *Sochineniia* (Moscow, 1994), pp. 13-168. A good introduction to Solovev's, and also Berdiaev's, thinking is Assen Ignatow, *Solowjow und Berdjajev als Geschichtsphilosophen. Ideen und aktueller Einfluss* (Köln: Berichte des Bundesinstituts für ostwissenschaftliche und internationale Studien 3–1997).
22 See especially Nikolai Berdiaev, 'Dusha Rossii', in Berdiaev, *Sudba Rossii. Opyty po psikhologii voiny i natsional'nosti* (Moscow, 1990, first printed in 1918 in Sankt-Petersburg).

When Berdiaev places universal mission at the highest point of the realization of the Russian idea and soul, he, in a way, develops Solovev's thinking in a more concrete direction. But these theories by Solovev and Berdiaev, in fact, only repeat the underlying arguments of the majority of works within Russian philosophical and political tradition. It is a widely shared view[23] that it has always been typical for Russian philosophy to cherish future utopias, to ascribe to Russia as its task and mission not only the destiny of Russia, but the fate of all humanity. According to this line of thinking, the peculiarities of Russian national psychology provide possibilities for Russia to accept this portentous mission. Thus, in the philosophical tradition of the Russian idea this dualistic thesis of Russia's universal task is widely spread. On the one hand the role of Russia is to save the West, especially from spiritual crisis. Without Russia's spiritual contribution the world is not 'whole', nor is it 'universal'. On the other hand, Russia can become the true Russia only through its connection to the West. Boris Grois, the representative of Russian postmodern philosophy, has remarked that this theme of Hegelian dialectic's materialization has charmed Russian thinking from the very beginning. Grois finds the same idea in Russian thought reappearing: the West is consciousness, reality, Russia is sub-consciousness; Russia is spirit, and the West is body, they are a woman and a man, whose cosmic marriage is possible only in Russia. Russia is the culmination of the Western Eros, the place to make Western fantasies of final synthesis a true, mystic-erotical ecstasy and sexual act, the view that had been blocked by the logic-dominated western civilization. According to Grois, this same refrain can be traced in slavophilist, *zapadnik* and religious philosophers' thinking, as well as in the thinking of Lenin, and Stalin.[24]

In present day Russian political thought it is not difficult to find strands of this sort of view. The most consistent example that applies Berdiaev's ideas in particular in the contemporary political sphere can perhaps be found in the texts of Sergei Kortunov.[25] According to him, nations are only phenomena of a transition period, a temporary phase

. . . . .

23 Already Berdiaev's contemporary, G.G. Shpet, for instance, advanced this claim in his 1922 analysis of Russian philosophy. See G.G. Shpet, 'Ocherk razvitiia russkoi filosofii', in A.I Vvedenskii, A.F. Losev, E.L.Rablov, *Russkaia filosofiia. Ocherki istorii* (Sverdlovsk, 1991), pp. 217–578, here p. 259.
24 Boris Grois, 'Rossiia kak podsoznanie Zapada', in Grois, *Utopiia i obmen* (Moscow, 1993), pp. 245–259, here p. 257.
25 Sergei Kortunov, *Rossiia: Natsional'naia identichnost' na rubezhe vekov* (Moscow, 1997).

in the development of ethnoses towards global and planetarian integration. However, this integrative mission needs a capable subject. Kortunov claims that Russia has all the qualities that are needed for the subject. Therefore, the historical mission of the Russian people, its *supermission* lies on the spiritual level, and it is the creating of an *interculture*. These messianic aspirations, that arise from the 'global universalism of Eastern Christianity', do not imply antagonism with the West, rather an alternative way of development for the West, as well. Western modernization knows subject but not dialectics, and therefore only Russia can bring the needed spirit into the technological post-industrial epoch. It is exactly Russia, with her centuries-old surface contact with all the other great cultures, that can bridge the gap between Europe, America, and the Asian-Pacific areas.

The West is naturally not ready to bestow Russia with the mission of creating the 'interculture'. In Kortunov's thinking, however, there is also the idea that the West will eventually reach the understanding that Russia is the place, or the mirror, in which the West can see its own perspectives, its diseases. But Russia is not a 'waste container' for the West, rather a 'cleaner', indeed it is a 'subsurface drainage' of the West. By closing this drainage, by hating Russia, the West also kills itself and the whole universe. Earlier, Kortunov claims, the West understood this, but today, in the euphoria of the victory of liberal values, the West has forgotten the all-human History and Culture. Nevertheless, even if without Russia the West has no Big Problem, it has no Great Culture, no Great Politics, and no Great History either. Kortunov's message is that without Russia there is no universe; Russia is the 'existential essence' of the world.

IN LIEU OF A CONCLUSION: CRIME, PUNISHMENT, AND THE POSSIBILITY OF REDEMPTION

According to an essay written by Nikolai Gogol in the 1840s, the *zapadniks* came so close in their criticism of the Russian reality that they were able to see only part of it. As in looking at a building, the part they could see they saw very accurately, but because of the overhang that decorates the wall, they could not see the top, the apex, the dome of the building, anything which does not stand further out.

The slavophiles, in their turn, went too far and could see only the facade but not the details. Gogol asked whether it would be possible to find the same language and scale, a common point of departure, and perhaps a compromise between the extreme views. He therefore advised the slavophiles to try to come closer, as time goes on, and the *zapadniks* to step a little further back.

However, as I have tried to show, this search for a common yardstick or scale for measuring Russia's past, present, and future resulted in even more bitter dissension. Gogol's own thoughts on the future of Russia also remained an unsettled dilemma. As is well known, *Dead Souls* ends with the absurd climax of Chichikov leaving the provincial capital N.N. The perspective shifts from the swindler to his troika-carriage, that flies through the step at a crazy speed; a reader moves aside together with other viewers, left to inhale the dust. Dostoevskii had a character of his remark that if Gogol's troika were hitched up to his own heroes, the Sobakeviches, the Nozdrevs, or the Chichikovs, then one would not get very far at all with that lot, whoever was the driver. However, we do know that Gogol had a solution in mind for Russia's future, similar to the one Dostoevskii had with regard to Raskolnikov. Gogol meant to augment Crime with Punishment and Redemption, to show that with the help of good people and through confessing his sins Chichikov will finally achieve piety and peace. But Gogol burned the last part of his *Dead Souls*. He destroyed his work of many years after realising, as Nabokov put it, 'in a final blinding flash of artistic truth' that no real improvement was possible for Chichikov.

Considering all this one and a half centuries later, one might once again ask whether the dominant direction of thought and practice in Russia will be Being instead of Becoming, whether spatial thinking will ultimately shadow time and progress. If so, will it be expressed in geopolitics rather than localisation, nationalism rather than regionalisation? Or perhaps it is this endless debate without common yardsticks, a postmodernist heterogenity, a lack of hierarchy and an absence of shared meanings that constitute the obscure space called Russia.

Heaven, Hell, Or ... Something in Between? Contrasting Russian Images of Siberia

Paul Fryer

Upon the mention of Siberia, the Asian part of the Russian Federation stretching from the Ural mountains to the Pacific Ocean, the image most often brought to mind is instilled with uncertainty and mystery. While the foreign perception of this vast 'space' may be accounted for by an almost total isolation from the region over the past 80 years of Soviet power, there are many starkly contrasting popular perceptions of Siberia in Russia itself, an odd combination of facts and fantasies, a product of both the former Soviet propaganda machine and of Russian literature's historical and contemporary portrayal of it. For the indigenous non-Russian inhabitants of Siberia, the sense of place is much clearer, though arguably the image is of the local surroundings – Eremei Aipin vividly recounts in his writings the Khanty's Siberian 'space' along the tributaries of the Ob' River in Western Siberia, while the Siberia of the Chukchi that Iurii Rytkheu represents is centred in Beringia.[1] Examples of Siberian tundra and taiga landscapes as

---

1 See, for example, Eremei Aipin, *Khanty, ili Zvezda Utrennei Zari* (Moscow, 1990), and Iurii Rytkheu, 'Irvytgyr, ili puteshestvie vo vremeni i prostranstve po Beringovu Prolivu', *Neva*, 1980, No.5, 49–110. An interesting critique of Rytkheu and his works is presented in Adele Barker, 'The Divided Self: Yuri Rytkheu and Contemporary Chukchi Literature' in Galya Diment and Yuri Slezkine (eds.), *Between Heaven and Hell: The Myth of Siberia in Russian Culture*. (New York, 1993), pp.215–226; A detailed history of aboriginal Siberia is found in James Forsyth, *A History of the Peoples of Siberia*. (Cambridge, 1992).

conceived by aboriginal writers can often be found in the journal for northern indigenous peoples, *Severnye prostory* – the aptly-named *Northern expanses*. Yet the majority Russian population, despite it figuring so prominently in Russian popular culture, continues to hold on to several contradictory images of Siberia, most often 'Othered' in terms of a 'Heaven-Hell' dichotomy.[2] In this paper, these two mutually exclusive 'romantic' themes will be explored, though it will also be suggested that an alternative can also be seen – one often constructed by Siberians themselves – and one that I will refer to as 'Home'.

SIBERIA THE ENTITY

By its very nature, the perception and conceptualising of the unknown, a process of mentally constructing an 'Other', implies a certain amount of subjectivity: the attributing of certain characteristics or qualities to something specific, yet foreign. As a result of this subjectivity, the end product may or may not be accurate, reached through the observations of others more often than not themselves without first-hand experience of the subject. There can exist as many mental images as there are individuals, though usually it is possible to observe some commonalities within the same occupational, gender, cultural, or ethnic groups.

This can be observed of Russian society in terms of Siberia, an important region if for no other reason than its vastness. Its total territory extends for 12,766,000 square kilometres, accounting for 74.8% of the Russian, and some 9% of the world's total land area.[3] This reality has led some sociologists to conclude that Russian culture has been a product of a 'northern' landscape – with Siberia the significant part of the Russian North.[4] Beyond the geographical

. . . . .
2 A dichotomy plainly represented in Galya Diment and Yuri Slezkine (eds.), *Between Heaven and Hell: The Myth of Siberia in Russian Culture* (New York, 1993).
3 Paul E. Lydolph, *Geography of the USSR*. 5th edition. (Elkhart Lake, WI., 1990).
4 Grigorii Agranat, 'Sever: zalozhnik i zhertva', *Svobodnaia mysl'*, 1998, No.1 (ianvar'), p.64; Tat'iana Iensen, 'Geografiia dushi', *Severnye prostory*, 1992, Nos.7–8 (iiul'-avgust), p.40; Franklyn Griffiths, 'The Arctic in the Russian Identity' in W. Brigham Lawson, ed., *The Soviet Maritime Arctic*. (Annapolis,

position of Russia in the northern hemisphere, a historical basis can also be established for this claim. Beginning in the seventh century, tribes from Central and East Asia swept across the Urals into the homeland of the early Slavs, forcing a migration northwards into the northern taiga. By the eleventh century, Slavs had reached the White Sea and, by the thirteenth, were trading with Western Siberia. By the end of the period of Asian occupation known as the 'Tatar' or 'Mongol Yoke', the formation of a distinct Russian culture had begun to form, for which the northern 'forests, lakes, rivers and snow-covered and icy expanses all acquired collective meaning...'[5]

Ermak's much-glorified expedition to and conquest of Siberia that began in 1581[6] opened up the territory to Russian colonisation, though the population has remained concentrated along the southern edge of the territory and had somewhat stabilised at 31,777,000, or 21.4% of the Russian total in 1996.[7] This figure is surprisingly low if one acknowledges that Siberia has played a significant role in Russian history, that Russian culture has a northern character, and that the region itself comprises such a large part of the country's land mass. Yet in reality this fact reflects the vastly contrasting images of Siberia, demonised and often mythologised by a Russian public blinded by the almost schizophrenic 'Heaven-Hell' image that exists, while overlooking another variant forwarded by a few. This latter 'grey-area', as a third alternative, does not quite fit into the over-simplified 'good-evil', 'black-white', or 'rich-poor' space constructed by the majority.

SIBERIA: A LAND OF NIGHTMARES

Ever since its first discovery, Siberia was foremost a place to be feared, and since has often been conceptualised as a virtual 'Hell' on earth. This mental image built out of fear is comprised of a number of

---

MD, 1991) p.85. For several geographical, historical, and socio-economic reasons, the Arctic and sub-Arctic lands of European Russia are often lumped together with Siberia in literature, referred to simply as Russia's 'North' or the 'Northeast'. Throughout, I have attempted to focus strictly on Siberia, though in many cases it is impossible to distinguish between the two areas.
5   Griffiths, p.81.
6   See Benson Bobrick, *East of the Sun* (London, 1992).
7   Goskomstat Rossii, *Demograficheskii ezhegodnik Rossii: statisticheskii sbornik* (Moscow, 1996), pp.26, 28.

different elements. Fundamentally, Siberia's vastness and remoteness from the early and greater Russian centres of 'civilisation' and 'progressive culture' has bred terror – a fear of the profane and unknown. The physical landscape itself contributes to this fear, as seemingly impenetrable taiga and vacant tundra wastelands cover the majority of the region, often attributed with the epic quality of 'continent'.[8] As the well-known Siberian writer Valentin Rasputin observes, the natural forces that have created this vast territory not only inspire awe, but also repel and frighten humans.[9] For centuries, Siberia was also the source of nomadic invaders who destroyed the early Slavic settlements. Consequently, these unknown tribes inhabiting Siberia contributed to the perception of fear. In his monumental poem 'Bratsk Station', Russian poet Evgenii Evtushenko laments Russia's trials at the hands of these Asiatic marauders, the 'Pechenegs' and 'Tatars',[10] uncivilised and uncultured 'pagans' that later would draw Orthodox missionaries east to bring about their enlightenment.[11] Russians could only guess at the uncertain horrors and violence that remained in Siberia, an image remaining until the present.

The Russian image of Hell has also been drawn from the often merciless Siberian climate. This is not surprising, as temperatures in the heart of Siberia can reach -70° Celsius, and the mean annual temperature is only 0° Celsius. Two-thirds of the area is covered by a layer of permafrost, a continuously frozen soil that annoys and thwarts the best of modern engineering, and Arctic ports are cut off as the seas and rivers remain frozen for up to ten months a year, a result of the long, cold winters.[12] This 'inhuman' climate has been recreated countless times in Russian literature, resulting in a mental vision of Siberia as a world 'forsaken by God', constantly blasted by ice and

---

8   The comparison to the discovery of the Americas by Columbus (see Stephen Watrous, 'The Regionalist Conception of Siberia, 1860 to 1920' in Diment and Slezkine (eds.) *Between Heaven and Hell...* pp.113–132) also finds a place in Bruce Lincoln's, *The Conquest of a Continent: Siberia and the Russians* (London, 1993).
9   As quoted in Griffiths, p.99.
10 Evgeny Evtushenko 'Bratsk Station', in *Bratsk Station and Other New Poems*. Garden City, NY, 1967), P.25.
11 See Yuri Slezkine, 'Savage Christians or Unorthodox Russians? The Missionary Dilemma in Siberia' in Diment and Slezkine (eds.) *Between Heaven and Hell...*pp. 15–31.
12 Alan Wood, 'Introduction: Siberia's Role in Russian History' in Alan Wood, (ed.), *The History of Siberia* (London, 1991), pp.1–16.

snow. There are countless passages from writers such as Fedor Dostoevskii and Anatolii Rybakov (to name but two) describing this frozen Hell, though Aleksandr Solzhenitsyn's *One Day in the Life of Ivan Denisovich* makes the point vividly:

> The cold stung. A murky fog wrapped itself round Shukhov and made him cough painfully. The temperature out there was -27 degrees; Shukhov's temperature was +37 degrees. The fight was on.[13]

Siberia is seen as requiring a constant struggle against the elements, and it is this battle that many Russians fear.

Yet the image of Siberia as a place of exile and imprisonment is perhaps the most prevailing stereotype in the Hell construct. Beginning in 1593 and lasting until this century, Moscow used Siberia as a place of exile for its political opponents and as a 'natural' prison for criminals, and was the most-favoured destination for the victims of Stalin's campaign of terror in the modern era An early and most famous example of these unfortunates were the Decembrists, and Russia's greatest poet, Aleksandr Pushkin, immortalised them in his poems 'Arion' and 'Message to Siberia'. This group of young army officers, whose 1825 revolt opposed the monarchy in favour of democratic reform, became an inspiration to the Russian revolutionary movement and is seen in popular culture as symbolic of the Russian nation's suffering under a series of absolutist and corrupt regimes.[14] By the mid-1800s, there were more 'criminals' and political prisoners entering Siberia than peasant settlers,[15] and a lasting image of Siberian exile under the Tsars has been impressed on Russian society by Fedor Dostoevskii's terrifying autobiographical tale, *Memoirs from the House of the Dead*.

The Siberian exile system was given a horrific new life under Iosif Stalin, who sent millions of ordinary Soviet citizens to exile, hard labour, and death in the notorious GULAG[16] camps of Siberia. After the terror of Stalin's rule, this period remains one of the most painful and vivid in the collective memory of the Russian people.[17] Exile in

. . . . .

13 Aleksandr Solzhenitsyn, *One Day in the Life of Ivan Denisovich* (Harmondsworth, UK, 1987), p.23.
14 Leonid Shinkarev, *The Land Beyond the Mountains* (New York, 1973), pp. 63-4.
15 Nikolaus Poppe, 'The Economic and Cultural Development of Siberia', in George Katkov, (ed.), *Russia Enters the Twentieth Century* (London, 1971), p.141.
16 GULAG, or Main Administration of Camps (*Glavnoe upravlenie lagerei*).
17 Veniamin Alekseev, *Siberia in the 20th Century* (Moscow, 1989), p.18.

modern times has been recorded in Russian literature in *One Day in the Life of Ivan Denisovich*, Varlam Shalamov's *Kolyma Tales*, and in Anatolii Rybakov's *Children of the Arbat* and *Fear*. Through works such as these, Siberia has become synonymous with exile, conceptualised as a frozen prison that rivals the tortures of Hades. Together or separately, these physical, climactic, and historical factors have contributed to a picture present in many Russians' minds of Siberia as Hell on earth.

SIBERIA: A GOLDEN EDEN

Despite this fearful image, Siberia has also found an idealised place in Russian culture as a paradise, a 'heaven' in many forms. To be sure, Siberia has often been the country's 'treasure chest', a frontier land of opportunity and natural riches that was conquered and bent to serve the individual and, more generally, the Russian nation. As James Gibson has outlined, social class had an influence in one's perception, and while the upper classes feared and despised the region, the lower peasant class saw opportunity, freedom and 'a fresh beginning' in Siberia.[18] In the early days of Siberia, a frontier mentality reigned in much the same way as in the American West, where people were, for the most part, unfettered by the state and able to own land. Many others were drawn in a spirit of adventure. This in mind, the frontier expanded in a quest '...to meet the sun',[19] an expression often used in describing Siberian history, instilled with the same emotions as the English expression 'to reach for the stars' – to go for everything, to attempt to obtain or achieve everything in one's dreams. Accounts of bold and reckless journeys and superhuman victories over 'wild' natives, beasts or the elements encouraged this,[20] and was later exploited and used by the Soviet state in its attempts to attract workers to develop Siberian resources.

. . . . .
18 James R. Gibson, 'Paradoxical Perceptions of Siberia: Patrician and Plebian Images up to the Mid-1880s' in Diment and Slezkine (eds.) *Between Heaven and Hell...*pp.67–93.
19 James R. Gibson, 'The Rush to Meet the Sun: An Essay on Russian Eastward Expansion', *Siberica*, 1990, Vol.1, No.1 (Summer), p.68; Bobrick, op. cit.
20 Griffiths, p.89.

As can be expected, a region of such an immense geographical size contains numerous and plentiful resources: the ever-expanding oil and gas fields of Tiumen' province, the coal deposits of the Kuznetsk Basin, and the most important of Russia's gold and diamond fields. Siberia alone contains more than half of Russia's raw material wealth, and much of Russia's foreign currency earnings from exports can be traced to the region.[21] Under the Soviets, Siberia's resources industrialised the state, supplied the country's industries during the period of forced isolation from world markets in the 1930s, and paid for the arms race. It is not surprising then, that Soviet press campaigns to draw labour to Siberia not only called upon the patriotism of its citizens, but also portrayed the region as one with inexhaustible resources ready for the taking, igniting imaginations and spirits of adventure with images of Siberian wilderness that could be and had to be broken and brought into production for the workers' state. These efforts led to thousands of Russians and other Soviet citizens streaming into Siberia to participate in the countless mega-projects from the 1930s onwards. Evtushenko's 'Bratsk Station' recounts and glorifies one of these projects, and reflects the almost mass religious zeal that the Russian people have held for expanding and conquering the Siberian frontier. Thus, the Russian perception of this 'golden fountain of resources'.[22]

Yet a deeper conceptualisation of the region that has been advanced by many writers constructs Siberia as 'salvation', or simply put as a 'Heaven'. Siberia has often been held as a sanctuary by the youth who came in their thousands in the second half of the twentieth century. Not only did the region provide a refuge away from the authority of older generations, but it also became their romantic dream, where youth believed they could play a role in constructing a new world for themselves.[23] The excitement and enthusiasm of Russian youth was encouraged by the state youth organisation, the *Komsomol*, which promised each person a hand in the building of the state and of their future. The *Komsomol*'s success in portraying this perception to Russian youth can be measured by the thousands making the move to Siberia to share in it. The city of Komsomol'sk-na-Amure in the Far East was named to commemorate this youthful fervour that helped to develop the region. Again, Evtushenko's 'Bratsk Station' describes just this very perception of youth's promised land.

21   *The Economist*, 21 November 1992, p.64.
22   Alekseev, p.58.
23   Idem, p.22.

Moreover, despite the region's history as a penal colony of Moscow, Siberia has also been seen as salvation, or as a 'beacon in the dark', for the persecuted. Beyond the reach of the governments in St. Petersburg and Moscow, the region's sparse settlement, slight development and loose administration suited those people who felt overcrowded and oppressed in European Russia.[24] Serfs fled their bondage for freedom in Siberia, and the hungry fled the famines in the 1920s and 1930s. In Russian literature, Iurii Zhivago fled east to the Urals for sanctuary from post-revolutionary chaos and dangers in Boris Pasternak's *Dr. Zhivago*. For religious sects, especially the Old Believers (*Staroobriadtsy*), the region became the proverbial promised land from persecution in Pharaoh's Egypt – in this case, Patriarch Nikon's post-church reform Russia.[25] Millions also fled to Siberian salvation from foreign invaders during the massive relocation undertaken during World War Two, as Russians, Ukrainians and Belarusans escaped the Nazis to relative security beyond the Urals. With these examples of Siberia offering salvation from persecution, it is no wonder that Russian society continues to hold such a mental image.

Most importantly, Siberia has often been perceived as Russia's salvation. The Orthodox Church has taught that the Russian people are God's chosen ones, and that the land in which they lived was similarly sacred. This holy place has consequently been constructed as the one last remaining Russian refuge from the outside world, one untainted by Western influences – namely Siberia. Both physically and spiritually, the endless and empty expanses of the Siberian tundra have been compared to the deserts of the Holy Land,[26] an inner Russian strength which inspires hope in the future of Mother Russia and of its children and which holds their salvation.[27] This spirituality is not a new phenomenon, as the sanctity of Siberia existed long before the coming of the Russians – the chants of shamans echoed throughout the landscape, and even today, sacred and taboo islands, woods, and territories continue to dot the country, coexisting and often blending with the Russian reality. Rasputin maintains that the

---

24 Bobrick, op. cit; Gibson, 'The Rush to Meet the Sun...'
25 See Bruce Holl, 'Avvakum and the Genesis of Siberian Literature' in Diment and Slezkine (eds.) *Between Heaven and Hell*...pp.33–45; Valentin Rasputin, 'Sibir', Sibir'...', *Nash sovremennik*, 1988, No.8, p.14; also the important memoirs of the schismatic and exiled Archpriest Avvakum.
26 Iensen, p.41
27 Shinkarev, p.233.

Russian way of life has been derived from and is sustained by the ancient Siberian landscape.[28] The natural beauty, majesty and vastness of Siberia uplifts the human spirit and bestows upon the chosen people, Russians, their greatness. Thus, salvation lies in this very natural environment which lends authentic meaning to the Russian existence. Aleksandr Solzhenitsyn echoes these sentiments, though also taking the opportunity to highlight this as a failing of the Soviet state:

> For half a century we have busied ourselves with world revolution, extending our influence over Eastern Europe and over other continents; ...with everything and anything, in fact, but developing and tending our country's chief asset, the Northeast. Our people are not going to live in space, or in Southeast Asia, or in Latin America: it is Siberia and the North that are our hope and our reservoir.[29]

In the reasoning of the 'salvationists', and in common with the views historically of the Slavophiles, what has made Russia great has been its differences from the West – and Moscow and European Russia have fallen too much under the sway of the West. Not only Solzhenitsyn and Rasputin, but many others continue to see Siberia as a last preserve of all of the good qualities of the Russian people – hard-working, simple, strong, and in harmony with God and nature. As Mehnert suggests, Siberia is 'the antithesis to the soulless urban civilisation',[30] a civilisation which was brought to Russia from the West by Peter the Great. For years Siberia did provide an earthly refuge or 'Heaven' for individuals and groups, and the implication is that Russia itself will be saved as long as the Siberia of old is not lost.

OUR HOME IS SIBERIA: REJECTING THE 'OTHER'

A common complaint of local Siberian inhabitants has been against the many Russians from over the Urals who came to the region with

---

28 Rasputin, 'Sibir', Sibir'...'; see also Griffiths, op. cit.
29 Aleksandr Solzhenitsyn, *Letter to the Soviet Leaders* (New York, 1974) pp.28-9.
30 Klaus Mehnert, *The Russians and Their Favourite Books* (Stanford, 1983) p.231.

no other intention than enriching themselves.[31] In the nineteenth century, this complaint spawned a Siberian *oblastnichestvo*, or regionalist movement led by the young Nikolai Iadrintsev, whose monograph *Sibir' kak koloniia* was a turning point in the way local Russians began to see themselves firstly as *Sibiriaki* – Siberians.[32] In the above-outlined constructed images of Siberia, this 'Heaven-Hell' dichotomy, Siberia is 'Othered' – objectified by those in Moscow and the European side of the Urals who have no real ties to the territory. Incredibly after over 400 years of inclusion in the Russian, then Soviet, Empires, Siberia has not come any closer to being really understood by Russians in the centre, understood for what these *Sibiriaki* have known and been attempting to convey for years – that above all else, Siberia is just another part of the country, a real, legitimate 'Home' not unlike elsewhere in Russia.

The regionalists under Iadrintsev were seeking to reject the colonial status of their home in the second half of the nineteenth century, in favour of something approaching the 'normality' found in other parts of the Empire – a university, local government, infrastructure. They were not seeking independence, or special rights, but just acceptance of their home, and in their writings, sought to show those in the centre and other inhabitants of Siberia that they were deserving of this.[33] Russians from Europe had constantly been using and exploiting the region, initially coming after the 'soft gold' of fur-bearing animals like the sable and fox, which led to the perception that the area could be harvested forever. This was embraced so enthusiastically that numerous animal species were almost killed off and left many parts of Siberia devoid of fur-bearers. The modern parallel to this has been the development of Siberia by the Soviets, and the reaction by local Siberians, especially writers like Rasputin, has been just as vehement in its denunciations. Locals attacked the centre for using Siberia as a place of exile and imprisonment, the imperial 'dumping ground' for the 'dregs' of society. A renewed regionalist movement can be seen in the post-Soviet rise and development of regional co-operation associations, such as the Siberian Accord, itself an attempt to give Siberia an equal, rather than a peripheral and 'Othered' role on the national stage much like Iadrintsev sought.

. . . . .

31 Dimitri Von Mohrenschildt, *Toward a United States of Russia* (East Brunswick, NJ, 1981), p.88.
32 N.M. Iadrintsev, *Sibir' kak koloniia v geograficheskom, etnograficheskom, i istoricheskom otnoshenii* (St. Petersburg, 1892).
33 See Watrous, op. cit.

It was especially in the latter part of this century that a rejection of the 'Heaven-Hell' stereotyping found a place among Siberian writers, part of the 'village prose' movement in Soviet literature.[34] David Gillespie suggests that in Borodin's novel *The Third Truth*, the author uses the conflict between the two central characters to illustrate a purely local situation, the 'Third Truth' of Siberia for its inhabitants.[35] This is not the 'truth' offered by outsiders, but instead something rooted in the Siberia of their childhood, innocent and free, but also turbulent and full of hardships. With the decline of post-Soviet Russia's economic fortunes, so too have those of Siberia. In record numbers, Russians are leaving the industrial centres of the far north,[36] a Russian 'exodus' of biblical scale, as living conditions deteriorate and the image of the Siberian 'heaven' fades into a reality of social and economic decay. To the *Sibiriaki*, the fact that these 'outsiders' are leaving supports their position – they came to Siberia with false impressions and never grew to see the land as what it really is – a home both harsh and cruel, but also rich and nurturing. To be certain, now more than ever the Russian government relies on the profits from Siberian resources to fill its coffers, but the arguments of environmentalists and Siberians such as Rasputin has begun to make an impact – the ransack of Siberia brings everyone, including Russia, closer to ruin. Perhaps the centre has been forced by the hard realities of the market economy to see Siberia for the part of the Russian home that it really is – not as something to be mythologised or demonised.

CONCEPTUALISING SIBERIA: THE NORTHERN CHIMERA

The above discussion can only be an introduction to the question of Siberia's conceptualised place in Russian society, and by no way precludes other possible interpretations. Whether it be 'Othered' as

---

34 Deming Brown, *Soviet Russian literature since Stalin* (Cambridge, 1978), ch.8.
35 David Gillespie, 'A Paradise Lost? Siberia and Its Writers, 1960-1990' in Diment and Slezkine (eds.) *Between Heaven and Hell...* p.270.
36 Agranat estimates a drop of almost 15 per cent in the northern population; Grigorii Agranat, 'Sever: zalozhnik i zhertva', *Svobodnaia mysl'*, 1998, No.1 (ianvar'), p.57.

immense frozen prison, cornucopia of natural wealth or a terrestrial heaven, Siberia will always invoke strong emotions in Russian society, not least a profound respect for the powers of this still greatly unknown giant. Several troubling and contradictory questions do arise. One is faced with the fact that Russians continue to both fear and hold Siberia sacred and yet, if accepting this premise, how can one reconcile this to the region's ruthless exploitation? This has been the negative consequence of the Siberian image – the mythologising of Siberia's endless landscapes and never-ending resources has led to reckless exploitation and desecration of the territory, leading to some of the most severe environmental problems facing the current Russian government, and the beginnings of organised opposition in bodies such as the Siberian Accord. It is this indiscriminate development of Siberia that Siberians themselves, such as Rasputin and Aipin,[37] have decried in their writings, attempting to enlighten their fellow citizens with a more realistic image of their Siberian 'home'. The very fact that these mental images, perceptions and preconceived notions about the region are conflictory and convoluted and are able to elicit such churning emotions in individuals indicate Siberia's vital 'space' in the Russian cultural landscape. This vast array of Siberian contrasts does suggest that the historic attempts to control information and independent thinking by both the tsarist and Soviet regimes have resulted in a social environment of mistrust and rumour, a major contributor to heavily-romanticised images. But it is, surely, time to escape the confines of the restrictive 'Heaven-Hell' dichotomy. The author Leonid Borodin has written that in Siberia, 'I shall discover for myself the essence of what is called the meaning of life'.[38] The opportunity now for Russians to deconstruct for themselves the images of Siberia is improving with the gradual opening up of post-Soviet society, though with this greater accessibility and knowledge the 'exotica' that once was Siberia begins to fade into the past. Though the love that Borodin, Rasputin and others have for this vast region will perhaps still echo in the hearts of their fellow compatriots for many years to come.

. . . . .

37 See, for example, Rasputin's 'Proshchanie s Materoi' in *Povesti* (Moscow, 1986), pp.155–326 and 'Sibir', Sibir'...', op. cit. or Aipin's 'Not by Oil Alone' *IWGIA Newsletter*, 1989, No.57 (May), pp.136–143.
38 Leonid Borodin, *The Year of Miracle and Grief* (London, 1984), p.185.

# The Soviet Communal Apartment[1]

Katerina Gerasimova

A dwelling is thought of as a space for private and family life, individual consumption, rest, and, sometimes, for work. As a rule sociology maintains that your housing is an indicator of social status. This point of view is typical of the Marxist, Weberian and structural-functional traditions. It proposes the study of social-spatial segregation and unequal distribution of housing among different social groups.[2] N. Elias has a different point of view. He examines not only the hierarchy of places of residence as a reflection of social hierarchy, but at the same time the internal structure of housing as an indicator of social structures.[3] Social-anthropological studies pay more attention to the internal structure of habitation. A classical example of this type

---

1   Originally published as "Sovetskaia kommunal'naia kvartira" in *Sotsiologicheskii zhurnal* #1–2, 1998. This translation by Jakub Lopatko.
    This work was supported by the Research Support Scheme of the OSI/HESP, grant no. 971/1998.
    The author would like to thank V.V. Volkov, D.A.Alexandrov, T.S.Baraulina, V.M. Voronkov, L. Kaufman, S.A. Tchuikina and other colleagues for their assistance in her work.
    The interviews which provide much of the basis of this work were conducted as a part of the project of M.A. Vitukhnovskaya "The old' and 'the new' Leningradians'. The informants are people who lived in Leningrad in the 1920s and 1930s, natives as well as migrants. The author of the project 'Assimilation of the nobles in a city (1917–1941)' S.A. Tchuikina has kindly provided the family stories used in this article.
    The documents and publications of the pre-war period, interviews and memoirs are used as the main sources.
2   For surveys of the theory of stratification, see A. Giddens *The Class Structure of the Advanced Societies* (London, 1981); J. Scott *Stratification and Power. Structures of Class: Status and Command* (Cambridge, 1996).
3   N. Elias *Die Hoefische Gesellschaft: Untersuchungen zur Soziologie des Koenigstums und der hoefischen Aristokratie* (Frankfurt/M, 1989), pp.68–102.

of study is the work of P. Bourdieu about the *kabile* house.[4] This work serves as an empirical basis for the conception *habitus* and the logic of practice. From ethnographic material Bourdieu has shown how the *habitus* (the predisposition to act in a certain way in certain situations) is formed through the structure of habitat (dwelling). The incorporation of the body into the space of the house, and the semiotic of this space brings about acquired habits of thinking and actions, which reproduce fundamental schemes of culture. So, the *kabile* house is organised on the principle of division into light and dark, masculine and feminine, open and secret and the whole world, according to *kabile* notions, has the same structure. And because of this the *kabile*s act in the outer world under the guidance of the models of behaviour appropriate to certain parts of the house.

The structure of your dwelling and relations between a person, between his body and his house are very important components of the organisation of daily occurrences. For every person the habitation is a category of vital importance which is linked with many relations and practices, from the education of children to interrelations with neighbours. A house is that space where everyday life takes place with all its problems, joys, tricks and compromises. The association of house and private life was formed in the consciousness of European peoples during the last five centuries. 'Privatisation' of the house is a part of the general process of 'privatisation' of life.[5] This process took place in West European states during the XV-XIX centuries and meant the growing separation of the individual firstly from the state, then from society, considered as social solidarity, and more later from the family. A house, associated with privacy, is outside of State power (the inviolability of the home) and the public sphere (in the words of E. Goffman, the house is a backstage.) But it does not mean that the house is outside of the process of creating and reproducing the social order. Habitation is a significant space where the rules of life are established in a certain society.

In the Soviet Union the housing problem was always one of the most important. The strategies of life of many soviet people depended on the so called housing question. Soviet people went to work in the northern and arctic regions in order to receive an apartment without

---

4   Kabile is an African tribe studied by P. Bourdieu. See P. Bourdieu 'The Kabile House or the World Reversed' in P. Bourdieu *The Logic of Practise* (Cambridge 1990), pp.271–283.
5   Ph. Aries and G. Duby (eds.) *A History of Private Life* Vol. II-IV (London, 1989).

waiting their turn, they contracted bogus marriages to acquire the right of residence, they gave birth to children in order to be included on the lists of persons who needed improvements in their living conditions. Townspeople lived for many years in family hostels and communal apartments. The subject of this article is the communal apartments of Petrograd – Leningrad – Saint Petersburg.[6]

Today 13,7% of apartments in St Petersburg are communal and 23,8% of St. Petersburg's inhabitants live in these apartments.[7] 'A communal apartment is an apartment in a house which belongs to the state housing fund of St. Petersburg or to the municipal housing fund...and in which some tenants live.' This is the definition given in the law 'On the allocation of vacant dwelling space in communal apartments in St Petersburg' adopted by the Legislative Assembly of Saint Petersburg on 12th February 1997.[8] But the communal apartment means more that just a juridical notion. It is a form of living together with strangers, and this form of living is unknown in other countries, it poses many problems for the present municipal power, and it is the most unprestigious housing, it is a part of the history of soviet daily life. In this article two questions are discussed. How did communal apartments appear in Leningrad? And what was the role of this type of dwelling in the creation and reproduction of the social order, incarnated in soviet daily life?

THE PROJECTS OF THE 1920S: 'THE REDISTRIBUTION OF HOUSING' AND HOUSE-COMMUNES

When the Bolsheviks came to power they abolished private property[9] and all available housing became municipal property. The state, through the local Soviets, for the first time in history obtained the

---

6 On the history, anthropology, and sociology of the communal apartment, see N. Lebina 'Kommunal'nyi, kommunal'nyi, kommunal'nyi mir...' in *Rodina* 1997, no.1, pp.16–21; V. Semenova 'Ravenstvo v nishchete: Simvolicheskoe znachenie 'kommunalok' v 30–50-e gody' in *Sud'by liudei: Rossiia XX vek* (Moscow, 1996), pp. 373–390; S. Boym *Common Places: Mythologies of Everyday Life in Russia* (Cambridge, Mass., 1994), pp.120–150.
7 *Chas pik* 1997, 7th February.
8 *Smena*, 1997, 11th March.
9 'Dekret VTsIK ob otmene prava chastnoi sobstvennosti na nedvizhimosti v gorodakh' in *Zhilishchnoe zakondatel'stvo* (Moscow, 1924), pp.3–5.

possibility of determining who has the right to build housing, what housing, when and where, and who, where and with whom one may live. The period from October 1917 until 1920 is characterised as 'an epoch of housing distribution according to class affiliation.'[10] All the enthusiasm for the 'redistribution of housing' is expressed in the slogan 'Palaces to the workers!' According to Engels' project on the obligatory expropriation of the apartments of the exploiters after the attainment of political power, the owners of two wealthy apartments, under the threat of confiscation of property, had to vacate one of them 'for the needs of poor inhabitants'.[11] A wealthy apartment was considered 'every apartment in which the number of rooms is the same or more than the number of permanent residents of this apartment.'[12] This started the process of *samouplotnenie* (the voluntary giving up of a part of rich men's dwelling space) and the formation of familial communal apartments. In March of 1918 there began the *uplotnenie* (reduction of living space) of the 'bourgeois' (meaning persons living on the profits from capital or owners of commercial or industrial enterprises with hired labour) by 'proletarian elements'.

The provision of living space at that time became the main index of living conditions, i.e. the number of square metres per person. The notion of living space had appeared in tsarist Russia, and in Soviet Russia it became not only an indicator of the quality of living conditions, but it also became the basis for fixing the rate of dwelling space. The setting of quotas of living space authorised for adult persons was a good way out of a difficult situation in which the authorities found themselves after the rejection of market relations. In the past one had a habitation for which one could pay rent. But now it was necessary to find a criterion of housing distribution independent of economic status. The biological needs of human beings for a certain amount of space, air volume, cleanliness, dryness etc. made up this criterion. The norms of these needs were fixed by experts in social sanitation and hygiene. For example 'hygiene has determined that the minimal volume of air' has to be 20 m^3 per one adult person, and

. . . . .
10 For details on the 'redistribution of housing' see A.I. Chernikh 'Zhilishchnyi peredel: politika 20-kh godov v sfere zhil'ia' in *Sotsiologicheskie issledovaniia* 1995, no.10, pp.71–78.
11 F. Engels, 'K zhilishchnomu voprosu' in K. Marx and F. Engels, *Sochineniia* (Moscow, 1935), Vol.15, p.19.
12 V.I. Lenin *Polnoe sobraniie sochineniia* (Moscow, 1965) Vol. 54, pp.380–381.

overpopulation leads to 'higher mortality, morbidity' etc.[13] In 1919 Narkomzdrav (the People's Commissariat of Public Health = Ministry of Public Health) approved medical norms of dwelling space, which is equal to 18 square arshin (Russian archaic linear measure = 71 cm.) per person. Social-structural factors are taken away, and all persons are equalised as biological creatures. On this basis there began the creation of a new system of privileges and advantages in housing distribution. This system reflected the formation of a new social structure.

House-communes were considered an ideal variant of housing. The ideas of the socialist Owen and the English engineer Howard about 'phalanstery' (prototypes of house-communes) integrated very well into Bolshevik ideology. House-communes appeared in 1918–1919. There were 51 house-communes in Petrograd in 1922. These house-communes ought to have been islands of Utopia realised, 'socialism in one building'.[14] It was supposed that these house-communes would be exemplary houses for working people, schools of collectivism, in these houses women would be free of slave housekeeping labour, houses should train people in self-government, should favour the withering away of the family and the reorganisation of modes of life. These houses were imagined as buildings for 5000 persons, with a system of rooms, with a common kitchen on each floor, a library, theatre hall, laundry etc.[15]

At the end of the twenties the question 'What sort of houses should working people have' was discussed again. Most architects, engineers and sociologists defended the idea of new house-communes for workers. The arguments were as follows: 1) It is impossible to renovate the modes of life in old houses 'we have to organise a new mode of life in old houses. All habitations inherited from the old tsarist regime are soaked throughout with mossy old ideas because all houses in old times were built with the purpose of isolating completely all families and households.'[16] And so it is necessary to

---

13 V. Stepanov, 'Perenaselennost' kvartir' in *Zhilishchnoe delo* 1924, no.2, pp.17–18.
14 This description was coined by Richard Stites. On house-communes, see his *Revolutionary Dreams: Utopian Visions and Experimental Life in the Russian Revolution* (Oxford, 1989).
15 'Obraztsovye doma' in *Krasnaia gazeta*, 1919, 3rd June, p.3.
16 P. Kozhanÿ 'Zhilishchnoe stroitel'stvo i novyi byt' n *Zhilishchnaia kooperatsiia*, 1924, no.5, p.4.

build houses of a new type for the collectivisation of life. 2) The economic point of view: collective houses are cheaper. The Economic Council in 1927 resolved to 'turn the attention of building departments of the RSFSR...to the expediency of the realisation of building new types of houses with collective use of auxiliary rooms (kitchens, dining-rooms, bathrooms, laundries etc.).'[17]

Economic demands coincided with ideological declarations: the socialist town has to overcome the opposition between town and countryside, it should be rationally organised, orientated towards industry, and the main idea is that it should resist capitalist influence and consequently it is impossible to orient an apartment towards a family. Ideas of socialist towns inspired architects, many of whom were under the influence of constructivism, to make Utopian projects and prognosticate the downfall of the family because according to these ideas the existence of the family contradicts the socialist way of life. The main characteristics of houses-communes became 'moving the functions of daily meals, child upbringing and laundering away from an apartment' and the demand that 'everybody has to live on principles of the most strict regulations and are subordinate to the regulations of a house.'[18]

Life in house-communes should be run under the strict control of neighbour-friends, and this control did not allow one to lead a reprehensible double life: 'one face in a factory or in an enterprise, with communist phraseology on the tip of your tongue, and another face, the face of vulgar Philistinism, at home, in the family.'[19] Vertical control (through the warden of the hostel and different commissions) and horizontal control (through neighbour-friends) made it possible to unmask the difference between a 'public' and a 'home' Self. By means of measures of social pressures a person should be only a 'public' person, open for constant control and observations.

17 'Postanovlenie EKOSO RSFSR o regulirovanii zhilishchnogo stroitel'stva... *Bulleten' finansovogo i khoziaistvennogo zakondatel'stva* (hereafter BFKhZ) 1927, no.15, p.540.
18 *Zhilishchnoe tovarishchestvo* 1927, no.29, pp.5–6.
19 'Partiinaia rabota v ZhAKTakh' in *Zhilishchnoe delo* 1928, no.3, p.4.

PROJECTS OF THE 1930S: HIERARCHY OF SPACES AND ISOLATED APARTMENTS

There were many projects for buildings house-communes, but only an insignificant portion of them was realised because of the shortage of investment. The attempts to realise the ideas of 'collective life' failed in practice: the construction of house-communes was very expensive, common dining-rooms were empty, there were month-long laundry-queues and the phenomenon of the family obstinately refused to disappear. A house-manager of one house-commune wrote that 'we have not enough education for collective life, in each of the house-communes there are interminable squabbles over the use of kitchens, laundries etc.'[20] In magazines the desires of workers to build isolated two or three-room apartments with all conveniences and kitchens were published. In 1931 ideologists had to admit that 'it is impossible to ignore the fact of the existence of the family in modern forms as habitual units of people in everyday life.'[21] Although the liquidation of private housekeeping and the family remained among the projects of the construction of communism, it was put off for an indeterminate time, and at the present time it was necessary to built habitations 'of a transitional period' where 'the forms of collectivisation of life can be realised only voluntarily.'[22]

At that time the change of trends in architecture took place, and architects turned from constructivism to 'Stalinist classicism'. The thirties were the time of the strengthening of a new hierarchy of 'spaces and men'.[23] The stratified system of soviet society and the structure of some social groups changed. First of all is the question of new social configurations of intellectuals and workers.[24] A new elite and middle class became firmly established in the social hierarchy through the capturing of values which were inaccessible for the main part of the population. High levels of soviet society 'became

. . . . .
20 *Zhilishchnoe delo* 1923, no.3, p.9.
21 *Voprosy kommunal'nogo i zhilishchnogo khoziaistva* 1931, no.6, p.7.
22 *Za sotsialisticheskuiu rekonstruktsiiu gorodov* 1933, no.4, pp.15-21.
23 An analysis of these two parallel processes is given in V. Papernyi, 'Kultura Dva' in *Novoe literaturnoe obozrenie* 1996, pp.100–143.
24 S. Fitzpatrick, *The Cultural Front: Power and Culture in Revolutionary Russia* (Ithaca, 1992), p.11; H. Kuromiya, *Stalin's Industrial Revolution: Politics and Workers, 1928–1932* (Cambridge, 1988), p.302.

bourgeois' and wanted to lead a 'cultural mode of life'.[25] In the conception of culture the main values were the family, a classical education, classical art, a good taste.[26] A comfortable life, consumption, social protocol and proprieties were important for the new elite. The frontier between the public and private spheres changed. In the twenties all displays of privacy and personality were condemned as counter-revolutionary remnants of the 'old life', 'Philistinism', 'petty bourgeoisie'. In the thirties privacy was not disapproved of as it was in earlier soviet times, but personal life (*lichnaia zhizn'* – the family, individual consumption) was very actively propagandised.[27] These social processes were reflected in housing ideology and in the practice of housing construction.

The common norms of housing projects adopted in 1931 divided all dwelling houses into four categories where the first category includes the building of avenues and squares of the capital city, and the fourth category includes provisional dwelling, mainly barracks. Although there was a permanent shortage of money for building, the Chief Directorate of Communal Building ordered: 'The main type of building for construction in 1931 is a dwelling house with individual apartments.'[28] This decree was explained by 'the changed cultural and everyday necessities of the working masses.' In 1934 the Presidium of the Leningrad Soviet inserted into 'The Addenda to the common norms of planning' the theses that the main element of the internal lay-out of a dwelling house is an individual apartment for families with different numbers of members.[29] The 1st and 2nd All-Union Congresses of Architects (1937, 1938) also issued directives to build small apartments.[30]

. . . . .

25 N. Timasheff, *The Great Retreat: the Growth and Decline of Communism in Russia* (New York, 1946); V. Dunham, *In Stalin's Time: Middle-class Values of Soviet Fiction* (Cambridge, 1976).
26 V.V. Volkov, 'Kontseptsiia kul'turnosti, 1935–38 godi: sovetskaia tsivilizatsiia i povsednevnost' stalinskogo vremeni' in *Sotsiologicheskyi zhurnal* 1996, nos. 1–2, pp.194–214.
27 O. Kharkhordin, 'Reveal and Dissimulate: a Genealogy of Private Life in Soviet Russia' in J. Weintraub and K. Kumar (eds.) *Public and Private in Thought and Practice: Perspectives on a Grand Dichotomy* (Chicago, 1997), pp.333–365.
28 'Instruktsiia GUKKh pri SNK RSFSR no. 64 from 7th April 1931' in *BFKhZ* 1931, no.17, pp.43–45.
29 A. Komarov, 'Zhilie iacheiki Lenproekta' in *Arkhitektura Leningrada* 1937, no.2, pp.54–59.
30 N. Brodovich, 'Malometrazhnie kvartiri' in *Stoitel'stvo Leningrada* 1938, no.3, pp.28–34.

In the thirties the isolated apartment became a kind of reward for great services to the country. The heroes of the Stalin epoch were the Stakhanovites and they were rewarded with apartments. 100 Stakhanovites of the Stalin automobile factory were rewarded with apartments as early as October 1935 (the Stakhanovite movement began in August).[31] Beginning from 1932 special houses for the specialists were built. One of these houses was the House of Narkomkhoz *(Ministry of the Economy)* designed by the architect Gal'perin in 1937.[32] This design for a model demonstration of a house of a 'higher type' was completely contrary to the projects of the epoch of 'the collectivisation of life'. The ideal house at the end of the twenties was a house for workers with a corridor system, without individual kitchens and bathrooms, with a common laundry, a day nursery, a Lenin's hall. The project of Gal'perin was earmarked for the elite specialists, and every apartment had a kitchen, bathroom, a room for washing clothes, a dryer, storeroom, one room for domestic servants and two entrances. They planned to place in the lavatory a bidet, a toilet table, a sofa and a little cupboard for toiletry articles. The door-keepers at the main entrances had to observe the coming and going of the tenants and their guests, and this especially indicated the high status of the inhabitants and the exceptional status of the house.

Housing policy, oriented to the building of isolated apartments, expressed the changes of the principles of stratification and the strengthening of the new social structure (workers as a privileged group in the twenties – elite specialists with great services to their country in the thirties), ideas about the role of private life (proclamation and negation of collectivism in the twenties – the family idyll under the control of the state and the public in the thirties), about the most important demands of habitations (economy and rationality, accordance to the norms in the twenties – comfort and culture in the thirties). The ideological orientation changed. The idea of the commune which was dominant in the twenties, was changed to the idea of an apartment for one family in the thirties. This change reflected the process of the privatisation of life and the strengthening of a new elite. But this process was reflected only at a 'high' level: in resolutions, orations, norm regulations, leading articles etc. If we look

. . . . .
31 L.H. Siegelbaum, *Stakhanovism and the Politics of Productivity in the USSR, 1935–1941* (Cambridge, 1988) p.188.
32 V.M. Gal'perin, 'Obraztsovo-pokazatel'nyi zhiloi dom Narkomkhoza' in *Arkhitektura Leningrada* 1937, no.2, pp.46–53.

through some court cases, letters to the magazines, helpful advice, instructions of NKVD (*Narodnyi Kommissariat Vnutrennikh Del* – People's Commissariat of Internal Affairs) etc. we can see that 'the protagonist' of the twenties as well as of the thirties was the same communal apartment with all its conflicts, regulations, partitions, space reduction, plenipotentiaries, hooliganism, common WCs, common kitchens etc.

In 1932 the *desurbanist* Ginzburg noted the stratification of housing when the elite had isolated apartments and the bulk of the population lived in communal apartments. He wrote: 'We know that only a very small strata of society are able to live in 3-room apartments. It is the highly paid section of specialists and workers. The majority of the population has only one room and a 3-room apartment becomes a kind of family hell because no less than 3 families live there.'[33] At the end of the thirties only 25 % of workers had isolated apartments, although the working class in the USSR was, ideologically, the privileged class.[34] How did the communal apartments which were no longer part of an ideological project and were considered as a provisional evil become the most widespread type of housing in pre-war Leningrad?

THE ORIGINS OF THE COMMUNAL APARTMENT

According to the ideological project the quantitative and qualitative redistribution of space should occur. But nobody hurried to realise these decrees of Soviet power. In March 1918 a newspaper wrote that 'the bourgeoisie cheat us in all ways. They invent non-existing tenants, register their relatives and familiars to defend their habitation from the invasion of 'working riffraff''.[35] In their memoirs many intellectuals of that time wrote about the fear of the commissions for the reduction of dwelling space.[36] People known as 'former persons' tried to defend their houses and their private lives, and if the reduction

---

33 'Protiv fal'sifikatorov i vul'garizatorov' in *Soregor* 1932, no.1, pp.25–27.
34 'O prave kazhdogo na samoyplotenie' in *Vechernii Peterburg* 1997, 1st August.
35 'Kvartiri spasaiut ot bezdomnykh' in *Krasnaia gazeta* 1918, 6th March, p.3.
36 See the examples in N. Lebina, 'Kommunal'nyi, kommunal'nyi, kommunal'nyi mir...' in *Rodina* 1997, no.1, pp.16–21

of dwelling space was inevitable, they chose as neighbours representatives of their social environment.

The workers did not hurry to move to a new place as well. The communist representatives organised meetings where they tried to convince the workers to use their right to occupy new apartments 'in the name of health and the happiness of their children.'[37] But for some reason the workers did not carry this out. The reasons were 1) economic reasons: moving to enormous manor-apartments demanded great charges for firewood and the transportation of property was excessively expensive. 2) Removal provoked psychological discomfort because of the unaccustomed great space, the abundance of unknown things and equipment, living together with 'the former' i.e. the shortening of physical distance, while at the same time keeping a social distance. Very often workers chose servants' rooms for living, and maybe not only for economic reasons: a small room without luxurious modelling on the ceiling was more usual for them. 3) the centre of the city was not convenient for the workers because their working places were very far away, in the suburbs. Many workers had their domestic cattle and kitchen-gardens, which it was impossible to imagine in the centre of the city.

By April 1919 the Petrograd Housing Commission had lodged about 36 000 workers and their family members.[38] They decided to evacuate 'the formers' from the centrally heated houses and to lodge workers there to economize on firewood during the fuel crisis which took place in the winter of 1919–1920. Evacuated 'formers' and tenants had to look for new 'bourgeois apartments to reduce space per person in living accommodation with the purpose of economising in fuel.'[39] If the evacuated bourgeois family has superfluous rooms 'they lodge other bourgeois families there.'[40] In Petrograd in October 1920 regional *troikas* (special three-member commissions) for the reduction of dwelling space were organised. The tasks of these *troikas* were to reduce space per person in living accommodation as much as possible on the one hand and to keep sanitary norms on the other hand.[41] They gave the apartment owners 2 weeks to 'look for cohabitants', the so called 'right of voluntary giving up of a part of a

---

37 'Doma-rabochim' in *Krasnaia gazeta* 1918, 28th August.
38 P. Starozhilov, 'Cherepashii khod' in *Krasnaia gazeta* 1919, 4th April.
39 'Pereselenie v burzhuaznye doma' in *Krasnaia gazeta* 1919, 5th September.
40 A. Bolotin, 'Pereselenie v burzhuaznye doma' in *Krasnaia gazeta* 1919, 11th September.
41 'O raionnikh troikakh po uploteniiu' in *Izvestiia Petrosoveta* 1920, 20th October.

dwelling space', and if they did not use this right, superfluous rooms were occupied by force. This meant that the social structure of certain apartments could remain homogeneous in such cases but there were the cases of 'social misalliance' when the former rich owner of the apartment lived together with lodged proletarians.

At the time of the 1923 census one family living in one apartment was considered the norm, but in practice only 48,4% of apartments were occupied by one family.[42] Most such apartments were in workers' regions because the apartments there were small. In 1926 only 23,81% of families lived in isolated apartments.[43] But a very small part of the remaining 76% lived in 'communal apartments' per se. The fact is that in the time of NEP many apartments were given for personal rent and for life ownership to their former owners or to persons who bought it at auction. The existence of the institution of apartment owners gave the local Soviets the possibility of saving the available housing stock from destruction and receiving rents regularly in spite of low levels of receipts from the inhabitants. The landlords lived in one or in some rooms and rented out the rest of the rooms. The landlords chose the tenants on the principles of personal sympathy. In this case they took into account the rate of rent, fixed for different categories. According to these rates landlords paid a sum to the house management, and the difference between the rent received and the sum paid gave the landlord rather good profits. Some landlords not only paid their own rent at the expense of tenants but lived on this money. This system functioned in the same way as the system of lucrative housing in pre-revolutionary St. Petersburg. In 1926 about a half of the Leningrad population had such relations with landlords.[44] The houses which were under municipal ownership and were at the disposal of Communotdels (Department of Communal Economy of local Soviets), and were nor rented, were called communal houses. It was possible to receive a room which belonged to the Trust of Communal Houses through local Soviets only, and

. . . . .
42 *Materialy po statistike Leningrada i Leningradskoi gubernii. Vip.* 6 (Leningrad, 1925), p.110.
43 V. Binshtok, 'Doma i kvartiry Leningrada i Leningradskoi oblasti po perepisi 17 dekabria 1926 goda' in *Biulleten Leningradskogo Oblstatotdela* 1929, no.22, p.57.
44 On 1st January 1927 the number of Leningrad inhabitants was 1 618 600. According to the data there were 197 518 apartment tenants and 668 990 room inhabitants. *XV let diktatury proletariata: Ekonomo-statisticheskii sbornik po gor. Leningradu i Leningradskoi oblasti* (Leningrad, 1932), p.97; *Zhilishchnoe delo* 1926, nos. 14–15, p.8.

there was a queue to receive dwelling space. The chief of a communal house was a specially appointed manager. It is most likely that the notion of 'communal apartment' came from the name of 'communal house'. In 1927 the Trust of Communal Houses was the owner of 301 buildings where 47,000 inhabitants lived.[45] At that time the 'communal dwelling space' was considered to be the worst kind of dwelling. Permanent quarrels between neighbours, dirt, damaged equipment, 'the odour of the WC changes the odour of pie', 'the house-manager leads the inhabitants to the WC' – such are the descriptions of these apartments.[46] The state of communal apartments is defined as 'unsatisfactory', and the conclusion was that 'the experience of communal apartments showed the absolute inexpediency of keeping them in further use.'[47]

In the middle of the twenties the term 'communal apartment' was used in Leningrad periodicals in the more broad sense, as a definition of apartments without landlords; i.e. apartments without an owner or individual apartment leaseholder who had the right to lease rooms as he thought best and who paid the house management according to the rent, fixed for different categories of tenants according to their social status. An especially appointed or elected plenipotentiary of the Housing Association had to observe general order in the apartment. In 1926–1928 a discussion took place about the necessity of keeping landlordism. Landlordism was opposed to the interests of Housing Associations which were the main form of house management in the twenties. This institution was an obstacle to the realisation of the policy of dwelling distribution, which was to the advantage of the authorities, and violated 'the class principle' of dealing with housing. At the time of the removal of NEP the institution of landlordism came to be considered as 'preserving capitalist elements' which did not conform to the political course and the question arose of converting all 'landlords'' apartments into communal ones. A description of this process is given in the article 'Mistress of the apartment'. An employee of the Russian Museum, a certain Mitropolskaya, living in Hertsen street (now Bolshaya Morskaya) was the landlord of a 233 m² apartment. She occupied 34 m², and the rest she rented to other tenants. 'The 'landlord' used free rooms as her own without paying

---

45 *Zhilishchnoe delo* 1927, no.14, p.39.
46 'Nakaz k nakazam vsekh komissii po vyrabotke novoi kvartirnoi platy' in *Zhilishchnoe delo* 1926, nos.14–15, pp.33–36.
47 *Zhilishchnoe delo* 1926, no.7, pp.22–24.

attention to the interests of the house management and the members of ZhAKT' (*zhilishchno-arendnoie kooperativnoe tovarishchestvo* – housing rent co-operative association). One Room became free in the apartment, and the house management wanted to give it to one of its members. But Mitropolskaya registered her sister as the tenant of this room and then rented it to 'an outside tenant'. The house management brought an action against Mitropolskaya The court deprived Mitropolskaya of her ownership rights and declared the apartment 'communal'.[48] In 1929 all free apartments were occupied for the sole disposition of house managements. The landlords were changed by the plenipotentiaries, or by appointed tenants,[49] and the apartments became communal. It was reported in an interview about the origin of a Leningrad communal apartment: 'The owners of this apartment in Pioneer street [a street in the centre of Leningrad – E.G.] lived there many years ago, but later on, when they began to separate, my brother,.....came in 1926, to take this room on lease. Probably, when the landlords were no more there, apartments became communal. Previously they rented these apartments and received money. And later they...became communal.' (The informant is a woman, born in 1914, who came to Leningrad in 1931, from a working-class family).[50]

The reduction of sanitary norms of square metres per person promoted the creation of new communal apartments and the reduction of living space in existing apartments. The sanitary norm for living space in 1926 in Leningrad was 13,5 m² per person, but it was reduced to 10m² per person in 1928, and to 9m² per person in 1931. This meant that it was necessary to 'reduce the living space according to the norms', or to move to a smaller room, or to register somebody in the room, or to change the lay-out of the apartment. The house management registered new rooms as 'above the norms'. So, the living conditions of inhabitants of Leningrad were becoming worse and worse, and new tenants were being lodged in the communal apartments.

Analysing the housing situation in the 1920s and 1930s it is possible to come to the conclusion that the Bolshevik project for solving the housing problem was unrealised. Everything stood against its realisation: the people, the structure of the city, and the buildings.

48 *Zhilishchnoe delo* 1928, no.1, p.39.
49 'Prava i obiazannosti s'emshchika' in *Zhilishchnoe delo* 1929, no.14, p.15.
50 In this case it is very interesting that this woman from a working-class family whose brother came to Leningrad from the provinces is talking about 'separating' but not about 'the reduction of living space', and it demonstrates the difference of perception of the same fact by people from different social levels.

This example shows how ideological projects were transformed in practice, how the strategy of the authorities was perceived and changed in everyday life. Although the variant of some families living together in one apartment was envisaged by the authorities, it was not considered appropriate as the ideological model or as the main type of habitation. The origins of communal apartments depended on many factors existing at the same time which had unforeseen results. We shall name the most important of these factors: 1) there were houses with large apartments of many rooms in the centre of the city; 2) the priorities of State policy (development of industry, militarisation) allowed no possibility of assigning enough money for housing construction; 3) large-scale migration to the city created housing problems and led to the reduction of living space; 4) the opposition of socialism to capitalism should mean that the mode of dwelling in the USSR differs essentially from the capitalist mode, and that led to the nationalisation of available housing and the right to distribute it; 5) the conception of living space made it possible to distribute apartments irrespective of family and the social status of tenants and apartment configuration, and to lodge aliens in one apartment.

If the notion of communal apartment includes such characteristics as several tenants living in one apartment, state ownership of living space, the impossibility of choosing neighbours, heterogeneous background of tenants, distribution of living space according to sanitary norms, rules of living imposed from outside, horizontal and vertical control, so this 'classic' communal apartment became the most widespread type of housing in Leningrad in the 1930s. The communal apartments did not correspond to the idea of the 'socialist city'. Its existence did not correspond to the 'permanent improvement of the material and cultural level of the working people', 'proclaimed collectivism', or 'the socialist way of life'. But the spontaneous origin of communal apartments did not mean that the authorities would not use the existence of communal apartments to achieve their own political goals. Stephen Kotkin, who researched the living conditions in Magnitogorsk, noted that housing was a very important field in the process of creating new regulations, in which the interrelations of the state and the individual were being defined, while the substance of everyday life and the new micro-order were being created.[51]

- - - - -
51 S.Kotkin, *Magnetic Mountain: Stalinism as Civilization* (Berkley, 1995), pp.160, 193.

SOCIAL AND POLITICAL CONTROL

Social and political control were introduced to the lodging of strange persons in one space, and the interrelation of these persons was regulated from outside. The status of senior plenipotentiary was established for it, who was responsible for maintaining the rules of registration and the sanitary rules of apartment maintenance. Usually the NKVD approved 'The rules of internal order in houses and apartments', and the relations in the apartment were regulated by these rules.[52] The Presidium of the Leningrad Soviet approved the rules of order in communal apartments in Leningrad. To control the realisation of these rules, besides the senior plenipotentiaries, observer commissions were established in communal houses.[53] After the adoption of these rules the personal responsibility for abiding by these rules by all tenants of the apartment was introduced. Vertical control was added to the horizontal control (neighbour on neighbour), and observation became asymmetric (both parties see one another but one of them has more rights). The plenipotentiary is responsible to the house management and administrative bodies. There was a point in the rules of internal order which obliged the tenants 'to give to the plenipotentiary true and exact information about their status and salary as well as about all changes in this respect.'[54]

In 1933 one-man management by the house-manager was established in houses in order to struggle against the absence of personal responsibility, and 'in order to establish real personal responsibility for the condition of apartments and places of common use'. The institution of responsible tenants which had to watch over the rules of internal order was also established.[55] The house management appointed the responsible tenants and made written contracts with them. All tenants after a certain time had to give certain commitments to the responsible tenant, and they undertook 'to obey the orders of the responsible tenant in respect of rules of internal order, care of equipment, repairs' etc. The responsible tenants had the right to summon the tenants to the comrades' court, and to demand

---

52 *Zhilishchnoe delo* 1927, no.3, p.13.
53 *Zhilishchnoe delo* 1928, no.2, p.14.
54 'Polozhenie ob otvetsvennikh upolnomochennikh i pravilakh vnutrennego rasporiadka v kommunal'nikh kvartirakh' in *Zhilishchnoe delo* 1929, no.1, p.8
55 'O merakh po uluchsheniiu upravleniia domami v g. Leningrade' *Postanovleniia i rasporiazheniia Lensoveta i ego otdelov* 1933, Vyp. 26, pp.1–10.

through the People's Court expulsion of tenants if they damaged equipment in the apartment or did not obey the rules of internal order. These plenipotentiaries were given preference for the occupation of free rooms in the apartment, and once every three years they could repair their own rooms at the expense of the house management.

Thus the basis was created for informing, which occurred on a mass scale after the assassination of Kirov in 1934. The possibility of improving living conditions encouraged voluntary informing and participation in the 'unmasking' of people's enemies. One woman, who lived in Leningrad before the war, talked about her woman neighbour, the former owner of the apartment, the director of a musical school. When she was asked 'Have the neighbours informed in order to improve their living conditions?' the interviewee woman (who was a responsible party worker at that time) answered: ' I think they have. Because housing was a very difficult problem. And that forced people. Ekaterina Pavlovna [the former apartment owner] was very afraid of it - they lodged me there and who was I, what was I? She was very afraid that I would inform. When they appointed her director I gave a positive testimonial (...) I remember that they invited me to the regional Committee several times (the director of the school was still one of 'the formers') and I always testified positively' (the informant M.I., born in 1908, came to Leningrad in 1927, with a secondary education). In this situation it was quite possible to slander a person out of envy, to take vengeance upon 'the former' because she looked down on her neighbours, or upon a neighbour because of quarrels in the kitchen. These calls to the regional Committee encouraged people to inform, giving them the chance to increase their living space.

NEIGHBOURLINESS

During the period of NEP and the redistribution of dwellings 'the formers' and 'the presents' tried to keep themselves spatially segregated. When at the end of the 1920s almost everybody was lodged in communal apartments, it then became very important, especially for 'the formers', to maintain a symbolic distance. In the communal apartments where people from different social levels lived it was a daily task to preserve the boundaries between them. A story of a noble family shows how this symbolic distance between 'the formers' and 'the worker' tenants was maintained if it was impossible to keep a physical distance. The style of life and the organisation of everyday life of the noble sisters reproduced the old social structure, preserving social distance. Even when living in the communal apartment the noble sisters tried not to do any of the 'menial labour' which the servant women living in this apartment did, the sisters wore peignoirs, made their 'ablutions with cucumber water or with rose-petal water', and created 'personal comfort' in the kitchen. 'The sisters began their day very late, at about 12. Then for half of the day they took coffee. In soviet times this order of life made a strange impression. Sometimes N.A. took her coffee in the communal kitchen. At one end of the communal table a white serviette was placed. Cups, a little plate, butter, sugar etc. were placed on the serviette.'[56]

In interviews people sometimes told about cases of social segregation in one apartment. In one case, where there were two social environments, 'ordinary' and 'intellectual', the female informant from 'the ordinary' environment did not know anything about her neighbours (her neighbours were professors). She knew only their names and professions, and she had never been in 'their part of the apartment'. Elswhere, when 'the formers' and 'the presents' coexisted they made a symbolic exchange – 'the news' gave to 'the formers' a kind of political defence (positive testimony in the party Committee) and helped them to do everyday work, and 'the formers' with their cultural capital educated 'the workers' who needed it for their successful soviet careers.

This is a citation from the previous interview: 'Ekaterina Pavlovna was a very educated and a very good person. She was very nice to me. And I helped her with her everyday work. She was not able to do anything; servants had done everything for her all her life. So she could not even cook a dinner...So, she was unpractical. It seems that she was this way by birth...I imitated many of her ways, much of her nobility' (female informant M.I., born in 1908, came to Leningrad in 1928, from a family of handicraftsmen, she made a good party career in the 1930s).

Industrialisation and collectivisation led to growing migration to the cities during the years of the first five-year plan. 3,5 million new inhabitants appeared in Moscow and Leningrad during the years of the first five-year plan.[57] The migrants brought with them 'the rules of

---

56 N.F. Zvorikina, 'Zapiski' (Unpublished family history, 1984).
57 M. Lewin, *The Making of the Soviet System: Essays in the Social History of Interwar Russia* (London, 1985), pp.218, 63.

internal order', i.e. class solidarity, representation of the individual through the family, the absence of privacy. Moshe Lewin refers to this as communal order.[58] Only 18,3% of all migrants arriving in Leningrad came from the towns.[59] They were settled in the centre of the city. While in 1926 21,5% of workers lived in the centre, in 1932 it was 60%.[60] Yesterday's peasants came to the communal apartments, the social structure of whose inhabitants was heterogeneous. On the one hand communal life with its mutual responsibilities, feebly marked distinctions between the private and the public, and the representation of the individual through one member of the family should have been congenial to 'the new Leningradians'. On the other hand, the communal apartment did not constitute a commune, it was a part of the urban society. 'The villagers' learned city life in the communal apartments. The communal apartments served as a kind of institute for the socialisation of young peasant girls employed as servants, for young people who studied in the FZU (factory and workshop professional school), for young workers who rented rooms or even a part of a room.

DISCIPLINE OF EVERYDAY LIFE

From the documents of the 1920s we get an impression that life in communal apartments was full of conflicts. Such a point of view on the communal apartments is reflected in the literature of the 1920s. I shall cite a description of a Moscow communal apartment from the novel 'Comrade Kisliakov' by Panteleimon Romanov. There were 27 tenants in the apartment. Two thirds of the families were intellectuals and one third were 'proletarians'. 'As far as relations between the inhabitants goes, it was not an apartment but a powder-magazine. Not a day passed without a powder explosion because everybody kept their powder dry...pretexts for explosions arose at every step. First of all it was the lavatory. In the morning a long queue of citizens

. . . . .
58 M. Lewin, *The Gorbachev Phenomenon: a Historical Interpretation* (Berkely, 1988), pp.35–37.
59 *Statisticheskii spravochnik po g. Leningradu i Leningradskoi oblasti* (Leningrad, 1932), p.12.
60 *XV let diktatury proletariata. Ekonomo-statisticheskii spravochnik* (Leningrad, 1932), p.124.

hurrying to get to work lined up there. Some of them were particularly impatient. And it was not possible for someone at the fron of the queue to go into the lavatory and shut the door before a dozen fists began to bang on the door reminding him that he was not in his own sitting-room... the next point of discord was the kitchen where, from the early morning, just as at a great factory, six primus stoves were blazing at the same time. Fights began in the kitchen almost every minute because of the dishes, slops etc... But the main source of discord was always the dirt in the apartment because nobody wanted to clean it up, and the places of common use which were left unrepaired. If it was not known who had scattered rubbish, it remained in the apartment. There was not a single day without pilfering. In the end they came up with a way of dealing with the dirt: taking turns to clean the apartment.'[61]

In this fragment the author has noted some important aspects of the organisation of life in the communal apartment. The necessity of living in one space and using the same things demanded the establishment of a roster of duties, so that there was a special regime of time in the communal apartment, and this type of regime is more common to public space but not to home life. A 'living' queue deprives an individual even of corporal autonomy. A person should be ready to defend a 'friendly person' and his rights, and at the same time to watch the behaviour of the others to 'catch them at the scene of the crime.' An woman interviewee told that her female neighbour, a former apartment owner, kept an eye on the cleanliness of the W.C. pan after the 'settled tenants' visited it. And if it was dirty, the woman would proclaim publicly her inclination to untidy the tenant's face. 'Everybody knew that she kept control, and so everybody tried to keep it clean...'

A period of conflicts and the joint elaboration of rules of communal life was inevitable in the making of such a social organisation as the communal apartment. People who had never lived together learned from their mistakes to organize the order of their everyday lives. There were plenty of housing cases in the courts of Leningrad and a special section had to be organized for it – the Chamber of Housing. In 1928 35% of cases in the Chamber of Housing concerned expulsion from the apartment because of the impossibility of communal living in one apartment, 31% concerned

---

61   P. Romanov, 'Tovarishch Kisliakov' in *Svetlie sny* (Moscow, 1990), pp.302–3.

expulsion from the apartment because of non-payment of rent, and 34% were mixed. In 1927 a special compromise-conflict commission was organised to solve small conflicts.[62]

In 1932 'everyday life discipline' appeared side by side with 'work discipline', 'self-discipline', and 'party discipline'. This kind of discipline regulated the order of everyday life.[63] It included the rules which are now habitual in every communal apartment, and is aimed at keeping order in several senses, such as sequence (cooking, roster duties, use of the places of common use); interactional order (interrelations between the neighbours); sanitation and hygiene (everyday cleaning, floor washing every 5-6 days, keeping order in the kitchen); administrative order (rules of registration), regimen (make no noise between midnight and 8 a.m.), equity (the sharing of repair expenses, payment for electricity according to the number of lamps); the structural order (responsible tenants, family representatives). The adoption of rules was only the codification of worked-out 'practices', and made it possible not only to take public measures against those who infringed the rules but also to take administrative measures as far as expulsion from the apartment.

In the 1930s the atmosphere in the communal apartments became calmer. And, what is more, the inhabitants of communal apartments of that time said that the relations between neighbours were quite normal and sometimes even friendly or 'familiar'.

PRIVACY IN THE COMMUNAL APARTMENTS

In the communal apartments the physical boundary between private space and public space is the door of the room, and the symbolic boundaries are secrets and intrigues. Bad sound-proofing (the partitions were made as cheaply as possible), the possibility of intrusion, vigilant neighbours watching visits by guests, often the lack of 'your own part of the room' because of a large family living there,

. . . . .
62 'Postanovlenie VTsIK i SNK RSFSR ob organizatsii primiritel'no-konfliktnykh komissii po zhilishchnym delam' *BFKhZ* 1927, no.16, pp.567–8.
63 'Obiazatel'nye pravila ukhoda za zhilishchem i vnutrennego rasporiadka v kvartirakh' in *Zhilshchnaia kooperatsiia* 1932, nos.21-24, pp.44-7.

made these borders very unstable and made rather an illusion of privacy.[64]

In a fragment of her memoirs a noble-woman describes the life of her family in the 1930s. 'All of us lived in communal apartments. It was very difficult. This is without speaking about the neighbours, who were all sorts of people, sometimes there were good persons, but more often they were strange and even alien to us, everyone had his own idea of what is good and what is bad. But even without neighbours it is very difficult to live with a large family in one room. Practically it means that the son-in-law is forced to take off his trousers in front of the mother-in-law, the children listen to everything they should not hear and do their homework accompanied by the conversations of their grandmother with neighbours or relatives. The middle generation is in an awkward situation too. It is impossible to say something sweet or to reproach, everybody hears everything...'[65] The way out of this situation was to divide the room by wardrobes or curtains into separate sections: 'dining-room' 'bed-room', 'children's room'. One woman told that she and her brother lived in one room, and when her brother got married, she spent a few nights in the room of a neighbour to leave the newly-weds alone. This model of privacy realised in the communal apartments can be called 'public private life'. In this case the characteristic of a house-commune where there is 'public private life' and the idea of isolated apartments for private family life are combined. In 1928 the author of the article 'Problem of a house' described the symptoms of a further 'great deviation' from the ideals of collectivism and the tendency to 'bourgeois life' in the communal apartments: 'And now, in the 12th year of the greatest revolution in the world we are building new houses (apparently at the demand of the working masses)...and are settling individual families in them, but very often 2 or 3 families live in one apartment because of the great demand for housing and the growing housing crisis. Bear in mind that elsewhere unauthorised and unorganised settlement has taken place... There is a private life in 100 separate apartments, bourgeois life is being renewed there, they acquire geraniums and muslin curtains, they are laundering clothes there and the housewife is chained to her stove...'[66] This shows the possibility of combining personal and

---

64 On privacy in the communal apartments see also S. Boym, *Common Places: Mythologies of Everyday Life in Russia* (Cambridge, Mass., 1994), p.121–50; S. Kotkin, op. cit., pp.170–9.
65 N.F. Zvorikina, op. cit.
66 V. Izmailov, 'Problema doma' in *Zhilishchnoe delo* 1928, no.22, p.8.

communal life. On the one hand there is family life, where people 'consume in a civilized manner', and create comfort, and on the other hand private life is controlled through the rules of internal order and the need to live together with other people.

CONCLUSION

In the middle of the 1930s the communal apartment was not considered 'the worst kind of dwelling' as it was in the middle of the 1920s but it was recognised as being in some ways advantageous and was adapted for living in. When everybody lives in communal apartments these conditions of living are considered the norm. Old residents say that the communal apartments were spoiled after the war when the inflow of a new labour force for the reconstruction of Leningrad was so great that the culture of the city could not resist this pressure and assimilate the migrants.[67] The communal apartment became 'quite horrible' in the 1960s when everybody (not only the elite) was able to obtain a separate apartment.

It was mostly single people, workers from poor enterprises which could not build their own houses, state employees who were on a waiting list of 10-15 years who did not obtain separate apartments. The social structure of the communal apartments was made up of *'limitchiki'* (a type of worker mostly in Moscow and Leningrad with limited rights of abode and working in these cities). The communal apartment was a temporary form of housing for many of them because they usually worked in a sphere of the economy (construction, industry and municipal services) where they had the chance of obtaining an apartment very soon. This changed the atmosphere of communal apartments and lowered the symbolic status of communal apartments. But many people, moving to the 'Khruchevkas' (cheep and rapidly-built houses of the Khrushchev era), sensed a feeling of loss and uncertainty because now they had no interlocutors who they could talk to about their joys and sorrows, none of the pleasant feeling 'that somebody is always at home' and 'they will always help'. This feeling is especially characteristic of people who have grown up in communal apartments or of older people. For them the communal apartment is a part of their life, of their youth, of their family and of their conceptions of the world.

Life in the communal apartments has changed after the collapse of the Soviet system. There is no more political control, no sanctions of the Communist Party to meddle in the life of neighbours, the district militia officers do not visit the apartments, and the responsible tenants have to pay general bills, nobody awards the title of 'an apartment of model maintenance and way of life.' But the coexistence of different families in communal apartments, which is not only a part of the old system of housing, but also of the need to reproduce some of the forms of everyday life of the Soviet society, continues to be an important element of the social structure of modern cities.

Traveling Maidens and Men with Parallel Lives – Journeys as Private Space During Late Socialism

Anna Rotkirch

Soviet citizens moved and traveled a great deal after the biggest social upheavals of the first three decades of Bolshevik power. The waves of migration to the big cities continued in the 1950s as well as smaller movements back to the countryside for holidays or to take care of sick relatives; or else elderly parents were moving to their children in the cities; adults moved around the country as work required; young men spent several years away from home while serving in the army; and with the growing living standards of the 1960s and 1970s holiday trips and leisure travel increased.

Some journeys were motivated by a need for private space. This need was both physical and psychological – everyday urban life was circumscribed by social conventions as much as by the crowded living spaces. On the basis of autobiographical accounts of 'ordinary' St. Petersburg citizens, this article looks at sexual experiences as part of Soviet domestic tourism. The two most frequently mentioned types of journeys are *vacations to the South* and *'komandirovkas'* or Soviet business trips. While both sexes made both kind of trips, the vacations figure in my material as an ambivalent symbol of women's sexual autonomy and dangerous (mis)adventures, while work related travel emerged as a typical male way of arranging a life style with parallel relationships. This chapter describes two cultural configurations – the traveling maiden and the man with parallel lives – typical for late Soviet society, which in this context refers to urban life in the 1960s-early 1980s.

ESCAPING THE EVERYDAY

The emblem of Soviet everyday life, including everyday sexuality, was the communal apartment.[1] With a family of two or three generations in the same room, sharing the kitchen and bathroom with the neighbours, sexual encounters required careful organization and spatial innovation in the form of self-made walls, secret places and borrowed apartments. The shame and frustration created by the constant lack of private space is, not surprisingly, a leitmotif in collected autobiographies about love and sexuality from Leningrad / St. Petersburg:[2]

> *Then the wedding – we had many guests: students, his friends and mine, in our one room in the communal apartment. We spent our wedding night on different beds, the place was full of drunken guests who stayed over night. The next night my mother left to her sister's place (it was the sister's idea) and we were on our own....Later everything happened in one room, with my mother and grandmother sleeping beside us on the little sofa. We waited for them to fall asleep in order to, as they call it now, make love....Practically all our private life took place before the eyes of our relatives.* (Woman, higher education, born 1937)

---

1   Svetlana Boym, *Common Places. Mythologies of Everyday Life in Russia*. (Cambridge, Mass., 1984)
2   The autobiographies were collected in 1996 through a competition organized by Alexandr Klyotzin and Liza Lagunova from the Institute of Sociology in St Petersburg. The material was part of the research project "Mosaic life. Transitional autobiographies from Finland, the Baltic States and St Petersburg", directed at the University of Helsinki by prof. J.P.Roos. Through an advertisment in the weekly newspaper *Chas Pik* and additionally distributed leaflets, people were invited to write about their love and sexual life "as they would talk to a close friend". The competition yielded 47 autobiographies, 24 written by women and 23 by men. The authors are in this article presented with pseudonyms and by reference to their sex, year of birth, and education or occupation.
    Sexual autobiographies have earlier been collected in a similar way in Finland (Kontula & Haavio-Mannila 1995 and 1996). For comparisons of the Finnish and the Russian materials, see Anna Rotkirch, 'Women's sexual biographies from two generations. A first comparison between Finland and Russia' in Voronkov & Zdravomyslova (eds.), *Biographical perspectives on post-socialist societies*, (St Petersburg, 1997) and Elina Haavio-Mannila and Anna Rotkirch, 'Generational and Gender Differences in Sexual Life in St. Petersburg and Urban Finland', *Yearbook of Population Research in Finland 1997*, XXXIV,(Helsinki, 1998).

In this description, the lack of square meters and proper beds is intertwined with both a lack of understanding support (the guests who won't leave on the wedding night; the mother who does not automatically leave the young couple alone) and an absence of (surviving) sexual vocabulary – nowadays people call it 'to make love', the author notes, but does not tell us what possible expressions she and her husband used at the time.

Another author remembers the joyous image of a newly wed couple which occupied the *kommunal'ka* bathroom on Tuesday nights with foam bath, laughter and loud music from the transistor radio. There are also the painful memories of a divorced woman who visited a man in his room and, because of the neighbours on the other side of the wall, was too ashamed to protest aloud when he made unwelcome advances and silently suffered from forced intercourse. Several examples present the classic Soviet problem of having new sexual partners while your ex-spouse is still living in the same flat. There is the traumatic story of a girl who hated overhearing her parents making love and, when she grew up, never could relax with her husbands or lovers because she wanted to protect her daughters from the same experience; etc.

Also for couples with their own, but tiny apartments, the proximity of parents or children was problematic. As a divorced, middle-aged woman describes one very satisfying relationship:

> *We met in order to have sex, which literally helped both him and me to live happily. I started to think about why this was happening, why we felt so good together, and I came to the conclusion that we could relax completely, nothing and nobody prevented us from making love. He had two small children at home, a young wife and a small uncomfortable apartment.*

(Woman, higher education, born in 1936)

The Soviet everyday both provoked innovations and new affairs, and created resignation and suffering.[3] In Soviet Russia journeys seemed to provide an especially important possibility for escaping conventional sexual morals and the surveillance of parents, spouses or children.

- - - - -
3   Survey data from urban Finland and Petersburg show that Leningrad/Petersburg citizens have had a higher number of extramarital affairs than urban Finns. The Finns were, however, generally sexually more active and reported a higher number of sexual partners and more sexual satisfaction than the Russians. (Haavo-Mannila & Rotkirch, 'Generational and Gender Differences...)

As in other industrialized countries, in Soviet Russia the 1960s and 1970s meant increasing liberalization and pluralization of sexual behaviour. But due to Soviet censorship on practically all matters of 'intimate life', the growing gap between the sexual experiences and values of the older and the younger generations was impossible to debate publicly. The norms of Communist ideology and those of the older generations coincided in supporting silence on sexual issues, abstinence from premarital sex, and a more permissive moral standard for men. Even when everyday family life diverged dramatically from this pattern, there was little space for young people in which to articulate other moral evaluations or elaborate new standards of behaviour. Of the few places available, many required traveling (we can also mention the pioneer camps for school children and student's yearly practice of leaving to work at collective farms during the summer). Additionally, travels of course provided the scarce commodity of private *physical space*, whether in the form of camping tents, train wagons, or hotel rooms.

Elena Hellberg-Hirn has sketched the dynamics of Russian space as arising from the opposition between the inwards, immobile center/home and a limitless, rapid move or escape away from the center. The secure and controllable home is in the Russian history of ideas especially preoccupied with borders and fences, the *zabors*. The centrifugal flight is of course connected with the vast steppes, and the vastness of the whole national space – *prostor*.[4] This basic spatial axis would also appear to be structuring the ways of remembering and writing in our autobiographical material. Soviet social practices further encouraged a division between *domestic* (silenced, controlled, routine) sexuality and *foreign* (outdoor, dangerous, unpredictable) sex.. The 'domestic' sphere here includes both life at home and in official Soviet public places (schools, working places). The 'foreign' alludes to less regulated, semipublic places, such as certain cafés, transport vehicles, or the usually official places at unusual hours.[5] Under the puritanistic surface of Soviet urban life, even short trips on public transport and taxis were loaded with the possibility of anonymous and potentially dangerous sex, or sex in exchange for material favours.

- - - - -
4   See Helena Hellberg-Hirn's chapter in this volume, pp. 49–70.
5   The term Soviet semi-public space was introduced by Elena Zdravomyslova (1997) in her analysis of the bohemian life style of café Saigon in Leningrad.

ANALYSING GENDERED TOURISM

Both in traveling practices and the metaphors of travelers, tourism is gendered. Or, as Soile Veijola and Eeva Jokinen express it, 'the tourist, the flâneur, the stranger and the adventurer ... are always embodied [relations] and, accordingly, sexed.'[6] Veijola & Jokinen speak of cultural configurations, 'a local relationship of time, space and power', which can affect or encompass concrete social subjects.[7] This article discusses the gender differences in connection with the cultural status and effects of the sexual encounters in the life course of men and women. I will also discuss the gendered differences in interpretation and moral evaluation through two types of cultural configurations, the Traveling maiden and the Man with parallel lives.

The journeys described in our corpus of autobiographies form two main types: *vacations to the South* and *'komandirovkas'*. Women and men tell about these types of journey with different emphasis and varying frequency. This difference in remembering and writing about journeys probably reflects direct gender differences in the amount of traveling. Soviet men were more likely to leave for longer working trips, as they had higher work positions and less caring obligations in family life. The women were more often tied to the home by the responsibilities of caring for dependent small children or elderly relatives. But also women could take one or two weeks of vacation, alone or with women friends.[8]

In analysing the travel stories, I will look at the interplay between three modes of experience: feelings, social practices, and cultural interpretations. This triad is based on C.S.Peirce's triad of experience

. . . . .
6 Soile Veijola and Eeva Jokinen 'The Disoriented Tourist: The Figuration of the Tourist in Contemporary Cultural Critique', in Chris Rojek and John Urry (eds) *Touring Cultures. Transformations of Travel and Theory*, (London, 1997), pp.23–24.
7 Idem, p.23.
8 Lyudmila Petrushevskaya's short story "Clarissa's story" describes a young divorced woman who first fights to get custody over her child, then leaves the child and travels to a sea resort. For this single mother "it was a pure feast when she after one year got a vacation, which she for the first time in her life spent completely alone in the South after having left the boy at a kindergarden in the countryside. Having arrived to the South Clarissa first felt the overwhelming concern for her boy typical for mothers, she felt guilty thinking about the sea, the tan and the fruits and remembered her child, who had been left in the pooring rain of the North. ... But the sea, the tan and the fruits of the South, which Clarissa bought because they were so cheap, had their effect and Clarissa's outlook changed once again (...) At this point a domestic pilot fell in love with her...." (Petrushevskaja 1989, 135, translation – AR)

as elaborated by de Lauretis, Määttänen & Simpura, and others.[9] I do of course not assume that 'feelings', 'practices' or 'interpretations' could somehow be clearly detached from each other or directly presented in a retrospective, written memory. My aim is to grasp the tensions and dynamics between bodily experiences, social norms, and cultural interpretations, as they present themselves to the authors at the moment of writing and to me as a reader. An example of this way of analysing excerpts was given already in connection with the first quote of this article, where I distinguished between the deplored lack of sex due to the social behaviour of friends ('practices') and parents, and the lack of linguistic expressions ('interpretations').

The autobiographical examples I will discuss are from two generational cohorts, those born between 1945 and 1960, and those born after 1960. The first generation had its formative years in the post-war liberal climate of Khruschev's rule. It represents the Russian *shestidesyatniki,* known for a specific life style, tone and political attitude, but not, like their Western counterparts, for making a gender or sexual revolution.[10] The second generation belongs to the so called period of stagnation, which actually coincided with the behavioural sexual revolution in Russia. It was during the Brezhnev-style late socialism that Soviet urban society witnessed a significant increase in premarital and extramarital affairs and a diversification of sexual behaviour.[11] The journeys described by both generations generally took place precisely during this behavioral revolution of the 1970s–1980s.

TRIPS TO THE SOUTH

For the younger generation of Leningrad women, growing up in the late 1970s and early 1980s, stories of vacations to the South stand for *sexual initiation.* This is one of the key events in the autobiographies

---

9   de Lauretis, Teresa: *Alice Doesn't. Feminism, Semiotics, Cinema.* (Bloomington, Indiana University Press, 1984). Kirsti Määttänen & Jussi Simpura: 'Transition, Transformation, Integration. Understanding European Social Changes from the Perspective of Experiential Time – Towards a Program of Comparative Research'. (unpublished manuscript, April 1998)
10 For comparisons between the Soviet and the Finnish sexual generations see Elina Haavio-Mannila and Anna Rotkirch, 'Generational and Gender Differences...' pp. 133–160.
11 See idem, and Anna Rotkirch, 'Women's sexual biographies from two generations...' pp.205–211

of both middle class 'Masha' (b.1954) and working class 'Valya' (b.1966). For girls the everyday at home meant pressure to behave strictly, even though values had already significantly loosened in the youngest generation.

In 1970 Masha was dating her first boyfriend. They did not go further than kissing, but her father eventually had a serious talk with the young man, who was some years older and from a lower social background. As a result, the boy ended his relationship with what she describes as the honest admission: 'I would like to go further, but that would be bad for your studies'. The father's regulation of his daughter's sexuality is accompanied with ignorance and disinformation: in Masha's childhood, the father told her she had been bought from a shop; and although she later learned she came from her mothers belly she had in her late teens no concrete idea of how human sexual organs look or function.

Masha's upbringing, including sexual education, was typical for a girl from the educated Soviet milieus.[12] By contrast, the permission or possibility to travel alone was something exceptional. At 18, she decided to quit her studies for a while and got the chance to work during four summer months at the Black Sea in 1970:

> There I was finally without parents, I was 18 years old, and I did not waste any time anymore. It is amazing [that nothing bad happened], I must have been protected by God! There I finally experienced my first intercourse with a man... (Masha, born in 1954, higher education)

Ten years later, in the 1980s, it is Valya's turn to travel to the Black Sea. Valya went together with a girlfriend. She had been there on vacations earlier together with her mother. But now she had started her vocational studies and moved away from home. And as Valya was living alone renting a room, nobody could prevent her from what she calls a 'summer of freedom'.

> I was so much in love with the South, that all my complexes, all my insecurity, all my timidity disappeared there. I'm now very often trying to recall that first night [of vacation], in order to experience those feelings again. The music was roaring below. And we descended towards it from the house on the hill. We walked as if everybody should immediately look on these

-----
12 Idem.

two snow-white young bodies, that attracted attention because of the lack of sunburn. I felt as if even the music fell silent. I really felt sensations like the ones in my frequent dreams about flying...I was overwhelmed by joy. (Valya, born in 1966, professional education)

For Masha, this was the summer of unashamed and loose behaviour. She recalls thinking she loved the local guy who soon became her boyfriend, but when he suggested they should marry she was 'not at all interested'. On the contrary, she reflects on her own feeling of social (and geographical) superiority vis à vis her friend: 'We were a few people from Leningrad there, like one group. We were supposed to be proud about being from Leningrad and feel a little above the local people. My lover was one of the locals.'

While dating one of the boys, Masha also flirted widely. She recalls how somebody asked:
'Is this your girl?' My friend answered, not without irony, 'yes, this is OUR girl'. I have to say that I was not actually hurt by that remark, but rather flattered. He could not downgrade me. Dirt did not cling to me.

During that summer vacation, Masha fully enjoyed reading, nature, and writing poetry. 'I was afraid of nothing then, I was strong and free. Imagine! [*Nado zhe*] I was happy then.'

Today, at the moment of writing, Masha is amazed that 'nothing bad happened'. But for Valya the adventure ended violently.[13] Already during the first magic evening described above, two local boys started clinging to her and her girlfriend 'with an iron grip':

Our young small heads could not even think about how this could end. That night they did not insist on their invitations to go to a café and accompanied us home...the [next] evening we went to the dances again. Now we had to be only with them. This time we went with them to a café. That was the first stupid thing to do. The second was that we separated into couples, when they accompanied us home. In the Caucasian darkness... Almost without any sudden movements and almost without using any force, the one who accompanied me pushed me at some suitable moment into some small building on the beach.

---

13 Valya does not herself use the word "rape" about the event. It would in contemporary Western terminology be labelled either rape or forced sex.

Before I knew where I was I was thrown down (it turned out to be the watch tower at the row-boat station). Later it seemed to me, that I simply did not resist all the way, that I didn't fight as much as I could... But it was an instinct of self-preservation, on the one hand, and the superiority of male force over female, on the other. And *my* curiosity...Then he helped me to get dressed and accompanied me home. My friend arrived just after me. The same thing had happened to her, but on the bare sand. We had nothing left to do but to laugh through half of the night over all the details of these events and our own foolishness.' (Valya, born in 1966)

THREATS TO THE TRAVELING MAIDEN

British feminists have analyzed the gendered differences in experiencing and telling about 'the first time'.[14] In their analysis, men and the norms of masculinity dominate the experience, leaving women with little space for feelings of autonomy and resistance:

> The two worlds of adolescent masculinity and femininity come together at the moment of 'first sex' in a way that powerfully confirms respective positions of agency and object, of doing sex and being done to. These meanings and positions are difficult to escape, despite the self-awareness and resistance expressed by many of our respondents....the only potential positions of female power appear to be negative and disembodied: either by saying 'no' or by ridiculing her partner's performance. [15]

In my reading, both Masha's and Valya's stories present a less simple picture. Certainly, we detect both contradictory and ambivalent relationships between the three levels of analysis I use: feelings, social events, and the (retrospective) interpretations and justifications. But it seems to me the Soviet stories both present strong evidence of at least

---

14   Janet Holland, Caroline Ramazanoglu and Rachel 'In the Same Boat? The Gendered (In)experience of First Heterosex', in Diane Richardson (ed.), *Theorising Heterosexuality*, (Buckinghman and Philadelphia, 1996), pp.143–160.
15   Idem, p.159.

partly successful female sexual autonomy.[16] At the same time, the desirability of such feminine independence was perhaps harder to justify in the Soviet Russian context than in Great Britain.

The Black Sea travel descriptions begin with colorfully described feelings of freedom and adventure. They obviously stem both from the lack of social surveillance and the exotic sensuality of the landscape, the food and the people. The strength of the feelings themselves remains important at the moment of writing. The summer is said to be one of Masha's happiest times, and Valya remembers that 'nevertheless, the summer left memories of warmth and light. As for my unconscious fear of men – how was I to know, that it would stem from precisely that summer.'

The initial happy feelings are then contrasted with the actual social interaction between young people. The first obstacle facing the *self sufficient travelling maiden* was the threat of irresponsible or violent men. The men's behaviour is on the one hand relativized and belittled – 'we had nothing left to do but laugh', writes Valya after what happened to her and her girlfriend. On the other hand, it is elevated to a continuous threat to ignorant young women, with (in Valya's case) unpredictable imprints e.g. on the unconscious.

This actual social threat is enforced by ethnic cultural stereotypes. Southern – Armenian, Georgian, Caucasian, Azerbaijani, etc. – ethnicity is in several female (but no male) autobiographies mentioned as an unsuitable trait in itself.[17] For instance, one woman who longs to get married rejected an Uzbek suitor whom she fell in love with only because of being afraid of living with an 'Eastern man' (*vostochnyi chelovek*); a young disabled girl's mother forbade her daughter to marry one of her few boyfriends, who was from Tajikistan. (In our material, accounts of harassment and rapes by Southern men also appear mostly in connection with exotic trips and 'foolish mistakes',

- - - - -

16   The difference between the conclusions of Holland, Ramazanoglu and Thomson and this article may reflect the ideology of the researchers, real cultural differences, and/or differences in the type of research material (Holland et al. made interviews with strong interaction between the teenager and the adult researcher, while the autobiographies I am using present fuller, more complex stories that are structured by another interaction – that between the teen and adult self of the autobiographical author). I suspect all three causes to be at work, but the scope of this article does not allow for a deeper comparison.
17   It is a great linguistic irony that 'kavkazkyi chelovek', literally "Caucasian man", in Russian is a strongly negative stereotype of a passionate, violent and often criminal person, while contemporary English uses the same word to describe a white, Western man.

although they were perhaps not less usual in domestic everyday settings.)

At the level of presenting interpretations and evaluations of their experiences, both Masha and Valya partly defend their right to, and enjoyment of, sexual adventures. Valya mentions her own curiosity about sex as one reason for not fighting more when she is forced to have sex. But the women also continuously moralize and blame their own behaviour. Valya describes her and her girlfriend's innocence and 'young small heads', thus casting herself both as a powerless victim and as a girl who should have known better. Valya also blames herself for not fighting more to protect her virginity – 'later it seemed to me, that I did not resist all the way'.

Valya also interprets her first violent sexual experience as being the root of her present 'fear of men'. Her current situation is certainly problematic, as she has started a long, complicated and unhappy relationship with an elder, married, sick and alcoholic man. Masha was, quite to the contrary, at the moment of writing living through a very experimental and exciting period of her sexual life. Nevertheless, she also judges her adventurous younger self:

> [My boyfriend] also liked to drink, and I was so unused to it I started drinking in big dosages. I am still amazed over how I did not get pregnant or infected from him with some disgusting crap...Now I remember myself with horror, wondering how that could have been me? I was very *porochna*: drank myself drunk, smoked, behaved extremely loosely [*raskovanno*], fucked with my boyfriend wherever we could. (Masha, born in 1954)

It seems that in Masha's retrospective evaluation, fitting into conventions – 'how could that be me?' – is almost as big a problem as the concrete social risks of pregnancy, venereal disease or sexual violence. Masha also continuously raises the theme of unjustly received, unearned happiness, of behaving in a too egotistic way.

> [My lover] arranged fantastic adventures for me. He took me to the mountains, let me ride on a yacht and a teplochod, took me on excursions....I did not think that my trip [on a yacht] was made possible by somebody's hands. I had not crossed one single finger [to help]. I got it for free. Why? I did not think that I had to pay for this in any way. I was irresponsible and *bezzabotna*, insouciant. I don't know who had to pay for that happiness of mine, nor how. (Masha, born in 1954)

In the British study, Holland et al. claimed the impossibility of fully autonomous female sexuality. The successful stories of women's resistance were, according to them, basically connected with denying pleasure – thus women present agency mainly by refusing to have sex, ending the relationship, and so on. The implicit assumption of the British researchers is that women would like to be (and be seen as) autonomous beings, and suffer from their passive role: 'The range of young women's responses reflects different approaches to the problems of managing their lack of agency. His achievement of manhood is her loss of autonomy.'[18]

As already said, I have less problems with detecting clear and sensual representations of women's autonomous sexuality from the Soviet autobiographies. In Valya's case, the autonomy is connected with the gorgeous surroundings and anticipating sexual adventures, while actual intercourse proves a dramatic and traumatic event. The young Masha fully realizes herself as a self-centered sexual subject. However, she cannot approve of this behaviour in retrospect. Her problems do not lie with initiating the sexual exploration, or telling her story, but with justifying it for herself and the readers. Even when psychological and physical space was found for young women's independent sexuality, there was not the cultural space available for expressing herself in positive terms.

Thus the second obstacle facing the traveling maiden is that too self-centered a life style is in itself culpable, not fitting into the ideal of a *self-sacrificing, altruistic woman.*[19] Also Valya is at the moment justifying her continuing current unhappy and worsening relationship by way of the man's heart problems and his need for her help and self-sacrifice.

In Soviet Russia, the self-approving, young and sexually active woman was a rare phenomenon. One of the social types dominating the corresponding Finnish autobiographical material - the single, childless, active woman in search of adventures and different partners – is all but lacking from the Petersburg material, both when we look at the authors themselves and the people they describe. But however rare, this type of woman did exist. One man with a previous broad

. . . . .
18   Holland, Ramazanoglu and Thomson., p.154
19   Annikki Verkkoniemi, Naisten asema ja selviytymiskeinot Neuvostoliitossa: analyysi Julia Voznesenskajan romaanista Naisten Dekamerone. (Unpublished paper, Department of Social Policy, University of Helsinki, 1998).

sexual experience describes his astonishment at meeting such a woman, Vika, during a tourist trip abroad. She was the one making sexual advances, and she was openly enjoying sex:

> Vika thought sex was a very important and central thing for a woman. Perhaps, as she did not have children, for her this substituted for children, and a regular husband. She dressed very well, but, the main thing I have remembered about her (and which was pointed out by the ladies in our group), was that she did not wear a bra. In those times (1975) it was against customs and conventions. (Man, born in 1930, construction worker)

Only one of the youngest women in our autobiographies (a physician born in 1972), describes a traveling life style, where the declared goal is self-fulfillment and pleasure, not responsibilities, marriage and children. Her sexual memoir is told in a detached and funny tone, with the amorous adventures in the US clearly separated from domestic everyday life back at home.

By contrast, somewhat older, middle-aged women give more examples of rich but unproblematic sex lives. Women of the middle generation have written accounts of Southern trips and exotic lovers where the threat of violence and the need for self-judgment and moralizing is absent. Thus a woman born in 1946, holding the especially prestigious (in Soviet times) position as the head of a supermarket department, describes her most recent love story as a beautiful romance at the Black Sea. The man was 16 years younger than she was, quiet, delicate, and very romantic. She took the initiative to have sex with him. The first problems arose only as she, when they parted, gave him her card encouraging him to contact her in Petersburg, and he froze when he understood her social position.

KOMANDIROVKAS

Soviet sexual practices during late socialism followed a 'double moral standard' in two senses: the declared ideological and social values were far from actual sexual behaviour, and the behaviour and morals of men differed from those of women. This double standard is exemplified in the autobiography of 'Vera', whose story also has the most detailed descriptions of advances made during train journeys.

(Night trains were famous for presenting good opportunities, as men and women shared the coupés on Soviet trains.)

> During one kommandirovka to Moscow I traveled with the head engineer of the project in a first class SV wagon, in a coupé for two After champagne, chocolate candy and mandarins, while a romance in Shalyapin's performance was playing, he, like a serpent-seducer, made me forget about everything. He was a 40 year old Armenian, a married man, who, in his own way, was deeply attached to his wife, and their daughters, but at the same time nothing could prevent the gossip of his new passion from spreading around the institute. I was seeing him for about one year. (Vera, born in 1937, secretary)

At that time Vera was herself married, and had already had some extramarital relationships. However, she wants to stress that she consciously had a 'taboo' against workplace affairs: several men were chasing her, while she maintained that 'you should never have relationships at work, in order to escape gossip, jealousy and misunderstandings.' Although the one-year affair described above is first depicted as romantically and sexually very satisfying, she now sees it as a 'stupid error' (*glupost'*).

> As we were both married, we basically met during working trips, which there were quite a lot of. When there were no trips we met at my place a few times, but that was not enough for him and he started to follow me at work, begging for a new meeting and insisting we should rent an apartment for our meetings. I refused his offer, because I was tired of his harassment and fed up with hiding, lying, and feeling ashamed, especially as he was a terrible coward in this respect (that nothing would come out, that nobody would see or think anything). (Vera, born in 1937, secretary)

The relationship ended brutally one Sunday, when they both had happened to come to work The man locked Vera in a room, threatened her and raped her. She was hurt and shocked, 'I felt like I would have been thrown away as garbage (*vyvalyali v pomoykach*). As they say, there is one step from love to hate.' After that, Vera escaped every kind of contact with the man, who eventually began an affair with another woman at the work place.

Vera's autobiography then continues with telling about how Vera successfully rejected another advance made on a train. Again, the man had arranged for a first class wagon for only two persons, and arrived slightly drunk to what he had planned as an amorous night. Vera found him disgusting and unattractive:

> When we met in the coupé I told him to be ashamed [for planning to sleep with her]. Then he started to make advances, and I said rude things to him and asked him to go outside. I quickly undressed and lay down on the upper bed, which surprised him when he entered the coupé, but he accepted my decision. However, in the middle of the night he woke me up, climbing to my bed and begging me to give myself to him. I was sleepy and at first did not understand what was happening. When I finally awoke, I was filled with such disgust at his spitty kisses, that I suffocated with anger. I pushed him away with all my strength and it was a wonder he did not hurt himself on the small table when he fell down from the bed. The next morning he excused himself. I told him to approach me only on work-related matters... (Vera, born in 1937, secretary)

Thus the only female autobiography in our material with detailed descriptions of affairs during *komandirovkas* is very ambivalent: Vera did not approve of work-place relations in principle, unwelcomed advances gave her long lasting memories of disgust, and a longer relationship ended in violence and mutual anger. She tells us she complained about the lying and hiding connected with her affair, while her lover on the contrary wanted to intensify the affair – and even to aggravate the lies by arranging a special apartment to meet in. Although Vera's personal feelings and her interpretations of adultery are not presented as very contradictory, she is explicitly criticizing the (male) social norms of organizing and conducting extramarital affairs for being morally unacceptable.

MEN WITH PARALLELL LIVES

For Vera's married male colleagues, by contrast, work place affairs and *komandirovkas* seem more like an *acceptable* way to arrange love affairs, a constant way of leading parallel lives. This impression is supported both by statistical comparisons and comparative analysis of autobiographies: while European men generally have more parallel affairs than women, St. Petersburg men more often demonstrate infidelity as a way of life, compared to Finnish and Estonian men.[20]

Infidelity in the form of consciously sought and upheld parallel lives is clear from this man's words of advice:

> It is evident that love affairs should not be conducted with single women, if you are married and cannot have a divorce. Single women always have the hope that you will be with her all the time, and it is not possible in most cases. You begin to feel guilty, and the meetings turn into family quarrels. Even the sexual meetings start to become monotonous. And, evidently, the affairs cannot last too long. It is better when they finish soon – you are left with the memories but no aftertaste of hurting each other. (Man, born in 1930, construction worker)

The prototype of a Russian Don Juan is found in autobiographies from the youngest generation, notably a rock musician born in 1960. This man is unfaithful to his wife before, during and after their wedding (they divorced soon afterwards), and the biggest part of the autobiography consists of hundreds of short encounters in hotel rooms and massage parlors. An almost identical sexual life story has been analyzed by Tatyana Baraulina. According to her, restless promiscuity is one of the paradigmatic forms for late Soviet and post-Soviet masculinity:

> As [the interviewee] continues to look for reasons for his polygamy, he runs out of explanations....[quote]: 'I don't know, why I do it, I can't explain it, I mean... I don't know, why do you, say, smoke – well it's like that and, well...'... The experience of one-night stands is the fundament on which the identity of the narrator is built. It is what he cannot explain, it is 'like smoking', it is what he is doing because he is – a Man.[21]

Of course, not all Soviet men were young seductive Don Juans, or married men in in high status professions. One of our autobiographical authors, 'Georgii', presents himself as a shy and socially

- - - - -
20 Elina Haavio-Mannila, J.P.Roos and Anna Rotkirch 'Types of Love and Male Infidelity in Finnish, Estonian and Russian autobiographies.' Paper presented at the 14th World Congress of the International Sociological Association, Montreal, July 26-August 1, 1998.
21 Tatyana Baraulina: 'Konstruirovanie muzhestvennosti cherez ee problematizatsiiu v biograficheskikh narrativah', unpublished magisterskaia dissertatsiia, European University of St Petersburg, June 1997, pp. 41–42.

awkward man. He was ruthlessly used by a woman, who left him once the trip was over. For Georgii, *komandirovkas* were among the few possibilities of meeting a new woman after he divorced his first wife in his early 30s. He participated in geological trips with the explicit (if failed) aim of arranging his sexual life.

> When I parted with [my first wife], I thought that changing woman would not be a problem and everything would go smoothly [kak po maslu]. There were no 'personal' advertisments at the time and my only source of contacts was the expedition in the summer...In the expeditions there were usually very short-lasting love affairs, they ended together with the expedition. But you don't think of that in the beginning, and the atmosphere of living together in field conditions facilitated the proximity of bodies and souls. The important thing is not to lose time when people are forming into groups...When the time came, [my girlfriend] parted and left only memories. After returning home from the expedition, I tried to continue our games, but she made it clear that she was not the least interested. I suffered for some time, but catching sight of a distant star in the sky one autumn evening, I understood how far we were from each other.' (Man, born in1949, various occupations)

Georgii's account of this *komandirovka* is just the opposite of the summer journey to the South told by Masha. Masha deplored her lack of love for the local guy she had an affair with and moralized over her sexual exploits. Georgii, by contrast, presents sex as the main (and completely acceptable) reason for starting an affair. Nevertheless, his suffering after being left – looking at the stars to console himself – unexpectedly reveals to the reader quite other feelings. In the next paragraph, however, Georgii again uses 'pure' sex as his only motive for starting to date. He tells us how after the sad end of his geological expedition, he finally managed to find a sexually available woman whom he says he used to call 'piece of meat' even in her presence.

Discussions about gender and autobiography have centered around the axis of 'autonomy' versus 'relationality'. Feminist scholars claimed that male autobiographers seem independent and heroic, while women authors tend to write about themselves as interdependent and part of surrounding social networks. Thus the autonomous self has been seen as typical for the classical Western male autobiography, while relational depictions are sometimes more easily found in women's writings.

In the descriptions of *komandirovki* related here, the Petersburg men also start from inside the the rhetoric of autonomy. As in the case of the construction worker quoted above, or in Georgii's case, the men often stress the instrumental and pragmatic aim of their social and sexual relations. The configuration of the Man with parallell lives is supported by an active, seductive man, who seems not to bother with more complex psychological and moral issues. (One could speculate to what extent this configuration was enforced by the perceived lack of control and autonomy – or Manhood – in other spheres of Soviet life. Leading parallell love lives and making ceaseless conquests would then appear as analogous to the obstinate refusal of Russian / Soviet men to wear car seat-belts – power is taken in the situations where it can be exercised.)

However, more recent contributions to autobiographical theory stress that the division between autonomy and relationality should not be applied too simply. In many texts, images of autonomy and relationality intertwine in both men's and women's autobiographies and vary according to what part of the life course is being described.[22] As we have seen, this is true for a closer reading of Georgii's story. He may long to be the sexual hero, but his experiences also touch upon relationality, the longing for love and a significant other in his life.

CONCLUSIONS

It has been said that Soviet culture did not perceive 'sex' as a separate sphere of existence. Instead, sexuality was understood as something embarrassingly banal.[23] Journeys, by contrast, seem to have provided both physical, psychological and cultural space for non-trivial sexual adventures. We have looked at two typical forms of Soviet domestic tourism, vacations in the South and business trips, in their gender dimensions.

The ultimate goal of traveling – transgression – is approached differently in the male and female autobiographies presented here.

. . . . .
22   Anni Vilkko '...'. In Matti Hyvärinen, Eeva Peltonen & Anni Vilkko (eds) Liikkuvat erot. Sukupuoli elämäkertatutkimuksessa. (Moving Differences. Gender in Autobiographical Studies) (Tampere, Vastapaino, 1998)
23   Boym, *Common Places*.

What the women found, and cherished, were autonomy, freedom, and the possibility of making sexual initiatives that were lacking and/or condemned in everyday domestic life. In the journeys to the Black Sea retold here, it is the allure of the foreign, of the rapid and risky 'letting go' that characterize the stories, which were often verging on the border to culturally culpable carelessness and physical risk-taking.

Similar configurations of 'Traveling maidens' can be found in other cultures (think, for instance, of the habit of Japanese girls of traveling to Europe or the US before returning home, marrying and leading the life of a proper wife). In Soviet Russia, traveling young women faced two main obstacles: the actual threats of violence, and the cultural difficulty of justifying a sexually self-sufficient and independent lifestyle. Even when there was, exceptionally, social space for women's sexual adventures, it could not be accommodated in the prevalent cultural configuration of the self-sacrificing Russian woman.

The men were, on the one hand, fulfilling the ideals of autonomy, initiative and freedom by dividing their lives into married domestic life and foreign traveling affairs. The configuration of the 'Man with parallel lives' of course fits into the much described absence of Soviet Russian men from everyday family life. On the other hand, one male autobiographer started from the assumption of autonomous exploits, but ended up telling about his longing for emotional proximity and deeper relationships with women. Here, the quest for space and foreign experiences was a getting away in order to come 'home' – escaping the everyday in order to look for a new centre.

Space in Russian (Soviet) Cinema: The Aesthetics of Censorship and the Case of *The Mirror*

Pentti Stranius

In the creation of the myth of Soviet power, cinema played a crucial role. In Russia we can clearly see that cinema cannot have a history purely and simply as cinema. All cinema has a special space in a historical context and this context can have various strands: the political or social, the economic or the aesthetic factors are all constantly at play. Furthermore, cinema always has a history behind the screen, because it has been made in some society. Every film production functions under certain conditions, under economic control or censorship – sometimes in very close connection with some ideology or big business.[1]

I am interested in these factors, the connections between cinema and reality, with the historical and social situation in Russia. In this article my topic is the place and space of Soviet cinema during the stagnation under Brezhnev – the limits of film-making formed by 'the aesthetics of censorship'.

Socialist realism represented only one way of describing reality. In Soviet cinematic art and literature its main principle was to show the world as it is, to describe some phenomenon as it happened. But as we know, this practice was already quite difficult to realize under Lenin.

---

[1] See, e.g. Richard Taylor, 'Red stars, positive heroes and personality cults' In Richard Taylor & Derek Spring (eds.), *Stalinism and Soviet Cinema* (London and New York, 1993), pp.69–89. Valeri Fomin, *Kino i vlast. Sovetskoje kino: 1965–1985 gody* (Moscow,. 1996).

The principles of *sotsrealizm* were formed and finally distorted during the Stalin era. In the 1930s cinema and literature started playing a more and more important role in the misinterpretation of actual Soviet life. The new reality, or the grand illusions of this '*sotsreality*', were created by means of mass agitation in the entire Soviet space: in art and the Red Army, in the schools and the houses of culture, in the theatre and on the screen, on the radio and the pages of books and newspapers, in sanatoriums and working places.

However, the Bolshevik leader Lenin was the first statesman to understand the full potential and the means of expression provided by cinematic art ('Of all the arts, for us cinema is the most important'). And he was the first power politician and Marxist political theorist to speak and write about the cinema as art. Many other Western thinkers, professionals and even the western intelligentsia considered cinema to be primarily a commercial entertainment for the masses. Of course, for Lenin the cinema was not only an art form, but the greatest means of mass agitation, which would help him and the new government educate the analphabetic people in the spirit of the new ideology.

The language of the new art was very easy to read, easy to understand, and always had a great and deep influence on the feelings and the subconscious of the ordinary people. Moreover, the language of the new Soviet cinema was very revolutionary in the 1920s. The first years after the revolution were still an avant-garde period in Russian art, theatre, literature and cinema. All these arts had a major influence on the cinema, which started to become a synthesis of all the avant-garde in the Russian arts.

The cinema of Sergei Eisenstein (*Strike, October, Battleship Potemkin*) seemed to be an ideal revolutionary process: the good heroes of the proletariat or the peasants were fighting against the evil Tsar, the military and the capitalists. The new 'intellectual' montage, created and used by Eisenstein, gave an illusion of continuous class struggle, the struggle between good and evil, between new and old. Life on the screen moved like a dialectical process, through conflicts between the classes to the victory of Communism. In this struggle the winner was always the new rising class, the Holy Proletariat - and, of course, its orthodox Bolshevik party. Little by little the world on the screen, the cinema itself, was changing, turning into a 'second' reality.

Very many viewers of Soviet cinema thought (even later, by watching TV), that the films of Eisenstein were documentary, a real history of the October revolution. The strikes and historical events which were filmed, for example, on the battleship Potemkin, seemed to reflect real life. The 'first' reality, actual everyday problems, disappeared from the pages of books and the screen. It was the beginning of the era of mythology, of massive mind control. The real paradox between *sotsrealizm* and Soviet cinema can be observed in the early 1930s. In the course of time a strange phenomenon appeared. New art, literature and cinema emerged so quickly and with such enthusiasm and ideological inspiration that the authors themselves did not completely understand how they created a new hero, the harsh, cruel Bolshevik in a leather jacket. In the 30s this hero stepped forth from the screen and the pages of books and took revenge on his creators through open terror and the censorship of socialist realism. (This new situation, the beginning of Stalin's terror in the early 30s has been shown in detail and excellently in two new perestroika films – *Without a Hero* (1987), directed by Tatiana Yurina and *My Friend, Ivan Lapshin* (1984), by Alexei German.) Mayakovsky, Fadeyev, Gorky, Sholokhov, Eisenstein and Dziga Vertov with his famous 'Cinema Eye' took an active part in the creation of this hero. And the principles of *sotsrealizm* were just the beginning of the total system of censorship in all the arts.

But the rules of censorship concerning cinema appeared much later than censorship in literature (the early 1920s in literature). Rules were almost unnecessary in cinema before the 1930s, because the financial side of the industry, on the whole, was in the hands of the Soviet state. New directors believed in Marxism and Bolshevism, many were party members or supported the Bolsheviks. Some escaped, emigrated to the West during the Civil War, while the older ones remained quiet, tried to live in peace and escape open conflicts with the new power.

The first conflicts between the state and cinema appeared in the 1920s, but more serious problems were awaiting directors in the 30s. For example, when Sergei Eisenstein tried to make an honest film about the Komsomol 'boy-hero' Pavlik Morozov, his project was stifled. The protagonist of Eisenstein's great work, *Ivan the Terrible*, was too close to Stalin, and the unfinished second part of the film was shelved.[2]

When the Writers' Union was founded in 1934, Stalin had a solid organization with a new elite, a *nomenklatura*, which was also interested in censorship. The members of the Writers' Union, under the leadership of the renowned writer, Maksim Gorky – who was specially invited from Italy, where he had lived since the 1920s – took

---

2   Naum Kleiman, 'Iivanan tragedia' in *Filmihullu* 1997, no.1, pp.28–32.

the lead in this ideological work. The Writers' Union was in fact the organization which started to control the other facets of cultural life, for example, cinema. In the 30s and 40s censorship was based on the ideology of Marxism-Leninism and the main role of the Chief Interpreter in this ideological game was played by Stalin himself and his inner circle. The fate of any film depended on the party leaders' opinion, and if the director had any friends close to Stalin, he naturally had a greater possibility of working.

The main issue was, however, how to control the film industry? In a country where literature had such traditional roots in cultural life, it was easier to refuse to release some screenplay written by a director or screenwriter, than to stop the whole process of production. Moreover, in the socialist society – where all finances were in the hands of the party-state, not private companies – Stalin had total power to either approve or reject money for some film project.

The State Film Committee – Goskino (originally Gosfilm) – was founded in 1938, the year after the coming of the Great Terror. The main duty of Goskino was the control of screenwriters' work. The controllers, who were responsible for the orthodox ideology, were famous writers, journalists, literary critics and other members of the cultural intelligentsia, who enjoyed the confidence of Stalin. The founding of Goskino was one reason screenwriting becoming a special art in the Soviet Union. Screenwriters became a special category of filmmakers in the industry – the same phenomenon, in principle, existed in Hollywood. Film-making started to become a factory process and Goskino's party leaders planned to create a real Soviet Hollywood in the south, on the Black Sea.

During the Stalin era we cannot yet, however, speak of specific censorship principles. First, the film industry was not very large, only 20–30 films per year. Film production fell from 148 in 1928 to 35 in 1933.[3] During the Second World War and thereafter, fewer than ten new films were made a year. Stalin had no problems controlling them. Second, after the Great Terror every normal human being, the intelligentsia in particular, feared for his life. The terror struck horror into scholars, writers and filmmakers, who began to recognize their 'space to manoeuvre'. Usually they did not even try to write, say or show anything dangerous. They started to develop a 'pre-ordained (or "internal") censorship' in trying to understand Stalin's taste, because

---

3 Richard Stites, *Russian popular culture. Entertainment and society since 1900* (Cambridge, 1992).

Stalin himself was the First Censor in the 1930s and 1940s: he always wanted to see the first copy of any film.

This situation changed in the late 1950s, after Stalin's death in 1953 and, especially, after the 20th party congress. The era of Nikita Khrushchev is often referred to in Russian historiography as a 'springtime' or 'the thaw'. In fact, many members of the intelligentsia with whom I have spoken about this time have stated that at the very beginning of the 1960s a euphoria gripped the younger generation. The main thrust against the rigid cultural system came from the artistic intelligentsia, writers in particular, but more and more from filmmakers as well. Cinema started to play a very important role in the formation of the new generation in Russia – 'the children of the 20th party congress' ('the 60s', 'the babyboomers' in the West).[4]

In the early 50s only five or ten films were made a year, by 1954 45 and by 1955 66. In the late 50s the centralized approval of film scripts was temporarily abolished, only to be restored under Leonid Brezhnev, ten years later. The Brezhnev period (1964-1982) was a reaction against Khrushchev's springtime. In Soviet history it was a quite stable period and for the most part was a peaceful time for the ordinary person, workers and peasants in the *kolkhozes* (except for Czechoslovakia in 1968, Afghanistan in 1980 ...). For dissidents, honest reformers and members of the intelligentsia it was the peace of the graveyard – a graveyard of ideas, openness and free expression, which had not seemed to be the case under Khrushchev.[5]

The Brezhnev era was a time of stagnation in the USSR for many reasons. Internal censorship – or 'controlled schizophrenia', as I call this phenomenon[6] – became a method for surviving and staying alive when trust in 'the shining future of Communism' disappeared. The aesthetics of censorship became a part of normal intellectual life. In these years, according to Alexander Solzhenitsyn, the Soviet intelligentsia started to think in one way, speak aloud in another way and do things in a third. It was 'life in a lie'. In the moral sense, it was a hard time for the creative intelligentsia, who had no place nor space for free speech in society.[7]

. . . . .

4   Peter Vail & Aleksandr Genis, *60-e. Mir sovetskogo tsheloveka* (Moscow,1996).
5   See e.g. Fomin, Stites.
6   Pentti Stranius, 'Intelligentsian kuolema? Älymystön omakuva Pietarissa ja Petroskoissa' In Ilkka Liikanen & Pentti Stranius (eds.), *Matkalla kansalaisyhteiskuntaan? Liikettä ja liikkeitä Luoteis-Venäjällä* (Joensuu, 1996), pp.151–161.
7   Alexander Solzhenitsyn, 'Na vozvrate dyhanija i soznanija' in *Novyi Mir* 1991, no.5, pp. 3–46.

In cinema the system of censorship had three levels, three interludes:

The first level in the aesthetics of censorship was to institute internal censorship among filmmakers, the so-called 'internal militia'. It was a state level, total ideological propaganda and, perhaps, the most important level of the entire system – self-imposed censorship.

By the 60s the whole population, the new generations, had been formally educated in the spirit of Marxism-Leninism; in practice, of course, it was the spirit of Stalinism, the interpretation of Russian Marxism. Real belief in this ideology started to disappear initially among the intelligentsia, among 'the 60s' generation, who knew quite well how to pretend to believe. The intelligentsia was now more educated, it had more information – and it received greater influence from abroad. But the writers, artists and film directors, for example, knew quite well their 'space for manoeuvre', the limits of the allowed and outlawed, the permitted and forbidden. If someone tried to overstep these limits, he was soon stopped by colleagues in the Writers' Union or in the Filmmakers' Union. Therefore the party-state, the Politburo or the Central Committee of the Communist Party tried to spread their influence to the filmmakers through their organization, through the Filmmakers' Union. The main idea was to build a system of internal censorship, to lay the foundations for the 'internal militia'. Under Brezhnev open terror seemed to be too cruel a method – the rigid internal militia technique seemed more human. It seemed like the result of Soviet education, like the normal behaviour of the new Soviet Citizen – Homo Soveticus.

Most of the declarations and orders pertaining to cinema written by the Politburo or the Central Committee were quite careful, more hints than direct orders or prohibitions. Most of all the party-state reminded the intelligentsia of a lack of patriotic and ideological content in art. This conflict between form and content was constant, permanent in ideological discussion since the early 1920s. For Soviet Stalinism, content was always more important than form: any play with form was often forbidden or censored. This is paradoxical, since the most talented film directors, Sergei Eisenstein and Andrei Tarkovsky, were always seeking new forms of impression. Very many orders were written about the importance of *sotsrealism*, the negative influence of subjectivism and a class line in art. These themes were repeated continuously in the 1960–70s.

I heard the term 'internal militia' from Joseph Heifiz, a very famous old film director in St. Petersburg. He was 85 years old when we spoke and he remembered this phenomenon vividly – from his entire life experience. Many other filmmakers and members of the intelligentsia who have lived under totalitarian systems in different countries have used such terms with the same content – and in the same context.[8]

The second level of the aesthetics of censorship was 'the Era of the Red Pens'. This expression, the red pens, is used by the film historian and author of the book *Kino i vlast* (Cinema and Power), Valeri Fomin. He works in Moscow, at the State Research Institute for Cinematic Art. Since perestroika, the period of Mikhail Gorbachev, Fomin has been working in the archives of the KGB with documents concerning shelved films.

According to Fomin every local studio in the USSR had its own red pens – trusted writers and film historians, sometimes film critics from the elite circle. They knew the tastes of the party-leaders (Brezhnev, Kosygin, Ponomariev, Romanov, Suslov) and they controlled filmwriting and the scenarios at the local level, for example, in Moscow, Leningrad, Kiev, Tbilisi or Tallinn. These studios were the most important in Soviet film production. Sometimes a screenplay was accepted at some studio, in Leningrad for example, and it was sent to Moscow. The highest level, Goskino, always wanted to have the last word: to release or reject it. In Moscow, the Goskino red pens often said '*njet*' and proposed some corrections in the screenplay to the local studio. These proposals, or corrections, were often made in red, with red pens. Then the scriptwriter, sometimes the director himself, went to work again and tried to take note of the proposals from the highest echelons of bureaucracy. Very often screenwriters and directors attempted to turn around the stupid rules of bureaucracy. They wrote one screenplay for the bureaucracy in Moscow and another for the film group, for the needs of the director. But this practice did not help for a long time. After the film had been shot, the Moscow censors at Goskino were the first to view the original copy. They had the last word: they could shelve the whole production.

Such practices in the censorship system could take very long, even years. It took a great deal of time to send screenplays and letters of introduction from the local studio to Moscow and then wait for the answers, send copies and organize showings at the local studio and in Moscow for the red pens, then to 'make the film better' by order of Goskino and await the final decision. Furthermore, film production

. . . . .
8   Markus Viljanen and Pentti Stranius *Elokuva vangitsee aikaa* Documentary film in two parts shown on Finnish TV on 26th October 1990, 2nd November 1990.

worked very slowly at the local studio and shooting a film, even a short documentary, might last for years. Therefore those films which were started during the Khrushchev springtime, were only finished under Brezhnev, in the late 60s, when the political situation had changed. The era of stagnation had already begun. It is the main reason why there are so many shelved films from the late 1960s: 'the children of the 20th party congress' tried to provide more 'space for manoeuvre' for cinema, but their works were put on the shelves.[9]

Many directors always had two or three screenplays on their desks. Sometimes, they waited for years for permission to start shooting their first film – or the second, if they had conflicts with the highest censors over their first film. Although they may have become famous directors at Western film festivals, and were good professionals and had graduated from the State Film Institute – VGIK – in Moscow, it did not alleviate the censorship of the party-state.

Sometimes a film was allowed to be made, but the censors interfered in the distribution of the copies. Usually 100 to 200 copies were made for the whole country, but if Goskino did not like some scenario or film director, they permitted the distribution of only 10–20. A controversial film might only be shown in small theatres, early in the morning, during the day, and with many critical reviews in the press.

The third level in the system of censorship, the last form of party-state control, was 'shelved films'. This practice was used very seldom, because the internal militia and red pens worked adequately, accurately and firmly. In this case, when a film was to be shelved, the original, negative material – and the copies, if they had already been made – were confiscated and sent to the Central Film Archive – to Gosfilmofond, near Moscow.

I have heard very many stories about film copies which have been smashed to smithereens. Of course, I can understand such exaggeration by world-famous film directors who were really personae non-grata in the USSR. For instance, one recalled that all the copies and the original of his best film were stolen one night from the studio and hacked to pieces with an axe. He was lucky enough to save one copy, which was hidden under his bed. The story was so interesting that I used it in an article. Then a couple of months later I heard the same story twice, from other directors.

. . . . .

9   Fomin, *Kino i vlast'*...

A year later I was visiting the Central Film Archive – Gosfilmofond – and I asked about these destroyed films (naturally, it was under Gorbachev). The originals of all these forbidden films, and sometimes many copies, were on the Gosfilmofond shelves, in good condition. Not even the Soviet censors or the archive staff were so stupid as would appear at first sight. They did not destroy forbidden films, they even tried to maintain and preserve copies in good condition.

The decision to ban, to put some film on the shelf, was always made at the highest party level, the Politburo. The proposal to prohibit might come from the KGB or the Ministry of Culture or Education, but the final decision to release or reject was made in the Politburo.

In the late 1970s Leonid Brezhnev was no longer interested in cultural life. He was often sick and his taste in cinema was quite close to Stalin's – western films, melodrama and comedy. Brezhnev had no time to think about any psychological or ideological details and meanings in new films. Power in cultural and ideological questions was wielded by other members of the Central Committee and Politburo, for example, Mihail Suslov and Alexei Romanov. Romanov was a party man who became angry at the slightest hint of sex in a movie, even when he saw bedclothes on the screen. Suslov was already responsible for ideological work among the masses. Therefore he was very proud of having the possibility of 'talking' (indirectly) with famous artists, writers and directors – and preparing and writing different directives and declarations about art.

The final decision to shelve a film was often made by telephone. Therefore we do not have so many documents concerning this level of censorship. Some member of the Politburo, usually Suslov himself, just took the phone, called Goskino or the local studio and asked to speak with the producer - not the director. Then he informed him very briefly about the shelving, without giving any reasons.[10]

But before the decision was made in the Politburo, the red pens had done a substantial amount of work in the State Film Committee – Goskino. The famous troika of red pens at Goskino in the 1970s included Vladimir Baskakov, Head of the State Research Institute of Cinematic Art, Rostislav Yurenev, a film historian and critic, and Sergei Yutkevich, an old film director. I have read many documents and letters signed by this trio. They liked to give advice to directors, 'to make your film better' or 'to help you with the bureaucracy', as

---

10   Valeri Fomin, 'Hyllytysten estetiikka' *Filmihullu* 1991, no.2, pp.42–47.

they used to say during private discussions or in letters they sent concerning some details in the screenplay.

Baskakov, Yurenev and Yutkevich were all very intelligent persons and had travelled a lot visiting every film festival in the West. As far as I know (I have met them all and talked several times with Baskakov and Yurenev), they believed that they really helped some directors through the networks of Soviet bureaucracy and really made many films better. They assured me they were powerless against the party-state and the orders and shelvings of the Politburo; even if they belonged to the cinema elite and were also members of the party elite.

This troika of the red pens had different tastes. Yutkevich (1904–85) himself filmed a number of stories about Lenin, but he was not inflexible towards experiments with form, if the director only knew and remembered the specific limits of *sotsrealizm*. In Finland Yutkevich was known as 'the Gentleman of Soviet Cinema'. Yurenev (1912–) and Baskakov (1921–) were representatives of traditional *sotsrealizm*: no play with form; the film must have patriotic, educational and ideological contents and a positive hero. Sometimes, when a production was shelved, the red pens sent a polite letter to the director: 'Considering these deep impressions given by your excellent film, it is so hard to understand why the story was not released .... We believe that the reasons were ...'

What were the reasons for rejection – or the main principles of the aesthetics of censorship?

Andrei Tarkovsky (1932–86) was one film director under Brezhnev who was in continuous conflict with Goskino. Like many others writers and film directors of his generation, he tried to find more space for manoeuvre for his art. Therefore, time in the screenplays for his films was sometimes either the past (history), or the future (science fiction). *Andrei Rublev* was a historical film which was put on the shelf in 1966 for three years. In this medieval story the censors saw too much violence, 'so many cruel episodes' and an incorrect 'non-patriotic interpretation of Russian history'.[11] Tarkovsky's next films, *Solaris* and *Stalker* were made formally in the style of science fiction (a very popular way to escape *sotsrealizm* in literature and cinema), but the subtext is filled with criticism of the Soviet system.

When I think about the place and space of Andrei Tarkovsky in Russian cinema during the stagnation, I am always very astonished at

---

11 Fomin, *Kino i vlast'*...

the fate of his autobiographical film – *The Mirror*. *The Mirror* seems to be an attack on all aspects of *sotsrealizm*, on the ideological and collective spirit of art and the 'holy-patriotic' values of Soviet society, on the history of the USSR. Nevertheless, Tarkovsky had the courage and the skill to shoot a film about his own life using his own 'biological memory'. The result was, that *The Mirror* was criticized everywhere in the Soviet Union, but – and paradoxically – it was not shelved.

In my opinion *The Mirror* may be the best example in the history of cinema of a real author-director using the real voice and memory of his own heart. In this way *The Mirror* reflects poetry, music and dream more than moving pictures, poetical language more than montage. This kind of cinema looks like a dream, and as we know the human memory also works like a dream. It lacks logic! How can this dream, this biological memory be touched? How can the forbidden political history of one's own country or one's hidden individual or sexual life, crucial events in one's existence be understood? In my opinion, we can understand history, our own fate and life sometimes better through art, poetic language, music and serious cinema than through established versions of historiography.[12] In Russian cinema *The Mirror* specifically represents this poetical genre in cinema – it sounds and moves like poetry or music, not only as flowing images.

Andrei Tarkovsky often used very long shots in his films. In the book *Zapetsatlennoe vremja* (*The Sculpting Time*), which is a collection of the most important writings about his cinematic art, Tarkovsky says that he is more a sculptor than a film director. More than writing or directing his films, he sculpts pictures of the time.[13] Time and space were very important parts of Tarkovsky's art. With long and slow shots and episodes he forced us to think more ... of what? Our own life – time and space.

When the Goskino's red pens saw the first version of the screenplay, they realized immediately that *The Mirror* had to be cut, to be 'made better' in many places. The main points in the official critique were that:

– *The Mirror* includes too much mythology and mystification – Soviet viewers cannot understand the director's meaning;

. . . . .

12 See Pentti Stranius, 'Problema "govorjashtshih golov" i russkaja intelligentsija' in V. Voronkov and E. Zdravomyslova (eds.), *Biografitsheskij metod v izutshenii postsotsialistitsheskih obshtshestv* (St. Petersburg, 1997), pp.26–30.
13 Andrei Tarkovski, *Vangittu aika* (Jyväskylä, 1989), pp.84–109.

- the opening episode of the film, 'the doctor-speech therapist' with the boy must be cut, since the beginning of *The Mirror* lacks any contact to the rest of the screenplay;
- the episode in the printing house lasts too long, the woman walks endlessly in the corridors, where the atmosphere is too dark and depressive;
- the war chronicle must be used more carefully – it is incorrect to compare the Great Patriotic War with the war in Vietnam and the events in China;
- the metaphor of the woman hanging over the bed is not understandable, it must be cut;
- the narrator of *The Mirror* continuously speaks in a very pessimistic tone and it seems that the protagonist of the film has lived his life in vain - he has worked in art for years and achieved nothing; a too pessimistic biography.[14]

After a long confrontation and struggle with the Soviet bureaucracy, Andrei Tarkovsky refused to make 'corrections' to *The Mirror*. In spite of this, the film was released, with almost no changes. Why?

First, in this case the Goskino censors probably decided that the Soviet viewers could hardly understand Andrei Tarkovsky's deeper meanings. On the other hand, although *The Mirror* was released, the red pens interfered in its distribution and organized a massive critical campaign in the mass media in 1975–76.[15] Furthermore, at first the film was only shown in small theatres, by day.

Second, the red pens realized, of course, that Andrei Tarkovsky was a very talented filmmaker – already well-known in the West. In the Soviet ideology an 'honourable' member of the so-called creative intelligentsia, such as Tarkovsky, played (often against his own will) an important role as a buffer not only between the masses and the party-state, but, in particular, in international relations between the Soviet Union and the West. And the incident with *The Mirror* followed shortly after the 'the case of Solzhenitsyn' (1974) and the European Security Congress (1975).

Third, the human factor also played a significant role in Tarkovsky's case. Andrei Tarkovsky himself realized very well that his cinematic language was not even understandable to many Soviet viewers. He did not work for the general public. The main principle in

---

14 Fomin, *Koino i vlast'*; 'Hyllytysten estetiikka'.
15 See e.g. *Iskusstvo Kino* 1975–76.

his art was no compromises of any kind. In Moscow all of Tarkovsky's colleagues – and the red pens – knew that he was absolutely free from the 'internal militia'. He had already managed to create and find his own poetical cinema-world inside 'sotsreality' in his first films.

The system of censorship usually worked very severely at the first and second levels. The internal militia and the red pens guaranteed a patriotic character and class-line in cinematic art, an ideological quality in Soviet films. These levels also guaranteed that every contested film production was stopped at the very beginning, when the screenplay was ready. Therefore, the Special Film Committee, which was founded in the late 1980s – under Gorbachev – did not find so many shelved films as the head of the Committee, the film critic Andrei Plahov, had supposed it would.

The number of shelved films totalled about 100. I have seen one-third of these films, perhaps 30–35. However, it is quite difficult to say why a specific film was shelved. Sometimes it is impossible to discover the real reasons, especially when there are no documents at all: no letters, no directives, or the directors or censors are already dead. Many things depended on ideological aspects, but even more on human factors – on the relationship between some director and his censors. Some critical thinker among directors sometimes managed to make a critical film about the social problems in the Soviet Union, if he had a protector, or patron, at the highest echelons of the Communist Party, in the Politburo.

For instance, Nikita Mikhalkov managed to make several fine films – and to handle deeply-seated social problems as well – during the very stagnation of the 70s (*The Slave of Love*, *Oblomov*, *Five Evenings*, *Without Witnesses*, *Lovely Relatives*). His father was Sergei Mikhalkov, a party-man who belonged to the intelligentsia-elite and to Leonid Brezhnev's inner circle. Moreover, for decades Sergei Mikhalkov led the Writers' Union and was known as an author of the Soviet national anthem. It was understandable that his son had more space for manoeuvre in the film industry than ordinary directors from 'Lenfilm' or 'Tallinfilm'.

But the main reasons which were commonly used for forbidding the distribution of some film were the same ones used in the other spheres of Soviet *'sotsreality'*. In cinema, for example, it was impossible to handle:

– forbidden themes ('black holes') or a new interpretation of Russian history;

– *personae-non-grata*, persons who were in or falling into disfavour;
– any criticism of national policy in the USSR;
– any criticism of the Politburo, Central Committee, KGB, Red Army or the work of militiamen;
– real life in the countryside, villages and provinces or working life in ordinary factories ;
– well-known faults in Soviet society – hard drinking, drugs, black market, abortion, prostitution, even jail jargon. Not only were sexuality, love-making or underclothes banned on the screen, but it was sometimes even impossible to show how ordinary people spent their free time – for example, in the spirit of a new genre, the French 'new wave' in the 1950–60s. The censors believed it had been a 'morality of wasting time';
– a negative hero... A negative hero in the main role was an impossible phenomenon in Soviet cinema, because a positive hero in art was a central part of the ideological education of the masses – one of the main principles of *sotsrealizm*;
– any experiments ('play') with form or the use of metaphors were considered 'subjectivism' in style. Formalism and subjectivism were the main sins in every art, very useful to attack and difficult to defend against.[16]

I have spoken with many Russian film directors (Vadim Abdrashitov, Alexei German, Joseph Heifiz, Elem Klimov, Nikita Mikhalkov, Alexander Sokurov ...) about the significance of the aesthetics of censorship on the Soviet cinema. Most of them wanted to mention some positive aspects. In lieu of final conclusions, I will try to at last summarize their opinions.

The cinema was always considered an art in the USSR, from the very beginning in the 1920s. Goskino, VGIK and the local studios tried to do their best in the professional sense. In the party-state system finances never ran out – once the shooting of a film had started. For example, Tarkovsky's *Stalker* was filmed twice, since the whole negative material in the first shoot turned out to be useless. All serious film historians and critics agree that Soviet cinema was usually very professional, but too ideological.

Thanks to the bureaucracy and censorship film-making was always a long process, during which many films really became better. The

---

16 Stranius, Pentti 'Hyllytetty elokuva – kätketty muisti' *Maailma ja me* 1989, no.8, pp.35–41; Fomin, 'Hyllytysten estetiikka'.

screenplays were often of a high quality, a special genre in literature. The censors, the red pens, even at the local studios, were not stupid people, but intelligent professionals. In Moscow they were, of course, ideological gatekeepers, who still sometimes really helped young directors to work inside the censorship system.

The censorship system became a special professional college for Soviet filmmakers. Censorship or the fear of censorship forced them to show important things below the surface, indirectly. The same phenomenon functioned in literature, theatre and art. Because cinema seems to be more or less a synthesis of all arts, this behind-the-screen-influence – imagined images, forbidden dreams, silent voices of conscience, interrupted talks – is even stronger than in literature. It was very useful to learn to present something indirectly. It really helped directors to develop their film language, their means or manner of expression in cinematic art. We can distinguish here two different styles of film-making: the overt, showing what happens – an action film – or the covert, hiding the actual meaning of the images, shots and episodes below the surface - an intelligent cinema, which always forces the viewer to think more deeply and profoundly.

In the same sense professional Soviet viewers tried to find some hidden meanings behind the screen. Educated and informed people became a very intelligent audience. Paradoxically, thanks to censorship, many quality Soviet films of the 1960–70s offered plenty of room for different interpretations. In their interpretation the role of an enlightened public was enormous. In addition, one of the functions of intelligent cinema – cinema by Tarkovsky, for example – was and is to permit different interpretations, to allow more space to think, to use human memory and imagination.

From Globalism in Confinement to Egocentrism Unbound. The Spheres of the Russian Intelligentsia

Timo Vihavainen

Katerina Clark in her seminal work *Petersburg. Crucible of Cultural Revolution* sees the Russian intellectuals' mission as one of a Hermes, who was to unbind the prisoners who could only see the shadow world, so that they might experience the true forms. Romantic anticapitalists as they were, the bulk of the intellectuals did not want to unleash as such the base instincts of the 'great Unwashed' (the masses in being), but to give them a 'new vision' *(novoe zrenie)*. In terms of space, Clark has it that after 1917 the October Revolution was figured in a way that took space to the foreground and de-emphasized time. Space was seen in a binary form, there was the polluted one on the one hand and the pure one on the other. A contrast was also seen between the surface, the here and now, and some other, authentic, pure space beneath or above.

The ultimate source of pollution was not the mass of toilers, but the lower middle class, incarnated by the abominable *lavochnik*. The proletarians, on their part, were not infrequently seen as -in essence- better intellectuals than the actual ones. The fierce Scythians might not have been intellectuals but they evidently did not belong to the contaminated world; they were of another breed than the 'world-wide philistine ... who is now destroying ... art in aestheticism, science in scholastics, life in stagnation, revolutions in petty reformism'.[1]

---

1 R. Ivanov-Razumnik in 1917 as quoted in Katerina Clark *Petersburg: Crucible of Revolution* (Oxford,1995), p. 52.

As regards Western Europe, for the intellectuals of the Silver Age it was a place severely contaminated and polluted by the philistine. Only North America was still more so. Although the Russian avantgarde seemed to be a very European phenomenon, there was not very much sympathy for Europe as it was. The dream of many outstanding representatives of the avantgarde was not to join Europe, but to surpass it. The romantic anticapitalists did not aspire to meeting Western Europe on common ground, but were anxious to retain the purity of Russia by keeping clear of the capitals of the philistine.

Of course, this stance was not new as such, it had been shared by the first generation of the slavophiles, by the panslavists and the *narodniks*.[2] For the nationalist wing of the Russian intelligentsia Europe, at its best, was no more than a cemetery, full of sacred memories, as it was in the case of Dostoevsky. Therefore, only Russia did really count. Europe was something that was to be avoided and surpassed. Paradoxically, it was just therefore – as the symbolic centre of depravity– that Western Europe became crucially important and always present.

If the philistine mentality was bred by capitalism and if its romantic enemies were free from it, then pure space was not confined to Russia proper -which was not completely pure either. Rather it was safe to suppose that purity could be found in commerce-free zones of the intellectuals even in other countries. Both the hopelessly poor and the really rich, as well as the aristocrats of mind among the *raznochintsy* were free of the crippling effects of economic calculation.

Having a huge population of poor peasants, a thin layer of idle aristocracy and a small embryo of a middle class, Russia was not totally pure, but it was likely to be better than most of the world. The best of Europe, for its part, was not worlds apart from the best of Russia, but more or less on the same level, even if surrounded by a sea of filth.

The Russian intelligentsia as a group can hardly be said to have thought in a very cosmopolitan way – let alone globally – before the revolution. There were of course some habitueés of the European spas and salons, but one cannot avoid seeing an air of otherness vis-a-vis Europe. Even for those, who were not nationalistically oriented, the main object of care for the Russian intelligents was always Russia.

. . . . .

2 About the slavophiles see Nicholas V. Riasanovsky, *Russia and the West in the Teaching of the Slavophiles*, (Gloucester, Mass. 1965), pp. 103–119; Tibor Szamyely, *The Russian Tradition* (New York Etc., 1974), pp. 160–61, 172–76.

Western Europe was the Other. Yuri Lotman speaks about values, which are linked to spatial oppositions, such as 'familiar – alien', 'safe – hostile', 'known – unknown', 'order – chaos', 'proper – improper', 'true - false', 'freedom – confinement', 'valuable - valueless', 'good – bad', 'own – alien', holy – sinful'.[3] Evidently, Western Europe did not always symbolize the worse side for the Russian pre-revolutionary intellectual. Whereas it might have been 'alien' and 'hostile', it nevertheless did not represent chaos or confinement, neither was it really valueless. Most important was that Western Europe was over there, not here. Basically, Russia stayed aside of Europe. If it politically adopted a French orientation towards the end of the 19th Century, this was just a matter of choice and more or less a way of getting money from a distant partner, whose worries were quite alien for the Russian, who could not care less about Alsace-Lorraine.

The bolsheviks' vision differed from this tradition in an important way. Ever since Lenin wrote his Imperialism, he irrevocably recognized that not Western Europe but Russia was secondary. Although the Bolsheviks were no less anti-bourgeois than any other Russian intelligents, their logic inevitably drove them into global thinking.

During WW I the bolsheviks were totally serious in their (albeit desperate) effort to change the world war into a civil war everywhere. After October the hopes of the Bolsheviks were attached to a revolution in Germany. A truly socialist society would supposedly be born from the union of the most advanced industrial centres of Western Europe with the more backward Russian masses. Only an international revolution would make a true socialism possible.

The bolsheviks always remained globalists. For practical purposes they supposed that the epicentre of the emergent world revolution was in Europe. More specifically, it was in Germany and not in the Anglo-Saxon world. The latter was the center of imperialism, but it was due to join the world of socialism only later. Between the world wars it was the German proletariat, nakedly oppressed by (Western) world imperialism, which was the natural ally of its Russian brethren. German, not English was adopted as the language of the Comintern. Before long all Russian workers learned the words 'rot Front', which soon surpassed the earlier 'Hände hoch' as the best known German expression.

---

3   Katharina Hansen Uve, *The Evolution of Space in Russian literature. A Spatial Reading of 19th and 20th Century Narrative Literature* (Amsterdam & Atlanta, 1994), p. 35.

The Bolshevik official myth supposed that Russia after October had become the vanguard of world history. The authenticity of all that pretended to be progressive in the world had to be gauged by its relation to Soviet Russia, baptised in 1922 the Soviet Union. True, for a lengthy period, anyway, even the Soviet Union itself was for the reigning bolsheviks a locus, which was left to a large extent impurified until the coming of socialism, which was supposed to happen by 1936. The ensuing purges just made a clean sweep of the 'pathetic remains' of the agents of world capital. After 1936 all of the Soviet Union was virtually pure. It had become a truly sacred land, which by the virtue of its very essence was connected to everything that was progressive and benign in this world and, accordingly, stood in diametrical opposition to everything that was oppressive, reactionary and evil. Just as in the socialist Soviet Union, there was no room and no place for an oppositionist party, neither was there room for impure thinking. If such thinking existed, it had its source somewhere in the surrounding sphere of capitalism and imperialism. All this necessarily confined the life and thought of the Soviet citizen to the sacred sphere of socialism. In this view, no real Soviet citizen wanted to cross the border or listen to foreign broadcasts and thus risk contamination from a depraved civilization - if someone did, he was no longer a Soviet man *(sovetski chelovek)*, which had a sinister ring about it. The Soviet man traced his descent from the proletarian, whose 'class purity' echoed Rousseau's notion of the 'natural man' as Andrei Sinyavsky has aptly remarked.[4]

The Soviet man, who in essence was a proletarian, was on the international level a representative of a class state and was supposed to share only the class interests of his proletarian brethren in other coutries. That is why he would have different problems from the bourgeois intellectuals, let alone the petty bourgeois masses of the capitalist countries. Evidently, he supported all those, who were fighting the forces of world reaction and avidly demonstrated his solidarity.

But could their problems really be his? *'Net chuzhoi boli"* was a popular cliché but, in effect, the housing problems of American inner cities or racial segregation in South Africa did not really concern the 'problemless' life of a Soviet citizen. The horrors of capitalism were

---

4   Andrei Sinyavsky, *Soviet Civilization: A Cultural History* (New York, 1997), pp. 142–47.

well advertised in the Soviet media, but this was just because they served well to remind of the axiomatic truth that elsewhere life was incomparably worse and that the Soviet new man was lucky to be separated from the horrors of capitalism. Apparently, then, he was also separated from his proletarian brethren in capitalist countries, but this only seemed to be so, for the highest incarnation of his class interests, the Soviet state, was promoting the case of the eminent class in the whole world in the best possible way. As Lotman has remarked, borders have a connecting as well as a separating function, they not only divide, but also bring together what is different. For the Soviet man the Capitalist world and the oppressing classes were always present, although the border protected the Soviet toiler from their direct influence.

After 1934 the world became politically more complicated in that now even the imperialists were depicted as potential allies in the struggle against the fascists, which embodied the darkest variety of the *nechistaia* α *chornaia sila.* True, capitalism and its offspring imperialism remained the real root and cause of all evil. For practical purposes, anyway, all were welcomed to resist fascism, even the abominable social democrats played a progressive role in popular fronts.

After the well-known pro-facist intermezzo of 1939–41 this constellation was once more reinforced. In fact, the capitalist West for some time played the part of a true friend, while the forces of the 'fascist' enemy embodied absolute evil: *'kak dva razlichnykh poliusa, vo vsem vrazhdebny my...'* as the popular hymn 'Holy War' had it. What had earlier been the antagonistic struggle of imperialism and socialism, now turned into an all-encompassing battle against fascism: *'s fashistskoi siloi chornoiu, s prokliatoiu ordoi...'.* Evidently, British and American imperialism also were on the right side in this battle, although they could hardly be elevated to the level of the main force of progress.

However, by 1946–48 all was put in place once more. Now a new system of 'popular democracies' was born, a territory, which soon was to be understood as a part of a world socialist system of equals, even if none else could be as equal as the Soviet Union, which was incomparably more developed as a socialist society. In the course of a couple of decades a hierarchical system of liabilities was born in the Soviet Empire. As the unquestioned center, the Soviet Union represented absolutely pure and orthodox socialism. As its antipode were the forces of imperialism, whose main citadel was the USA. However, in their most dangerous and perfidious form they were represented by China (a preposterously 'red' China!) with its allies. Among the purer countries, there were the peoples' democracies, then there were the socialist countries of the third world and last but not least, the non-aligned and benevolent countries like India, Yugoslavia, and Finland, whose policy was free from anti-communist influence.

In the divided world, understood in the Soviet way, the avant garde role of the Soviet Union was not questioned by anyone, save by the Chinese and their hacks. Even the USA and its allies acknowledged it. This amounted to saying that the Soviet Union was not just a country, but had a global nature. If Dostoievsky and the slavophiles had contended that the Russian people are not just people, but mankind, the communists -and virtually the capitalists also- testified that this was the case. True, departing from their class-point of view they made the reservation that only a part of mankind was immediately connected to the Soviet Union, while the other part fought it.

Indeed, those who were 'red' in any country, had a touch of 'Russianness'. They were often suspected of considering the USSR their true fatherland. and this was not always an ungrounded suspicion.

Officially, the realm of the Soviet man was extended to the utmost in the post-war years. From the 1950's, it also comprised Outer Space, into which the imperialists succeeded in intruding only later. The language of the progressive world was no more German – let alone English – it was Russian. From Cuba to Vietnam, from Korea to black Africa, a Russian could feel at home, everywhere he could speak his vernacular and meet Lenin's smiling face. China was an exception from the 1960's, but even there Stalin's face reminded one of the Soviet connection.

The officially supposed globality of the Soviet space had important implications: there were no narrowly domestic issues at all. Everything that was done in the Soviet Union had global meaning. It might be building the BAM or sending rockets to outer space, it might be building up Soviet defence or conquering the virgin lands which were obviously tasks of global consequence. But even the meanest of everyday tasks merged into the common whole, be it milking the cows, be it felling the trees or digging ditches. The supposedly huge output of Soviet industrial production was always announced with utmost accuracy, as this made it possible for everybody to see, where the (world-historical) meaning of his labour was situated: there are the 30 litres of milk which I milked, there is the extra tree, which I felled during that certain subbotnik and so on.

The importance of all this was tremendous: everything that one was doing in his everyday work, was supposed to have a world-wide significance. Therefore, it had an almost sacral nature and, accordingly, the Soviet citizen was also supposed to work hard. Work and battle were always mentioned together and this did not happen by chance. The socialist world was in antagonistic conflict with imperialism and the battle was being fought in workshops and farms. Imperialism was doomed to lose the battle, but this was to happen just by virtue of the heroic work of the socialist peoples, with the Soviet Union as their undisputed avantgarde. (The fact that it was disputed, did not belong to the real world, but was part of capitalist ideology).

This ideological stance resulted in a curious merger of the international and the domestic: mere thinking about national problems, as dissociated from their international context, was banned. Alexander Solzhenitsyn, who bemoaned the fate of the Northern villages, not seeing that their fate had to be submitted to the primacy of the global tasks of the Soviet Union, was unavoidably heretical. No less heretical was Andrei Sakharov, who discussed foreign matters without subordinating them to the interests of the incarnation of world progress, the Soviet Union. The kernel of the problem was that no universal values existed. What was valuable was so because of its utility for the principle, which was incarnated in the Party.[5]

The procrustean bed of orthodox Soviet thinking became more and more uncomfortable in the 1970s, in the days, when – in the expression of the Paris emigre paper *Russkaia mysl* – a spectre was haunting Eastern Europe, the spectre of scientific-technical revolution. The official Soviet ideology began to be challenged by more and more intellectuals after the sixties.

The intellectuals reacted to the official demands of Soviet ideology in various ways. The *refuseniks* bluntly refused to share the public space, which was filled with the official *poshlost*, and established for themselves private plots of their own. Being non-political was, anyway, a highly political choice. It meant that one rejected the role that had been designed for a Soviet citizen from above. In the spheres of the emerging new right, a current for the 'nationalization' of the officially 'international' Russian space emerged. Analoguously, in some national republics the elites wanted to build up 'national' borders against the Russian 'internationalists'.

173

---

5   See Vladimir Slapantokh, *Soviet Intellectuals and Political Power. The Post-Stalin Era* (London & New York, 1990), pp.162–64.

This all meant rejection of the pseudo-global thinking that had been imposed on the Soviet intelligentsia. In fact, practically any critical thinking was doomed to be 'dissident' because the official Soviet dogma had become utterly rigorous. If one recommended that the Russians should first take care of their own house or that they should recognize the fact that many problems of world politics had no ideological content at all, he was inevitably a dissident, and thus belonged to the camp of the enemy.

It was a real sensation, when Gorbachev introduced the concept of 'new thinking' in foreign policy in the mid-80's. He did no more than recognize the self-evident truth that all of humanity, independently of 'class', was interested in avoiding both nuclear and ecological catastrophe. Anyway, this recognition of 'general human' *(obshechelovecheskie)* values destroyed the cornerstone of Soviet logic.

If everybody really had the same kind of problems, then international class antagonism was not universal. Then also the universal role of the Soviet Union and the very idea of (and need for) its universal presence – as a counterweight to imperialism were dubious. If the greatest tasks were common for all humanity, then it was not plausible that it was necessary to overcome the imperialist antagonist at any price. It would make more sense if everybody would work for their own benefit, rather than to counterweight the antagonist.

If the toil and endurance of the Soviet people were thus deprived of their universal importance, then it was just possible to compare their life with that of their fellow humans elsewhere. This comparison also became unavoidable.

Retreating from globality, Gorbachev wanted to make a halt at the borders of Europe. Quite a lot was spoken about a common European house (or home), where every nation had its room. This was no more global thinking and there was no more room for the global antagonism which entailed the presence of Russian troops in all of the 'brother' countries and along the East-West border. In practice then, the European house proved to be no home for the Russians. Deprived of their mission, the Soviet troops left Eastern Europe – which immediately became Middle Europe – but in return the Russians got just a bunch of Deutsche marks. No genuine Russian integration to the rest of Europe, in either the political, economical or military sense followed.

The new, post-communist Russia prided itself on its alleged 'return to civilization'. It professed the creed of globalism, now understood in its capitalist form and at this time not entailing any Russian presence in every corner of the world. 'Civilization' was now understood as westernism, which for the new elite meant obtaining high-class imported articles and living the once-accursed life-styles of the opulent idlers.

The new Russian now meets the Westerner on even ground. This happens much in the same way as his precedessors, the wealthy nobility, met their peers in the European spas of the last century. According to this thinking, Russia is now a part of the world economy and, like any country, it is bound to reward its best sons according to their desserts. If it will not, then the money will flee to a better place. The world of the new Russian is truly international in the sense that he grabs the money from his country and spends it abroad. As regards domestic issues, they must and can be resolved only in the context of, and subordinated to, the demands of the global economy. For the new Russians, the new borders are semi-transparent and allow a kind of osmotic one-way penetration. Borders which guard the property of the new rich from the taxpolice do exist, but on the other hand, there are no protective borders, which would inhibit their way of doing business.

For the post-Soviet masses, things look less beneficial. The burden of global socialist responsibility has been released from their shoulders, but it has been replaced by the capitalist global imperative.

In practice, the borders have opened and the Russian state is no more trying to separate its subjects from the West or of any other parts of the world. The common man can now cross the border, and he quite often does. He can buy commodities which were forbidden to him in the past. Now they are a normal part of everyday life and bear no stigma of the Antagonist. For anybody, without exception, it is also now possible to enjoy the fruits of the Western industry of entertainment: TV programmes, literature, journals, much of which is unabashedly bad, but has no air of the forbidden about it. In fact, though, the world of the common man has not been enlarged, let alone globalized. In a way, it has greatly shrunk. The world of socialism was always supposed to be the pure space, which in one way or another, reached all corners of the world. The Soviet man was always the lord of the planet and the future of mankind belonged to him.

Now, the Russian poor toiler looks no more than another poor toiler. Moreover, in hindsight it very much seems to be the case that he has also been abused and hoodwinked. The border, which once connected the common man to the whole world has vanished. Only the vast distances remain and the capitalist economy tends to make travelling more expensive than it used to be, although there are no formal restrictions.

The plight of the common man has suffered vastly in terms of grandeur. It may be that he is, by and by, beginning to be treated better by the bureaucrats, he may even be better off in terms of available commodities. Anyway, alas, nowadays his poverty and suffering are nothing more than his personal poverty and suffering. The new order of things has even deprived him of the value of his past labour and hardship. In the post-communist world even the solidarity of the working people in the home country has lost its meaning. A Russian toiler may nowadays even be referred to by the infamous word 'loser', which entails a whole world of naked capitalist value nihilism. In a way, this is a new kind of 'atomized' society. The totalitarian society, which supposedly also was atomized, did not forsake its citizens, but was endlessly interested in them.

On the other hand, as the reality of the singular human being and his restrictedness is affirmed, at the same time it will also be possible to claim for him unlimited worth, as Dostoevsky did. Only the source of his dignity can no more be the immanent and global nature of his material activity.

Now, it is possible to consider the individual as independent, the personal sphere as apolitical, to conceive of one's here and now as absolutely significant as such, but this presupposes a nonmaterialist approach, which is not being ranked highly by the new ruling class.

From the point of view of consumerism the individual will never be worth very much, while from the point of view of communism his existence and activity always had a pseudo-transcendent importance. This importance, however, always remained restricted and was subordinated to the primacy of the laws of history. The individual's worth consisted of his being a part of the larger wholes, serving the interests of the world proletariat and the will of the god of history, in the last instance.

Dostoevsky's Ivan Karamazov, who did not forgive God for the sufferings of a single child, would have been equally angry at the communists. Happiness for all in the future was promised by the communists, happiness of the greatest number here and now seems to be the creed that post-communist Russia professes. If so, it may mean that a certain number of innocent children may well be sacrificed, if the result will be the happiness of a certain greater number of new Russians.

For the Soviet man, the space which he inhabited was at the same time both totally open and tightly restricted. It necessarily embraced the whole world, but the intelligent Soviet citizen was supposed to understand that this implied consenting to narrow limits, for had not

Marx said that freedom was equal to consenting to necessity, for no other option existed?

Now, options exist, but for most people they exist only as a possibility. The real space of the post-communist *obyvatel* is, where his peers live.

Now, it seems to be that the Russian *obyvatel* inhabits much the same kind of local space as he did before socialism. The powers that be are claiming for Russia a place in world affairs, but more or less accepting the fact that Russia is now not much more than a European power, whose economic capacity equals that of Finland. In a curious way, the Russian economy has, hitherto, not really opened up to the world. Even though it formally encourages international economic cooperation, Russia in practice shirks foreign capital. The new business elite seems to understand globalism as a protectionism against foreign capital combined with an export of Russian capital.

The opposition, for its part, preaches a restructuring of the economy and a retreat from globalism. Instead, the Russians should restrict the supposedly perilous effects of economical openness and concentrate their efforts on Russia (or 'Eurasia', practically the former Soviet Union, at most).

From what is left of the once so important layer of the Russian intelligentsia, it seems to be the case that quite many support the policies of the government, which has infuriated, for example, Andrei Sinyavsky, who considers it a historical treachery and an end of the intelligentsia.[6] The opposition, including Solzhenitsyn, who is loath to join any group, opposes 'mondialism' (globalisation) and preaches the concentration of forces and attention on Russia or the Eurasian continent (minus Western Europe). One can hear very little talk about the Russian message for the whole world, rather, Russia is seen as the victim of the West, of the Jews or its unspecified domestic quacks. Rather than being an example for others it has been seen as needing spiritual as well as material healing before entering the international community.[7]

Quite a few are unhappy about the relentless flow of mass culture from the West, but few dare to recommend the introduction of censorship. As a whole, Russia is seen as a receding geographical and

---

6 Sinyavsky, op. cit.
7 For example, Alexander Solzhenitsyn. See his *The Russian Question at the End of the 20th Century* (London, 1994).

spiritual entity, which needs recovering first and only thereafter may gain its due place abreast of the other Western countries – a place which it never really aknowledged before, considering itself either vastly superior or immensurably inferior. The intellectual, for his part, no more regards himself as a Hermes, going to emancipate the lower depths and to bring about a new kingdom of God, but rather as a doctor, who is trying to heal what can be healed of the wounds inflicted by the guardians of the heavens. It may be, as Dmitrii Shalin has suggested, that the Russian intelligent is now finding a medium half-way between facile intellectualism and emotional excesses.[8] But the intellectual cannot help confronting the present with the past. For him, the past may look glorious and sublime, but much of it is also perilously near to the ridiculous and the pathetic.

His lot is not unlike that of a doctor who, during a hunting party, happened to send pellets into the hips of his comrade and, while tending the wounds, uttered: 'Certainly you were lucky to have a doctor with you'!

---

8   Dmitri N. Shalin (Ed.) *Russian Culture at the Crossroads* (Westview Press), p. 91.

Studia Historica 62
Sacred and Secular Space Intertwined...
A Case Study:
The Bilateral Ecumenical Negotiations between the evangelical Church of Finland and the Russian Orthodox Church – Space for 'Useful Idiots' and Sincere Kebisty

Arto Luukkanen

The questions of collaboration have been discussed in post-Soviet historiography in great *extendo*. However, the collision between the Western and Soviet understanding of private and public space has rarely been examined. The difficulty of this dilemma is especially visible in religious life. In Western countries religion has usually been understood from the days of the Enlightenment as belonging to the private space of life. But in the Soviet system the situation was quite the opposite; the secret police interfered and mingled in the activities of religious organizations and Soviet visiting delegates of clergymen were totally subordinated to Soviet ideology and policy. The Western 'useful idiots', to use Lenin's expression, were totally unaware of this.

This short case study sheds light on the 'bilateral doctrinal negotiations' which were launched between the Evangelical Lutheran Church of Finland and the Russian Orthodox Church in the 1970's. The emphasis is on the political background of these negotiations, which became closely entwined with Finnish foreign policy during the Cold War. The most recent meeting between the churches was held in October 1997 in Lappeenranta, Finland.

THE BACKGROUND OF THE DOCTRINAL NEGOTIATIONS

The Russian Orthodox Church (the ROC) has traditionally been very conservative in its ecumenical activity.[1] In the 20th century the reason for this has been obvious: since 1917 the ROC was under constant oppression from the communist authorities, and the greater part of its energies were directed at simple survival.[2] However, the war against Germany revived the activity of the ROC, until Khrushchev's policies started a new era of suppression. The change that occurred under Khrushchev is a paradoxical illustration of his political aims; exposing the sins of the ideological gods, such as Stalin, and putting an end to the Terror, all demanded a new ideological justification – a new *credo* for the Soviet system. Khrushchev's message to the Communist Party was plain and simple: even if Stalin had gone too far, the time was ripe for a return to the legacy of Lenin.[3]

Khrushchev's new ideals became clear in the third party manifesto of 1961. This document expounded that the Soviet Union would attain the ultimate stage of communism around the year 1980. Naturally such an endeavour would require the disposal of 'the survivals and

. . . . .

1 For some historical background to the the ROC's attitude,see: Peter Fenell, *A History of The Russian Church to 1448* (New York, 1995). p. 103; Janet Martin, *Medieval Russia 980–1584* (Cambridge, 1995) p.257. See also S.F. Platonov, *Venäjän historia* (Helsinki, 1933). pp. 251–252.
2 The following are recent works on the relations between the the ROC and the Soviet authorities: Valeri Alekseev, *Illjuzii i dogmi*(Moscow, 1991.); John Anderson, 'The Council for Religious Affairs and the Shaping of Soviet Religious Policy', *Soviet Studies*, 1991, Vol 43. No. 4; A.Bessmertnyi-Anzimirov, 'The Legal Status of Religious Organizations and the Clergy in the USSR' in Nicolai N. Petro (ed.) *Christianity and Russian Culture in Soviet Society* (Boulder, 1990); John Shelton Curtiss, *The Russian Church and The Soviet State 1917–1950* (Boston, 1953); Nathaniel, Davies, *A Long Walk To Church A Contemporary History of Russian Orthodoxy* (Boulder: Colorado, 1995); Arto Luukkanen, *The Party of Unbelief. The Religious Policy of the Bolshevik Party, 1917–1929* (Helsinki, 1994); see also by the same author, 'The Rise and Fall of Trotsky in Soviet Religious Policy', *Journal of Trotsky Studies*, 1996; Terry Martin, 'Cults Commission' in *The Modern Encyclopedia of Religion in Russia and The Soviet Union.* Vol. 8. (New York, 1995); Daniel Peris, 'The 1929 Congress of the Godless' *Soviet Studies* 1991, Vol 43. No. 4; see also by the same author: 'Commissars in Red Cassocks: Former Priests in the League of the Militant Godless', *Slavic Review*, 1995, Vol. 54. No. 2. summer; Edward Roslof, 'The Renovationist Movement in The Russian Orthodox Church, 1922–1946', (Unpublished Dissertation, University of North Carolina. 1994).
3 Wolfgang Leonhard, *Kreml Stalinin jölkeen* (Helsinki, 1965.), pp. 121–124, 137–139, 150–164.

superstitions of capitalist society'. The Church became an obvious target. In one of his speeches a triumphant Khrushchev promised to show the last Christian on television in 1980.[4]

When Khrushchev was ousted in 1964, religious policy was once again changed. Vigorous persecution was replaced by regular bureaucratic control. In 1965 the Council of ROC Affairs, which had been founded during the war, became part of the Cults Commission. This was renamed the Council for Religious Affairs (CRA), which illustrates the ruling elite's desire to harmonize the activities of the churches with the policies of the Communist Party.

THE SOVIET PEACE OFFENSIVE AND THE ROLE OF THE COUNCIL FOR RELIGIOUS AFFAIRS

The publicity value of the CRA had been appreciated by the Soviet leaders at an early stage. The Council's ecumenical activity, begun in 1959, can be seen as part of the new offensive of Soviet foreign policy in Europe; the grand design for the 'stabilization of peace' in Europe.

The Korean War had clearly shown that the Western Alliance, with the United States in the lead, was prepared to engage its arms with the East, and that any advances in Europe would require an armed conflict. Thus the tactics had to be changed. The slogans of 'peaceful coexistence' and 'detente' were created. One of the priorities was the cultivation of 'good will' among the Western intelligentsia, as well as among the Western masses. This was intended to weaken the inner cohesion of the Western military alliance. One of the major thorns in the Soviet side was the rearmament of West Germany, as well as its integration with the West. It is noteworthy, that negotiations between the churches initially began with the Evangelical Lutheran Church of Germany(EKD).[5]

. . . .
4   Leonard Schapiro, in Leonard Schapiro and Albert Boiter (eds.)*The USSR:. An Analysis of The New Programme of the CPSU* (Munich, 1962), pp. 255–312.
5   The researcher Adam B. Ulam has termed this post-1952 period in Soviet foreign policy 'The Grand Design'. See Adam B. Ulam, *Expansion and Coexistence. The History of Soviet Foreign Policy, 1917–67* (New York, 1968), pp. 580-581, 628–629. See also Charles Gati, 'The Stalinist Legacy in Soviet Foreign Policy' in Stephen F. Cohen, Alexander Rabinovich and Robert Sharlet (eds.), *The Soviet Union Since Stalin* (New York, 1980), pp. 281–282, 296–297.

Thus the ecumenical activity of the Russian Orthodox Church was not inspired by the 'beautiful eyes' of the Western churches; it was a logical part of Soviet foreign policy.[6] According to the ideologies of the Central Committee of the Communist Party of the Soviet Union, the World Council of Churches (WCC) was a tool of 'Western political interest groups'.[7] As such the Soviet churches' participation was justifiable only in the context of the protection of socialism and its interests. One of these ideologues, N.S. Gordyenko, expressed his view that it was quite impossible for the WCC to be a neutral forum where the churches could look for answers to ecclesiastical dilemmas. On the contrary, the WCC meetings should be an arena where 'Western capitalist ideas and Eastern communist ideas would challenge each other and would collide'. Thus the ecumenical activity of the representatives of the socialist camp should have three major aims: 1) to struggle with the forces of reaction; 2) to represent socialism; 2) to thwart anti-communist tendencies.[8]

Another communist ideologue, Y.V. Kryanev, stated that the Western churches were inclined to create an anti-communist, anti-Soviet atmosphere. According to Kryanev, 'the leaders of Western reactionary churches, goaded on by imperialists, constantly seek to play on the human rights questions.'[9] It was precisely for this reason that the connections with the Finnish Evangelical Lutheran Church were optimal. No distracting comments on human rights violations in the East were heard, while the Western violations were brandished freely.[10]

So why did the Soviet Union and the KGB wish to carry out ecumenical negotiations? Felix Corley, a researcher of Soviet church policy at Keston College, has pointed out that the representatives of the Russian Church were needed to convince Western audiences that religion in the Soviet Union was free from persecution. Also, the PR-men of the church were needed in the ideological struggle with the opponents of the Soviet system. However, the most important duty of the ROC was to take part in the 'Grand Design', meaning the Soviet peace offensive, and to win support from the more idealistic

6 Evangeliche Kirche in Deutschland.
7 Around this time Metropolitan Nikodim suggested negotiations to the Archbishop Salomies. Compare with Sakari Virkkunen, *Arkkipiispan muotokuva* (Jyväskylä, 1977). p. 283 and Saarinen, Faith... pp. 20–21.
8 N.S. Gordienko, *Contemporary Ecumenism* (Moscow, 1972).
9 Y.V. Kryanev, *Khristianskii Ekumenizm* (Moscow, 1980).
10 See e.g. Sinappi, p. 25; Järvenpää1, p. 44, p.49.

members and leaders of religious movements. West Germany was a natural target for this offensive. Thus Finland, another bastion of Lutheran denominations, gained importance.[11]

One must bear in mind that the Russian clergymen were in a highly uncomfortable position in the ecumenical negotiations. They had no chance of expressing their personal opinions or of veering from the roles assigned by the KGB. The church leadership had been formally recruited into the KGB. They had code names, and they received instructions from the Council of Foreign Affairs. Above all, the church leaders were obliged to inform and explain all their actions to the security officials.[12] The statements of the Soviet representatives in the WCC had to adhere to the party line.[13] In this way the plight of the

.....
11 Felix Corley, *Religion in the Soviet Union. An Archival Reader* (Basingstoke, 1996) pp.171, 280.
12 See J.A. Hebly, 'The State, The Church, and The Oikumene: The Russian Orthodox Church and The World Council of Churches, 1948–1985' in Sabrina Petra Ramet (ed.), *The Religious Policy of the Soviet Union* (Cambridge, 1993). The following churchmen of the 70s and 80s should be familiar to many...here are some of their agent names: 'Abbot' – Metropolitan Pitirim (Volakolamsk), 'Adamant' – Metropolitan Juvenali (Krutitsy), 'Antonov' – Metropolitan Filaret (Kiev), 'Drozdov' – the present Patriarch Alexei II. On the other hand, although all the church leaders were under strict KGB control it should be remembered, as Corley comments, that the quantity of collaboration, and the enthusiasm for it, varied among the agents. It must also be noted in particular that the so-called First Directorate of the KGB (responsible for foreign intelligence) usually played a part in the planning and excecution of the clergymen's travels. The middleman in the 70s and 80s was Colonel Vladimir Fitsev. After Fitsev's death in 1985 the position was inherited by Colonel Jevgeni Milovanov. Supervision of religious communities was delegated to the 5th Directorate of the KGB, and especially its 4th contingent. See John Barron, *KGB, The Secret Work of Soviet Agents* (London, 1974) pp. 49–50, 100–101; Felix Corley, *Religion in The Soviet Union*, p. 361. According to Felix Corley the clergy of the the ROC had no chance of engaging in genuine ecumenical intercourse. '...Foreign propaganda visits by the delegations from the Soviet Churches played an increasing role in promoting Soviet interests in the international religious sphere... far from representing a genuine ecumenical desire to work together on the part of the Churches, such delegates were cobbled together in the offices of the CRA (Council for Religious Affairs)'. Corley, *Religion in the Soviet Union*, p. 274.
13 See the Furov Report: V.G. Furov, 'Cadres of The Church and Legal Measures to Curtail Their Activities' – *Religion in Communist Dominated Areas*, Vol. XX, No. 1–3, 1981. This report, which was leaked to the West, testifies to the ROC's complete dependence on the State. The collapse of the Soviet system paralyzed control for a while, and certain churchmen, such as Gleb Jakunin, moved to call for an exposure of the collaboration. The ROC has rejected such demands for public scrutiny. On the other hand it has adopted the mission of defending Russian ethnic interests in neighbouring countries, especially in the Baltics, and remained loyal to the State during the war in Chechnya. An honest look at the Soviet period may yet be far in the future. Nathaniel Davies, *A Long Walk to*

Finnish intelligentsia during the years of Finlandization is very similar to the tragedy of the Finnish ecclesiastical negotiators; reaching out to their Soviet peers, they were met by the security police.

So, what was the true function of the ecumenical negotiations from the Soviet point of view? Who pulled the strings? It is a tricky task for the historian to try to give simple answers to such questions. Nevertheless, it can be stated with certainty that the Soviet side did enter the negotiations at the initiative of the Council of Foreign Affairs and the KGB's department of foreign affairs. Or, ultimately, at the initiative of the Soviet Communist Party. The Finns either could not or did not want to comprehend this;[14] official suspicions were never voiced. Quite the contrary, many Finnish negotiators considered the peace cause particularly relevant.[15]

Church, pp. 46, 70–78, 95, 211. See also Kimmo Kääriäinen, 'Venäjä ja Eurooppa – ylittämätön distanssi? – Kirkot ja Euroopan murros' in Matti Kotiranta (ed.) *Studies presented in the November 1995 symposium of the Finnish Association of Theological Literature (STKS)* (STKS Annual, STKS 203, 1997), p. 59.

14 As Docent Timo Vihavainen comments in his book *Kansakunta rähmällään* (A Nation on Its Knees), Finnish politicians did not always realize the theatrical quality of the content and form of Soviet ideology. Vihavainen makes good use of the Russian word *'pozlost'*, which refers to dishonest smarminess, self-conscious pomposity, pretentious authenticity, and the use of outrageous jargon. The Finns were completely taken in by *'pozlost'*. For example, in the 1980s the Finnish Centre Party presented the Soviet Communist Party with earth from the Finnish village of Lepikko (birthplace of president Urho Kekkonen); 'the best, most genuine soil we have'. Timo Vihavainen, *Kansakunta rähmällään. Suomettumisen lyhyt historia* (Helsinki, 1991), pp. 220–222.

15 For example, see the Reverend Jouko Martikainen's letter to Maunu Sinnemäki, Licentiate in Theology, 3.2. 1970 in Sinappi, op. cit. What happened to Russian churchmen who strayed from the rules of ecumenical contact? One example was Metropolitan Nikolai (Jarushevich), who got into a tangle with the Kremlin after writing a speech for Patriarch Aleksei, to be given at a conference for disarmament in 1960, which was 'too positive'. The consequences were tragic; in July 1960 the Holy Synod relieved Nikolai of his duties as head of the foreign affairs department of the the ROC, and accepted his request to be relieved of the office of Metropolitan of Krutitsky and Kolomna. Nikolai resisted these measures, and contacted the International Peace Movement for support. After a brief house arrest he passed away in the Boktin Hospital, Moscow, cared for by state doctors. Those who had been close to him were denied access. Rumours abound that he was in fact poisoned by state security officials. Davies, pp.37–38.

A FEAST OF RESOLUTIONS

Official relations between the Church of Finland and the ROC, and the beginning of bilateral negotiations, kicked off in 1960. In public, the Finnish church officials have claimed Finnish initiative for the negotiations, and this misconception has prevailed in the media as well.[16] However, only 18 years ago the official story was quite different. In those days, it was still advantageous to accord the merit of first contact to the Soviets. In a 1980 edition of the Finnish Theological Review, Simo S. Salo described the history of the negotiations, giving a grand account of the Metropol Nikodim, the ROC's head of foreign affairs, bringing up the subject with Archbishop Salomies. After which Salomies gave Martti Simojoki the job of 'developing the consolidation of the interaction between the churches'.[17]

In these negotiations the method was to accept a common statement at the close of any dogmatic or ethical discussion. In one instance, during the Zagorski negotiations of 1971, the parties agreed on a resolution which stated: 'permanent civil peace cannot be achieved where human dignity is denied. Therefore the Christian's obedience to the authorities has its limits. Permanent international peace cannot be built on imperialist lobbying of self-interest.'[18]

. . . . .

16 See Risto Cantell's official version of the negotiations. '...the negotiations were initiated by Archbishop Martti Simojoki... still it's hard to believe... that the Russian clergy are acting on the orders of the KGB', '...The Finnish Evangelical Lutheran Church has acted according to its own faith and ecumenical imperative in the course of these negotiations...' SK 1995, No 7, p.48.
17 See Saarinen, pp. 20–21; TA 1980, No. 6, p.505.
18 TA 1972, No. 4, 321–327; TA 1980, No. 6, 509. As the Finns and the Russians went on with their doctrinal negotiations, a different kind of dialogue was going on in the Soviet Union. In November 1965 two Moscow priests, Gleb Jakunin and Nikolain Eshliman, had sent an open letter to Patriarch Pimen. In this letter the priests criticized state interference in the life of religious communities. This started a veritable wave of samizdat-writing. The dissidence peaked in 1975, when religious dissidents attempted to exploit the Helsinki Accords to guarantee freedom of religious practice. The KGB wasted no time; dissidence was to be silenced by any means. Many were locked up in prisons for the criminally insane. It is not quite clear whether the Finnish church leaders knew of such goings-on. The Church has often emphasized that during finlandization it was nigh impossible to get a clear picture of conditions in the Soviet Union. On the other hand, according to church counsellor Risto Cantell, the Finnish Church was well informed about the religious situation in the Soviet Union; according to Cantell the contents of the Furov Report, for instance were known. See SK 1995, No. 7, s. 48.

This resolution, with minor changes, could well have been accepted by the Finnish far left. It is one of the most radical documents in the history of the Finnish Church. The contents could be interpreted in such a way, that as the Soviet Union viewed itself as a progressive state, the imperialists were the Western democracies. In other words the Finnish clergymen condemned their own country, and all Western democratic states.[19]

These political statements were followed up in 1974, when Bishop Vikström presented the Soviets with his own special 'formula for peace'. Peace, so important to the Soviets, was defined by Vikström as being either 'negative peace', meaning the absence of war, or 'positive peace', which means that the relations between people and states are marked by justice. This formulation had been meant as an introduction to more general discussions. It seems that Vikström did not understand how compatible his theses were with Soviet ideology.[20]

Questions of war and peace have received Christian treatment for centuries. Vikström's rhetoric, however, was surprisingly close to that of the Soviet writers, who strove to express their 'class-based' conceptions of peace, as opposed to the 'bourgeois, value-free' definitions. At the same time the Bishop's words tie in nicely with the communist idea that true peace begins with political change, i.e. through world revolution. The Bishop expounded that the path to positive peace would be traveled by using the associative method, which meant that nations would be brought closer together.[21]

The statement of the Zagorsk negotiations was highly political: '...in accordance with the experience that we have gained through the

. . . . .
19 Among the groups using such rhetoric about the imperialist governments were the Western terrorist organizations, such as the Baader-Meinhof group. These offspring of protestant ministers were inspired by the demand for justice. Their Christian obedience reached its limits in the use of explosives.
20 See Järvenpää, pp. 52, 54-55. In his newer book published in 1992 Vikström speaks of the dissociative and the associative paths to peace. '...modern conflict research has proved that the latter path is the better'. See John Vikström, *Myös maan päällä. Artikkeleita, esitelmiä ja puheita sosiaalietiikan alalta. Suomalaisen teologisen kirjallisuusseuran julkaisuja 176.* (Helsinki, 1992), p.221.
21 TA 1980, No. 6, p. 509. This closely resembles Lenin's recipe for guaranteeing the mutual good will of nations. According to a later Soviet version, the special nature of each nation would blossom just prior to their merging. This policy, known also as Russification among Western scholars, was carried out successfully in Estonia and Karelia, among others. A large number of Russians were moved to these areas to enforce the noble ideal of the unity of nations.

consolidation of our countries' political, cultural and ecclesiastical lives, we are convinced that active interaction between peoples and countries in as many fields as possible, as well as ecumenical cooperation, will facilitate the achievement of permanent peace.'[22]

In 1980 the negotiations reached their peak. The negotiations in Turku, Finland, were attended by several theological heavyweights: Mikko Juva, A.T. Nikolainen, Kalevi Toiviainen, Kauko Pirinen, Tuomo Mannermaa, Fredric Cleve, Samuel Lehtonen, Maunu Sinnemäki, Juha Pihkala, Simo S. Salo, Lorenz Grönvik and Risto Cantell. Peace was once more at the top of the agenda. And what a current topic it was, as the Soviets had just attacked Afghanistan in the previous year. This was a violation of international law, and 'an unrighteous deed' from a Christian point of view. The Finnish delegation was unperturbed, and Afghanistan was never mentioned in the negotiations.[23]

The negotiations had taken place in the most formal of settings. In accordance with an old Soviet custom, an excited telegram was sent to the great leader, in this case President Urho Kekkonen. At the same time the Soviet-style liturgical rhetoric reached new heights in the many slogans that were bandied about in the documents of the meeting: '...it was noted with great satisfaction', '...the themes were organically constructed...', '...atmosphere of mutual trust', '...the meeting would most certainly consolidate the relations between the Finnish and Soviet churches and people in the spirit of Helsinki (CSCE)'.[24]

THE CASE OF AMBARTSUMOV

This bigwig ecumenism had its equivalent in the more humdrum ecclesiastical contacts which were cultivated by the Soviet system. Most of these visits are recorded in the form of travel journals in the Soviet National Archive (GARF), *fond* 6991.[25] This *fond* is a true

. . . . .
22 TA 1980, No. 6, p.510.
23 The theses on peace condemned the evils of the arms race, among other things. On the other hand it was written down that: '...the credibility of the message of the church requires solidarity with those who suffer from injustice, deprivation of freedom, and the constricting of human rights'. Turku, 1980, p. 57.
24 TA 1980, No. 6, pp.514–517.
25 The ROC's archive guide gives a succinct definition of the fond: Sovet po delami religii pri Sovete Ministrov SSSR 1943–1977. Dokumenty po delam religii pri SM SSSR.

treasure-house for students of Soviet ecumenism. I will here present just one ensemble of documents, which sheds light on the routine activities of the ROC's department of foreign affairs.

During 1963, the Russian priest Evgeni Ambartsumov traveled extensively in Finland as an emissary of the ROC. These trips are covered in the documents. Among his duties was to gauge the Finnish Lutheran willingness to engage in ecumenism as well as in peace activity. He made contacts among Finnish church leaders, and wrote reports to his superiors about the relations with the Finnish Evangelical-Lutheran Church., as well as consolidating ecumenical contacts. He also met representatives of the Theological Faculty of the University of Helsinki, with whom he had several conversations. Professor Nikolainen (the Dean), Professor Pirinen and Professor Lauha were among them.[26]

Ambartsumov was particularly excited about meeting Archbishop Simojoki. According to the report, the Archbishop spoke about the inevitable consolidation of church relations, and confessed to being a russophile. Ambartsumov also confessed that conversations with the university theologians did not strike a promising chord. Professor Pirinen in particular had proved to be a tough nut; the Russian priest felt he had emerged as the underdog in debating with the quick-witted professor, and demanded better intellectual preparation for future meetings. But he also stated that these contacts were extremely interesting in regard to future peace activity.[27]

This extract from the archives raises many questions. What was Ambartsumov's true status? Did the visitor find it necessary to exaggerate the Archbishop's russophile comments? Who were the goats, and who were the sheep? How were the priest's initiatives dealt with in different Soviet instances? At the same time, the archives and its documents are intriguing; in the same *fond* and *opis* one can often find records of communication between several churches. The curious

. . . . .

26 On the basis of the archive material it seems clear that that the Russian clergymen were expected to single out friends as well as potential enemies in the Orthodox Church of Finland as well as among the Lutherans. The main thrust of Soviet ecclesiastical contacts after the war was directed at the Orthodox Church; the ROC put severe pressure on the Finnish Orthodox to join the Patriarchate of Moscow.

27 Gossudarstvennyi Arkhiv Rossiiskoi Federatsii, f. 6991, op. 2, d. 521 ll. 3–5, 18, 64, 66. Professor Pirinen's expertise on Russian church affairs was, and still is, exceptional among Finnish theologians. A good example is his article 'Neuvostoliiton ortodoksisen kirkon pappiskasvatuslaitokset' (The Institutions of Clerical Education in the Soviet Orthodox Church), TA 1964.

scholar may compare meetings with German and Scandinavian ecclesiastical figures. The most interesting era seems to be the 1970s; the CSCE stirred up a flurry of ROC representatives into hurrying abroad.

Researchers have only recently begun to comprehend the history of the international relations of the Finnish Evangelical-Lutheran Church. The Church itself has been less than enthusiastic about the research. At a press conference of the synod held in the autumn of 1996, the Archbishop John Vikström declined to comment on the subject. According to the Archbishop, it was facile and being wise after the event for the critics to condemn the Church's activity in a different context.[28]

Referring to the spirit of the times has been the major defense of the church authorities. Others include lack of information, and the desire to help Soviet Christians. On the other hand it has been pointed out that the negotiations prevented the Finnish Church from succumbing to the lure of the Prague Christian Peace Conference (CPC).[29]

Nevertheless, the international relations of the Finnish Evangelical-Lutheran Church include facets that require historical investigation. Since Finland became an independent state in 1917, the Church has always adhered to the prevailing political conjunctures and followed state policy, rather like a weathercock. During the early years of independence the church strove to cultivate connections with the Nordic countries and the Anglo-Saxon world. Later on some clergymen felt drawn to National Socialist Germany. In regard to the later contacts with the Soviets, it is interesting that the Church did not find it convenient to engage in doctrinal negotiations with the Nazis, or with the Nazified Reichekirche.

After the Second World War, close contact with the Western victors looked like a safe bet. In the Brezhnev era the aforementioned bilateral negotiations increased in importance, and the list of Finnish

. . . . .
28 There are many examples, (some could call it hypocrisy, or ignorance). Take for example the former Archbishop Simojoki, who complained about the Lutheran World Federation's general assembly, which was to take place in Brazil in 1970. According to Simojoki, the '...social conditions are unrighteous' in Brazil; Virkkunen, p. 227.
29 The Soviets were fond of Lenin's definition of Western idealists as 'useful idiots'. To read more about these political dilettantes, see Paul Hollander, *Political Pilgrims. Travels of Western Intellectuals to the Soviet Union, China, and Cuba 1928–1978* (Oxford, 1981).

clergymen attending the meetings read like a Who's Who of the Finnish Church.

Since the collapse of the Soviet Union the contacts with the Russian Orthodox Church have strangely faded. Telegrams to the President are a thing of the past. In the negotiations that were held in Kiev in 1995, the previously heartfelt mutual understanding was not reached. On the contrary, the Finnish Church has once more flung its eyes to the West. The Porvoo Confession is a practical communion with the Church of England. At the same time, contacts with the Church of Rome have been moving in a favorable direction.

CONCLUSION

As can be observed from this small case study, the totalitarian state was able to intertwine the sacred and secular space together, and to exploit the counterprevailing notions of private space held in the west to their own foreign policy ends. On the one hand, Soviet citizens and the whole of society with its organizations were obliged to subordinate themselves to the authority of communist ideology. On the other hand, foreign democracies and their citizen could not comprehend the ways of totalitarian society or its double-morality; where there was no clear distinction between the private and public or the sacred and secular space of Soviet society. This is of course quite understandable because the whole context of civil society and a free civic space was an unknown entity in the Soviet Union.

'A Place without Taverns': Space in the Peasant Afterlife

Chris J. Chulos

Death is one of the basic organizational motifs of life. Filled with notions of fiery netherworlds of demons, devils, and goblins, as well as radiant landscapes of angels, cherubs, and saints, beliefs about life after death reveal much about the temporal reality from which they come. Sometimes perceptions of the afterlife are the result of conscious intellectual creativity when leading cultural or political minds attempt to reorder cosmology; but on the whole, the deeper meanings and significance of beliefs in the next world are left to others to decipher and interpret. In a tour de force, Jacques Le Goff argued that the emergence of the belief in purgatory in the twelfth century was about the 'spacialization' of thought that was part of an intellectual revolution 'associated with far-reaching social change . . . .about the other world [that] was related to specific changes in this one.'[1] In a more folksy way, the Russian peasant whose utterance about hell as 'a place without taverns' was speaking about this symbiotic link between beliefs about the afterlife and temporal reality.[2]

In the late imperial period, Russian peasant perceptions of the afterlife were shaped by religious, political, and social spatial demarcations that can be broken down into the good (we), the bad

. . . . .
1   Jacques Le Goff, *The Birth of Purgatory*, trans. Arthur Goldhammer (London, 1984), pp.1–2, 4.
2   Th. Polikarpov, "Bytovye cherty iz zhizni krest'ian sela Istobnogo, Nizhnedevitskogo uezda, Voron. gub.," *Pamiatnaia knizhka voronezhskoi gubernii*, otd. 3 (1906), p. 25.

(they), and the not-so-good/not-so-bad (those with vague identities). In peasant idiom the afterlife was painted in materialistic hues that reflected peasant struggles to influence, mollify, and gain control of the fates belonging to the chaotic and unknown 'other world.' The result was an otherworldly order that mirrored political, social, and national distinctions of temporal reality.[3] Key to this other existence was the *geography of the afterlife*, or how peasants mapped heaven and hell.[4]

GEOGRAPHY OF THE AFTERLIFE

According to Orthodox theology, earthly life was a reflection of the paradise lost by Adam and Eve, an imperfect image of that primordial world, as well as the beginning of the Kingdom of Heaven which was not limited to another time and place, but began already in this life.[5] Like Eliade's mythical center where heaven and earth meet, peasant notions of heaven resembled a combination of the temporal and extraterrestrial. A sense of geography emerges in the ways peasants spoke about heaven and its complementary opposite, hell. Some peasants used the more educated word *rai* (literally paradise or Eden which is related to *raion*, the word for region or area), to refer to heaven. Most, however, preferred the more concrete *zagrobnaia zhizn'* (life beyond the grave), *tot svet* (the other world), and *budushchii vek* (the coming age). These words acknowledged the 'natural' physical boundary between the world of the living and that of the dead. For the righteous, older beliefs were based on the myth of the Moist Mother Earth whose warm embrace nestled those who had not

---

3   Russian peasants were not unique, but were doing what many others had done since time immemorial. See Mircea Eliade, *Images and Symbols: Studies in Religious Symbolism*, trans. Philip Mairet (Princeton, 1991), pp.37–38; and idem, *The Myth of the Eternal Return, or Cosmos and History*, trans. Willard R. Trask, Bollingen Series XLVI (Princeton, 1954; Princeton/Bollingen Paperbacks, 1991).
4   This is similar to Le Goff's "spacialization" and Eliade's "mythic geography" which assigns "location" to Heaven, Earth, and Hell. See Eliade, *Images and Symbols*, p.39.
5   Stephen Lessing Baehr, *The Paradise Myth in Eighteenth-Century Russia: Utopian Patterns in Early Secular Russian Literature and Culture* (Stanford, 1991), pp.14–16.

blasphemed her by violating the ancient laws of nature.⁶ The Christian version of heaven was located somewhere in or above the clouds or beyond a rainbow. It was 'a radiant place, where trees with beautiful fruits (such as apples, for example), flowers, and berries grow.' It was the permanent residence of the redeemed who were escorted there by the angels and the saints, and thereafter lived under angelic guard far from the suffering of demonic souls.⁷ For the damned, hell was 'a dark, terrible place in whose depths burns an inextinguishable fire' guarded by devils who ensured that no one escaped. It was found in the nether regions of the earth which was conducive to fiery rivers, boiling cauldrons, and unbearable heat and darkness. This was the place to which sinners were led directly after death, under the escort of unclean spirits gleefully shouting, 'One of ours, one of ours!'⁸ For those whose eternal status was unclear, a sort of purgatory (*chistilishche*) existed among some peasants who believed it to be situated on a large precipice between good and evil. Russian purgatory, like its western counterpart, gave the not-so-saintly/not-so-damned an opportunity to expiate their sins before the final judgment.⁹ Heaven (and presumably hell) maintained the religious and political boundaries of the world. In addition to the three regions of the afterlife, further distinctions were made according to the national and religious characteristics of the soul, with Russian

. . . . .

6   Olga Semyonova Tian-Shanskaia, *Village Life in Late Tsarist Russia*, ed. David L. Ransel, Indiana-Michigan Series in Russian and East European Studies (Bloomington, 1993), 137; Joanna Hubbs, *Mother Russia: The Feminine Myth in Russian Culture* (Bloomington, IN, 1988), chapter 3; and Elena Hellberg-Hirn, *Soil and Soul: The Symbolic World of Russian* (Aldershot, 1998).
7   The quote is from Rossiiskii gosudarstvennyi muzei etnografii (hereafter RGME), f. 7, op. 1, d. 536 (Kaluga province, 1899), l. 1. On the location of heaven, see ibid., l. 1; ibid., f. 7, op. 1, d. 556 (Kaluga province, 1898), l. 2; and B. M. Firsov and I. G. Kiseleva, comps., *Byt velikorusskikh krest'ian-zemlepashtsev. Opisanie materialov etnograficheskogo biuro Kniazia V. N. Tenisheva (na primere Vladimirskoi gubernii)* (St. Petersburg:, 1993), p.146. Throughout this article, many examples could be given for references to the afterlife. I offer a selection which, although representative, is not exhaustive. Readers interested in more examples are directed to the archive of the Ethnographic Commission of Prince V. N. Tenishev. These materials are housed in RGME.
8   The quote is from RGME, f. 7, op. 1, d. 536 (Kaluga province, 1899), l. 1. On the location of hell, see ibid., f. 7, op. 1, d. 556 (Kaluga province, 1898), l. 2; and Firsov and Kiseleva, *Byt velikorusskikh krest'ian-zemplepashtsev*, p.147.
9   Ibid., p. 147. The idea of purgatory was not widespread, although it seems to be less of an aberration from the usual black and white view of sin than one might think. Throughout Russia it was customary to pray to ease the suffering of the deceased and, in the case of less grave sinners, to ensure their eventual passage to heaven.

Orthodox Christians (*russkie pravoslavnye*) having a purer, more radiant content, followed by non-Orthodox Christians living in Russia and elsewhere (*inovertsy*), and non-believers (*neveruiushchie*) having slightly tarnished essences, and, finally, the dark and sinful (*osuzhdennye*).[10]

With the location of heaven and hell generally agreed upon, what did they look like? To begin with, the soul, immaterial and invisible in earthly life, now became corporeal and took on features of the body just before death. Age, gender, and physique transferred to the next life.[11] Physically, heaven resembled the good life (*vse khorosho*) reified, with its large and sumptuous gardens of all the best the earth had to offer. It was a place of endless delights free of earthly hardship, sorrow, and need. Apples (a peasant favorite) featured prominently as did images of golden houses for all inhabitants.[12] In short, it was a happy, toil-free eternity filled with all the comforts one could imagine with the additional benefit of justice for all. Hell was nearly the opposite in that suffering and want were enforced by Satan and his minions, the innumerable unclean spirits and demons who tormented the living and tortured the dead. It was a place of relentless punishment and dark iron houses. There, people eternally boiled in tar, some to their knees, others to their waists, others to their necks, depending on how sinful they had been. Specific punishments were added for swearing and blasphemy (conveyance to hell by the tongue), for spitting in someone's face (torture by licking a scorching pan), for theft (hanging by the hands), and for lascivious dancing (*pliaska*), especially on the eve of a holiday or during a fast period (foot beating with nails), to name just a few.[13]

. . . . .

10 RGME, f. 7, op. 1, d. 556 (Kaluga province, 1898), l. 1; ibid., f. 7, op. 1, ed. khr. 530 (Kaluga province, 1898), l. 2; ibid., f. 7, op. 1, d. 484 (Kaluga province, 1898), ll. 15–16; and Firsov and Kiseleva, *Byt velikorusskikh krest'ian-zemplepashtsev*, p.145.

11 Exceptions to this were the sectarian *molokane* and *khlysty* whose souls were believed to transfer to animals, people who died violent deaths and continued to roam the earth tormenting the living or occupied the bodies of sorcerers and witches, and animals who were not thought to have souls. See RGME, f. 7, op. 1, d. 556 (Kaluga province, 1898), l. 1; ibid., f. 7, op. 1, ed. khr. 883 (Olonetsk province, 1899), l. 2; and Firsov and Kiseleva, *Byt velikorusskikh krest'ian-zemplepashtsev*, p.145.

12 RGME, f. 7, op. 1, d. 536 (Kaluga province, 1899), ll. 1–2; and Firsov and Kiseleva, *Byt velikorusskikh krest'ian-zemplepashtsev*, p.147.

13 RGME, f. 7, op. 1, d. 536 (Kaluga province, 1899), ll. 1–2; ibid., f. 7, op. 1, d. 631 (1898), ll. 53–54; Firsov and Kiseleva, *Byt velikorusskikh krest'ian-zemplepashtsev*, p.147.

In the end, regardless of how firmly peasants believed in life after death, they lacked actual proof of postmortem realities. One source of comfort was the myriad of rituals that created an image of continuity between the fleeting present and the endless future.

SPACE IN THE AFTERLIFE

Educated Russians often observed that peasants lacked the ability to think abstractly, something that carried over to their notions of the afterlife. In the words of ethnographer Olga Semenova Tian-Shanskaia, 'The peasant God is something material, very much so, in fact. He is the giver of rain, of drought, health, and sickness,' and 'Both heaven and hell are understood purely in material terms.'[14] The endemic smugness of educated Russians festered in the memory of peasants until extreme misfortune (epidemics, droughts, crop failures) led to unrest when socially conscious aid workers, often in the form of *zemstvo* medical personnel and agronomists, offended local sensibilities with their scientific solutions.[15] Notwithstanding the critical tone of observations such as Tian-Shanskaia's and many like her, peasants indeed based their understandings of the afterlife on what they knew best, the world around them which was chock-full of uncertainties and unfairness. Life and death were not circumscribed by degrees of materiality, but were understood to be two complementary spheres constituting an integrated whole. Between the spheres were fruitful and damaging relations. Space in the afterlife included the living and their milieus. The only distinction between them was an eternity that resembled earthly life.

Although death separated peasants physically from their departed friends and relatives, the spiritual relationship between the deceased and their survivors was treated with great care. Proper relations between the living and the dead were an insurance policy for the future of the community. A proper burial provided peasants with a

---

14 Tian-Shanskaia, *Village Life in Late Tsarist Russia*, p.136.
15 For example, see Ivan Stoliarov, *Zapiski russkogo krest'ianina*, Récit d'un paysan russe. Préface de Basile Kerblay, Notes de Valérie Stoliaroff ave le concours d'Alexis Berelowitch, *Cultures & sociétés de l'est* 6 (Paris, 1986), p.25; Gosudarstvennyi arkhiv Voronezhskoi oblasti, f. I–6, op. 1, ed. khr. 80 (1892), ll. 9–58; and Rossiiskii gosudarstvennyi istoricheskii arkhiv, f. 1284, op. 194, ed. khr. 54 (1910), ll. 10–10 ob.

good start to relations with the deceased. According to peasant belief, a proper burial would send the deceased on to the next life, placate wandering and disturbed spirits, and safeguard against a premature or painful end to life. It was not for naught that peasants uttered phrases reminding of this duty: 'Put a piece of bread and salt under the table on which a dead person is lain, and death will stay away from the family for a year;'[16] 'A father should not carry his own child to the cemetery . . . otherwise after that his other children will die.'[17]

Upon death, and sometimes just before, the corpse of the deceased was washed, dressed in new clothes (unmarried girls were dressed in the wedding costume) which assigned identity markers (gender, class, social status, marital status). Coins, vodka, and food were also buried with the dead to help their passage into heaven (as payment for sins, possibly a reflection of the way absolution was usually dispensed after payment to the confessor), as well as magical cloths and belts which were to protect against unwanted encounters with evil spirits. While physical separation between the household and the departed began with the burial, spiritual contact between the two was believed to continue for thirty-nine days while the deceased walked the earth before beginning eternal life on the fortieth day (just as Christ ascended to heaven after forty days of wandering among his friends and relatives). Throughout this period, the needs of the deceased were considered to be nearly the same as in earthly life, and special porridges were left at the icon shelf or on the table, cups of water were left on the window sills, chimneys and *fortochki* (hinged window panes) were left open, and the bedding of the deceased was moved to an outer building, all so that domestic life would not be disrupted when the dead person returned every night after a day of wandering.[18]

Memorial services on the 9th, 20th, and 40th days after death, as well as on the six month and subsequent anniversaries, reinforced

- - - - -
16 "Poslovitsy, pogovorki, krylatye slova, primety i pover'ia, sobranny v slobode Sagunakh Ostrogozhskogo uezda," *Zhivaia starina*, vyp. I–II (1905): 154. The custom of laying out a dead person at home before the Church funeral and burial usually lasted one day, during which friends and relatives paid their last respects.
17 I. Selivanov, "Etnograficheskie ocherki Voronezhskoi gubernii," in *Voronezhskii iubileinyi sbornik v pamiat' trekhsotletiia g. Voronezha*, 3 vols. (Voronezh, 1886), 2:112.
18 D. K. Zelenin, *Vostochnoslavianskaia etnografiia*, trans. K. D. Tsivinaia, with an afterword by K. V. Chistov (Berlin and Leipzig: Walter de Gruyter and Co., 1927; Moscow: Nauka, 1991), 345; and A. Fon-Kremer, "Obychai pover'ia i predrassudki krest'ian sela Verkhotishanki," *Pamiatnaia knizhka voronezhskoi gubernii* (1870–1871): pp.277, 280.

links between the living and the dead. In addition to private prayers, remembrance of the 'forefathers' was often passed from generation to generation in the form of communal commemorations of the dead on the Saturday before *maslenitsa* (carnival before Lent), on Easter, the second Thursday after Easter, on St. Dimitrii's Saturday ('Relatives Day') at the end of October, and other days according to local custom.[19] These memorials took place in church graveyards and were accompanied by gifts of food and drink, as well as fellowship and merriment that strengthened communal and family bonds by supporting the idea of eternal unity and permanence of the group over the individual. These activities were essential for the maintenance of supernatural links with the world beyond the grave, and their chief venue was the overlapping space of the living and the dead.

Above both spheres of existence was the belief in the final judgment of God, who acted as the supreme judge and organizer of space in the afterlife. For most peasants, God was an omnipotent and omniscient *batiushka* (father) of jealous and impatient temperament and severe countenance not unlike the God of the Old Testament. He spent his time rewarding and punishing people for their obedience and disloyalty. Assisted by the archangels and myriad of lesser angelic beings, God was the bearer of happiness and fortune to the faithful; but for those who strayed, his wrath knew no limits. In the scheme of eternity, justice would prevail in God's final judgment of all souls. Those who disagreed with the verdict could, in typical peasant fashion, 'petition' God through their own prayers and those offered by their relatives. But, it seems, God remained a strict and fair judge and was seldom moved by these last-ditch efforts.[20] Despite this image, in some peasant minds, through the ages God had become more compassionate. According to one peasant woman,

> Before, God was not as he is now. . . . .Before, he did not separate good people from the bad, and all people went to hell because Satan was strong then. And when Christ was born, he [God] began to separate people: the good to heaven, the bad to

---

19 RGME, f. 7, op. 1, d. 556 (Kaluga province, 1898), l. 2; Ioann Putintsev, "Selo Dimitrievskoe, Korotoiakskogo uezda," *Voronezhskie eparkhial'nye vedomosti*, no. 14, unof. pt. (1868): p.465; Zelenin, *Vostochnoslavianskaia etnografiia*, pp.346–57; RGME, f. 7, op. 1, ed. khr. 883 (Olonetsk province, 1899), l. 2; and Selivanov, "Obychai pover'ia," pp.277, 280.
20 RGME, f. 7, op. 1, d. 536 (Kaluga province, 1899), l. 3; and ibid., f. 7, op. 1, ed. khr. 1486 (Saratov province, 1898), l. 17.

hell. Now, if a person is good, nothing will happen to him. Maybe he will have a few sins, but the Lord will forgive him. And so he who causes harm to others, corrupts, and steals will be hung by his ribs from iron hooks.[21]

He was like a tsar exponentially multiplied, someone to be loved unquestioningly, whose power and domain were best left unchallenged in order to avoid undesired consequences from high and faraway places. God was as much a material as supernatural being who ruled the world as a great lord who intervened in the course of history.[22]

HEAVEN ON EARTH

At the beginning of the nineteenth century, village space in the afterlife was challenged by a growing number of peasants who no longer saw the need for a deity or heavenly justice. Blasphemy, mockery, and insubordination were part of growing disenchantment with the regime ('[I] save and will be a savior.' 'There is no God. He never was and could not be.' 'What is the Sovereign? The Sovereign is nothing.' 'We do not need a Sovereign.').[23] They also threatened the religious frameworks that supported the belief in the afterlife and its spatial organization. Radical changes in spatial attitudes toward the afterlife, however, began with the revolutionary furor of 1917 and the miserable institutional emasculation suffered by the Orthodox church, while the Christian idiom continued to appeal to broad segments of the population regardless of social status, religious affiliation (or lack of it), ethnic background, or gender. In the midst of extreme physical, spiritual, and psychological upheavals, the ideas of heaven/paradise, eternal life, hell, and damnation offered consoling images to the masses who were recoiling from revolutionary dislocations that had

. . . . .
21 RGME, f. 7, op. 1, d. 631 (1898), ll. 53–54.
22 I. Taradin, *"Zolotoe Dno": Ekonomika, istoriia, kul'tura i byt volosti tsentral'no-chernozemnoi oblasti* (Voronezh: Izd. Voronezhskogo kraevedcheskogo obshchestva, 1928), p.3.
23 Gosudarstvennyi arkhiv Voronezhskoi oblasti, f. I–1, op. 1, ed. khr. 182, l. 1 (1902); ibid., f. I–6, op. 1, ed. khr. 730; ibid., f. I–6, op. 1, ed. khr. 161 (1895–1897), l. 10 ob.; and ibid., f. I-1, ed. khr. 598 (1904), ll. 5–5 ob. Many more examples can be found in the Archive of the Tenishev Ethnographic Commission.

turned their world on its head. As Richard Stites has argued, one of the three main utopian visions in the 1920s was rooted in the peasant notion of a righteous world – justice, community, and rebellion (when necessary) – and all of these were salient aspects of peasant religion.[24]

The influence of images of the afterlife persisted throughout the 1920s from the highest echelons of political power to the lower depths of the impoverished urban working classes. The near deification of Lenin not only drew upon the tradition of the life of Christ, but it repeated familiar rituals in Christianity, especially those associated with the enshrined holy person whose remains served as a Mecca for devout believers.[25] As Mark Steinberg has recently pointed out, the importance of religious imagery, especially in the survival of those unsettled revolutionary years, can in part be attributed to the lower urban classes' understanding of them in eschatological and millenarian terms. If nothing else, the end appeared to be near, and religious frameworks offered a 'humanistic, comforting, inspiring, moral, and possess[ed] a quality of mystery and destiny.'[26] As the Godseekers and Godbuilders settled their scores and the League of Militant Godless stormed the heavens, the symbolism and imagery of religion proved resilient in the creation of a socialist paradise not too unlike the Orthodox teaching on the Kingdom of Heaven on earth. The afterlife, transformed and disguised, was an eternal reproduction of earthly models that made the new Soviet society everlasting.

24 Richard Stites, *Revolutionary Dreams: Utopian Vision and Experimental Life in the Russian Revolution* (New York: Oxford, 1989), pp.14–19.
25 Jay Bergman, "The Image of Jesus in the Russian Revolutionary Movement: The Case of Russian Marxism," *International Review of Social History* 35 (1990): pp.220–48; and Nina Tumarkin, *Lenin Lives! The Lenin Cult in Soviet Russia* (Boston, 1983).
26 Mark D. Steinberg, "Workers on the Cross: Religious Imagination in the Writings of Russian Workers, 1910–1924," *Russian Review* 53 (April 1994): pp.213–39.

Studia Historica 62

Distance and Logistics as Problems – Their Soviet Solutions

Jarmo Eronen

THE SOVIET APPROACH TO THE LOCATION OF PRODUCTION

Empires are by nature expansionist, and the areal acquisitions of the Russian empire were especially impressive in the East and North, where enormous territories comprising seemingly limitless natural resources were annexed to the state. The idea of Russia as a land of almost inexhaustible natural resources rested very much on the Siberian potential, as shown by the famous saying *'Mogushchestvo rossiiskoe prirastat' budet Sibiryu i Severnym okeanom*' (Russian might will increase thanks to Siberia and the Arctic Ocean). However, the cost of opening up these almost uninhabited areas was prohibitively high and during the tsarist era the industrial exploitation of Siberia remained modest compared to what happened in European Russia.

The Soviet regime brought about a radical change in how the national economy was developed regionally. More balanced location of economic activity between regions was a high priority objective of the regime. Lenin himself stressed, that the rational location of productive forces required the shifting of industries nearer the raw material resources in the East and North.[1] The market oriented location of manufacturing industry, a legacy from the tsarist era, was

---

1   V. I. Lenin *Polnoe sobranie sochineniia*, t. 36, pp.188, 288, cited in *Planirovanie razmeshcheniya proizvoditelnykh sil SSSR*, 1, (1985), Moskva, "Ekonomika", p. 17.

not considered rational. The idea was not new of course but its realization had been hampered by lack of capital and high costs. Also some Soviet economists raised the cost issue in the late 1920s referring to the Weberian location theory, which states that cost minimization is the optimal criterion for industrial location. As this theory obviously could not legitimize the high cost of opening up Eastern and Northern areas it was soon dismissed and did not become a guiding principle in the areal allocation of resources.[2] The so called Leninist principles of socialist location of production became prevalent including:
 – the more even distribution of productive forces
 – the creation of industrial bases in the Eastern part of the country
 – the cultural development of all regions
 – the creation of new towns
 – considerations of the defense potential of the country

The cost factor was also present. Different investment projects were compared by means of coefficients like the pay back period or yield of investments.[3]

Although these principles were called Leninist they were formulated in the late 1920s and early 1930s. Their implementation started during the first and second five year plans when the centrally planned economy had been established, after the experiment of NEP. The location principles were an integral part of the Stalinist industrialization strategy, in which considerations other than cost prevailed. The share of the Urals and Siberia in investment outlays and total production increased constantly until the war. This tendency was further emphasized during the war years as a large number of industrial enterprises was evacuated to the East from the areas threatened by Germans. The Eastern regions were favored in investment allocation during the post war period as well. Emphasis was laid on the development of the energy and forestry industries, whose share increased in Siberia (fuel output also increased in Central Asia and Kazakhastan, see Table 1). In most other branches of the manufacturing industries a market orientation and the European part of the country remained dominant. Geopolitical considerations obviously also played a role especially in the development of the Soviet Far East facing the potential Chinese threat.

. . . . .
2   V. V. Kotov 'Iz stanovleniya otechestvennoi teorii faktorov razmeshcheniya promyshlennosti' *Izvestiya AN SSSR*, Seriya Geogr. 1980, Nr. 4., Planirovanie i razmeshchenie ...pp. 55–56.
3   *Planirovanie razmeshcheniya* ..., pp. 47, 52–53.

Table 1   Shares of Eastern Regions in the Soviet Economy 1960–75

	Siberia, Far East		Central Asia, Kazakhstan	
	1960	1975	1960	1975
	- % -		- % -	
Population	11	11	12	16
Production of Crude Oil	1	31	6	8
Natural Gas	1	14	2	33
Coal	28	35	8	15
Roundwood	25	34	0.6	0.5
Rolled Steel Products	10	10	1	4
Chemical Fibres	16	12	3	4
Concrete	13	12	8	10

Source: V.A. Vinogradov et al. (eds.), *Istoriya sotsialisticheskoi ekonomiki SSSR. Sed'moi tom. Ekonomika SSSR na etape razvitogo sotsializma (1960–1970-e gody)* (Moscow, 1980), p. 428.

The share of Siberia and the Far East in the population and output of the Russian Federation increased constantly (the share in the total population did not change much due to the higher nativity of the Moslem dominated republics). The result was longer haulages and rising costs.

SOVIET SOLUTIONS TO THE DISTANCE PROBLEM

Solutions had to be found to address the problem of the high costs of operating in remote areas. The following deserve to be mentioned in the first place:

1) Expansion of transport infrastructure. This meant above all building railways and later, since the 1960s, pipelines mainly in Western Siberia. The expansion of the railway network was a key element in integrating remote parts of the Soviet empire with the core areas and opening up new raw material sources. In the 1920s lines were built in the Urals, Central Asia and Southern Siberia (the Turksib mainline). In the European North the Kotlas-Vorkuta railway was completed in the early 1940s. After the war most of the new railway

projects were started east of the Urals. Lines parallel to the Transsiberian mainline were built in Southern Siberia. Expansion to the North started in the 1970s with the Tyumen-Surgut-Nizhnevartovsk-Urengoi-Yamburg line connecting the oil and gas fields with the Transsiberian.[4] The last giant project was the Baikal-Amur mainline (BAM) completed in 1984. Since then investments into new railways have practically stopped.

Large scale building of oil pipelines started in the late 1950s. Of prime importance was the connection of the West Siberian oil fields by pipelines with the consuming areas. Major investments into the gas pipelines were carried out in the 1970s and 1980s.

Improving river and Arctic sea port facilities, building roads and flight connections were also part of the strategy. Still, most of Central and Northern Siberia remains beyond the reach of land routes.

2) A supply of cheap labor through the Gulag system was important for a certain period. A large number of logging camps and mining communities were founded as prisoners' settlements, the most important being Norilsk and Magadan.. This kind of labour recruitment became rare after Stalin's death. Predominantly economic incentives had to be used to attract labour to remote regions, which meant, that the period of cheap labour was over.

3) Freight rates were subsidized by the state; this concerned railway freights especially but also, for example, passenger flights. Periods of especially low railway freight rates included war communism, when transports were free of charge for the state, the years 1934–38 and 1945–85.[5]

4) Territorial production complexes (TPC) as instruments of shifting resources to the periphery. Areal concentration of economic activity creates locational advantages (market potential, access to transport and social infrastructure, a common energy source), which attract industries and enterprises. Weber called this economies of agglomeration, which he considered one of the key location factors along with markets, raw material and labour sources. In the Soviet system of planning location decisions based on the benefits of agglomeration (as contrasted to isolated production sites) also became

- - - - -
4   A. T. Khrushchov (ed.), *Ekonomicheskaya i sotsial'naya geografiya Rossii* (Moscow, 1997) p. 291.
5   G. A. Golts and V. N. Filina, 'Tarifoobrazovanie na zheleznodorozhnom transporte: sovremennoe sostoyanie i problemy', *Problemy prognozirovaniya* 1997, no.4, pp.89–90.

evident although the Weberian concept was not used. When opening up new regions for economic exploitation the main resources would be concentrated in territorial production complexes, which by including a common transport, energy and social infrastructure and facilitating inter-industry linkages was considered an efficient method of regional development in the periphery.

The implementation of the TPC concept started during the five year period 1971–75, when resources started to be shifted especially to the following complexes: in European Russia Timano-Pechora (Komi ASSR), Kursk MA and Orenburg TPCs, in Siberia Kansk-Achinsk, Sayan and Bratsk-Ust'Ilimsk TPCs, and a separate TPC in Southern Tajikistan. After the completion of the BAM the South Yakutian TPC would be a priority project.[6] Much was accomplished within these complexes in the 1970s and early 1980s but the stagnation of the Soviet economy in the 1980s and collapse in the 1990s put an end to the development of the TPCs. The real efficiency of this concept can be questioned as in the initial phase the complexes required enormous capital outlays for building the infrastructure. The cost benefits attributed to agglomeration effects would come later but in many cases they were hardly able to compensate for the high real cost caused by enormous distances (e.g. in the case of the Bratsk-Ust' Ilmisk or southern Yakutia TPCs). Actual transport fares were naturally subsidized.

All this combined with important investment outlays served the objectives of the Soviet regime well: new raw material and fuel sources were tapped in the East and North, production volumes rose, new settlements were erected, people migrated to these inhospitable regions. Population growth spurred by migration was especially rapid since 1950 in the Komi ASSR, Tyumen, Magadan and Kamchatka provinces, and the Yakut ASSR. Giant enterprises were built at locations which would have been inconceivable in a market economy; recall the Vorkuta coal mines, Norilsk metallurgical combine, the Bratsk forest industry integrate and aluminium factory, the Ust'-Ilimsk pulp mill etc.

At the same time inefficiencies increased, the cost of maintaining people in inhospitable conditions (creation of new social infrastructure, paying higher salaries) and the cost of delivering goods rose as haulages became longer and longer. Low value industrial raw

---

6   Vinogradov, p. 428; *Planirovanie razmeshcheniya proizvoditelnykh sil SSSR*, no.2 (Moscow, 1986), pp. 86–89.

materials (ores, wood, pulp, construction materials etc.) hauled by railways are especially sensitive to transport costs. Oil and gas can be transported rather cheaply by pipelines, once the infrastructure has been built the transport cost is not a problem. Also river transport is cheap but the navigation season is only 3–4 months in Siberia. For high priced products like gold or diamonds transport costs are not a problem. However, for most of the industrial raw materials to be supplied from the East and North the only alternative is the railways. Subsidized freight rates blurred the real costs, however, and excessively long haulages (3000–5000 km) of commodities like roundwood or coal were not uncommon. In market economies distances of 500 km are rarely exceeded for these goods. As the real railway freight rates diminished during the whole post-war period until 1985 the volume of irrational transports increased in the Soviet economy.[7]

During the Soviet period a large number of towns and settlements dependent on a single enterprise were erected. Distances to markets were typically very long and these settlements had also to be supplied from remote industrial and agricultural regions.

When the Soviet system collapsed Russia was left with a legacy of non competitive industries and agriculture, which produce low quality or wrong products (like military hardware) at high costs, due to inefficiency or wrong location. The Soviet strategy of areal economic expansion was not based on sound economic foundations as it was not able to create enough competitive industries and enterprises to keep settlements viable. Too many of the production facilities and settlements created in remote areas were dependent on state subsidies, which are no more available. They are doomed to fade away. Such solutions to the distance problem as large scale subsidies or state financed territorial production complexes are not viable any more. However, the Soviet period also left a legacy of impressive transport infrastructure (railways, pipelines, roads, airports, ports) which will be essential for the future development of the Northern and Eastern regions.

. . . . .
7   Golts, p. 90

Space of Survival: The Soviet Evacuation of Industry and Population in 1941

Robert Argenbright

The Soviet evacuation of industry and population in World War II was a radical restructuring of the country's economic geography which stretched to the limit the state's abilities to organize its territory.[1] This often chaotic and brutal process altered the lives of millions of people, in large part by changing the places in which, and by means of which, they lived their lives. The paper argues that analysis of the evacuation, the re-establishment of industry, and the re-settling of evacuees offers insights into the Soviet state's fundamental approaches to administration and transformation of territory. Study of this issue, moreover, furthers understanding of the principles and practices of Soviet territoriality, which largely has been overlooked in the historical literature.

The first section of this chapter outlines the conceptual approach drawing largely on the work of Robert David Sack,[2] although it unfortunately is impossible to do justice in such a summary form to the richness and complexity of his framework. Then the discussion turns to past and current views of the evacuation. Then the chapter takes a new look at the evacuation both as a vast attempt to transform the spatial organization of the world's largest country and as a complex place-transforming process realized at a range of geographical scales.

---

1 The archival research for this product was funded by the International Research Exchanges Board (IREX). The author is grateful to Patricia K. Kerig for helpful comments and computer aid.
2 Robert David Sack, *Homo Geographicus: A Framework for Action, Awareness, and Moral Concern* (Baltimore, 1997).

SPACE, PLACE, AND TERRITORY

For many people, the image of Russia begins with some impression of a great space. In *The Cambridge Encyclopedia of Russia and the former Soviet Union*, the first sentence of the first chapter refers to 'territorial vastness.'[3] Nicholas Riasanovsky's classic history text begins with a 'geographical note,' which describes this 'enormous territory.'[4] John M. Thompson's text similarly begins with an interpretation of the importance of 'the vast expanse of territory.'[5] Popular 'coffee-table' books on Russia are similarly inclined. For example, *A Day in the Life of the Soviet Union* starts by describing how the 'sheer distances are breathtaking.'[6]

For some, mention of the vastness of Russia or the USSR is a matter of following convention, for others it is a 'hook' with which to capture the reader's attention. However, some have employed the concept of space prominently in the elaboration of overarching principles which would define Russia. For instance, George Vernadsky argued that 'history provides no clearer example of the profound influence of geography upon a culture than in the historical development of the Russian people.'[7] Yet such a perspective may be too Olympian for empirical research either to confirm or contradict.

If geography is important in human life, to a great degree it must be because it is there all the time, constantly, yet most historical and social-scientific perspectives scarcely take this factor into account. A different approach to the concept of space starts by arguing that in the attempt to understand human affairs, such as Russian history, it is not so much *space* that is of interest, but *place*. As put forth by Robert David Sack, this perspective, among many other things, clarifies geographical concepts by distinguishing more carefully among terms. In his view, *space* should be reserved for the fundamental dimension of the universe, which here on earth 'has an effect in that distances

. . . . .

3   G. Melvyn Howe, "The Natural Landscape," in *The Cambridge Encyclopedia of Russia and the former Soviet Union*, eds., Archie Brown, Michael Kaser, and Gerald S. Smith, (Cambridge, 1994), p.2.
4   Nicholas V. Riasanovsky, *A History of Russia*, Third Edition, (New York, 1977), p.3.
5   John M. Thompson, *Russia and the Soviet Union*, Fourth Edition, (Boulder, CO, 1998), p.1.
6   Harrison Salisbury, preface to *A Day in the Life of the Soviet Union* (New York, 1987), p.10.
7   George Vernadsky, *A History of Russia*, (New Haven, CN, 1949), p.6.

between things, in conjunction with the medium through which interactions travel, affect the intensity and degree of interactions.'[8] If one were concerned to fence off a fragment of space in order to look at the objects distributed within it, the fragment could be called a place, but in Sack's view this would evoke a secondary meaning of place: 'The objects in space are present and interacting, and space (albeit relationally) is having an effect on them.'[9] However, it is the *primary* meaning of place that makes possible a different way of understanding the world, one that inter-relates *nature*, *social relations*, and *meaning* without a priori privileging one sphere over another or reducing one to another.[10]

> When place, and not only the things in it, is a force – when it influences, affects, and controls – it is a primary place. Primary places involve human actions and intentions and have the capacity to change things. Unlike a secondary place, which can be re-placed without remainder by substituting the objects and interactions in its area, a primary place cannot be re-placed. Primary places are delimited, they possess rules about the things to be included and excluded, and they have meaning.[11]

Place in this sense – demarcated, rule-governed, meaningful – can also be described as *territory*.[12] However, it would further clarify matters to reserve 'territory' to signify the dimension of place that is shaped by power.[13] 'Territory' then appropriately may serve as the companion to *territoriality*, which Sack defined in his seminal work on human territory as 'the attempt by an individual or group to affect, influence, or control people, phenomena, and relationships, by delimiting and asserting control over a geographic area.'[14]

. . . . .
8   Sack, *Homo Geographicus*, p.31.
9   Ibid., p.32.
10 At present, most geographers who consider such issues speak of *construction of social space* or *social production of space*, which would tend at the onset to privilege the realm of social relations. For a particularly insightful and influential example of such an approach, see Henri Lefebvre, *The Production of Space* (Oxford, 1974).
11 Sack, *Homo Geographicus*, p.32.
12 Ibid., p.272, n. 1.
13 By power, I mean *power over* others, not the *power to do* things. See: Dennis H. Wrong, *Power: Its Forms, Bases, and Uses*, (Oxford, 1979), pp.1–20.
14 Robert David Sack, *Human Territoriality: Its Theory and History*, (Cambridge, 1986), p.19. Human territoriality is distinct from animal territoriality because it involves intentionality, not just instinct. And that is why territory is primary, not secondary place. See Sack, *Homo Geographicus*, p.275, n.11.

Following from this, Sack has further developed his thinking on how places 'act as forces or causal agents.' The idea that place could be a force, even a cause, may appear extreme at first encounter, as if geography were reverting to the discredited doctrine of environmental determinism. Yet to say that a place is causal force is not to argue that it is alive.[15] Places obviously can reflect human consciousness or else there would be no point to architecture or landscape design. Moreover, places may embody specific intentions, as does a minefield, for example. This is not to say, of course, that all interpretations of place or all consequences of the forces of place can be predicted or controlled, any more than the poet can anticipate all reactions to the poem.

Sack discusses three interconnected types of relationships which are inherent in places and which may act as forces. Each of these inter-related 'loops' is also connected with one of the main realms of place: the 'in/out-of-place loop' is linked with social relations; 'spatial-interaction' embodies the natural or physical dimension of space; and 'surface/depth' relates to the meaning of place.[16] Let us briefly consider the Soviet Union as a place in this regard. Most clearly 'in/out-of-place' relationships were vitally important, as was shown by numerous displays of power such as the downing of the Korean Air Line passenger plane in 1983. This topic has recently been extensively addressed in Andrea Chandler's study of Soviet border controls.[17] One could continue to cite examples through a series of scales that evoked in/out rules, until reaching the scale of the body, for example metro seats reserved for children and disabled people.

Sack regards the power to govern in/out relationships as the basis for human territoriality because these relationships are the most distinctly linked to social relations.[18] However, the links are interconnected. In the real world, and perhaps especially in the lost world of the Soviet Union, power could be exercised in place by the ability to control or change spatial interaction and to impose specific meanings on place. In this regard, it seems that if there is a weakness in Sack's framework, it is an inadequate allowance for the great range of capacities, especially in the modern period, of social institutions

- - - - -
15 Cf. the "Gaia hypothesis," see: James Lovelock, *The Ages of Gaia: a Biography of Our Living Earth*, (New York: 1988).
16 Sack, *Homo Geographicus*, pp.88–126.
17 Andrea Chandler, *Institutions of Isolation: Border Controls in the Soviet Union and its Successor States, 1917–1993*, (Montreal, 1998).
18 Sack, *Homo Geographicus*, p.272, n. 2.

and agencies to affect and use place. Sack describes how an individual may shift focus from place to space by *distancing*, either as s/he moves rapidly through the world or by exercising rational thought, i.e., by a mental process of abstraction.[19] However, a person or agency may also relate to space rather than place because a powerful location in the social structure enables the agent to maintain, (re-)structure, or perhaps even obliterate places from afar. In the case of the monopolistic, centralized Soviet state, every decision concerning changes in spatial interaction benefited some places and entailed opportunity costs which affected other places. For example, a new railroad linking Siberia and Turkestan may well have meant that Ukraine would have to wait for infrastructural improvements. In countless similar cases, the regime asserted a territorial prerogative to transform space for its own purposes, with scarce regard for the impact on places.

Similarly, the surface/depth loop is highly constricted in a non-pluralistic, closed society. The regime was able to broadcast its interpretation of the construction of the Turksib railroad, and countless other major projects, to every 'bear's corner' in the land. Everybody, everywhere was 'building socialism,' and in that effort they were expected to be inspired by the heroic example of this or that key project. The party/state's symbols were installed and its rituals enacted in all kinds of public places. Virtually every place had its narrowly-defined significance which was supposed to replace older meanings and eliminate the possibility of other interpretations. Of course, the regime was unable to impose its interpretations of everything to the exclusion of all alternative understandings, everywhere all of the time. But, the ubiquity, intensity, and persistence of the effort affected virtually all places in the immense territory and, by thus circumscribing the significance of the places in their world, influenced the people as well.[20]

To be fair, Sack's topic is place, not the state. Evidently, in his view, the state would primarily fall under the heading of social relations, which, as he recognizes, may overshadow nature or meaning in the make-up of many places. Yet, to look at the state more closely, this appears inadequate generally, and especially so in the case of a

. . . .
19 Sack, *Homo Geographicus*, pp.85–86.
20 For an important example, see Nina Tumarkin, *Lenin Lives! The Lenin Cult in Soviet Russia*, (Cambridge, MA, 1997), pp.207–251.

Communist state which is eager to transform nature at every scale, from the continental to the body, and to dictate the proper interpretation of everything. The state, even one more 'normal' than the USSR, is much more than just another social institution, primarily because of its unrivaled territorial powers. Of course, other institutions will engage in some sort of territoriality, but usually this is peripheral to their main functions. As Cox has argued, no theory of the state or study of a state would be sound without a discussion of territoriality.[21] In this regard, Michael Mann has developed the idea that state power 'flows principally from the state's unique ability to provide a territorially-centralized form of organization.'[22] This form of organization is inherently ambiguous, as Mann explains: 'The state contains two dualities: It is place and persons and center and territory.'[23] Sack knows well that there are places *within* places. If we adopt Mann's view, then the state is not only the largest of the nested *matrioshka* dolls, but also *the* place that is in *all* places within state territory, at least potentially. State territoriality then appears as the exercise of power in (every) place, by means of place.

HISTORIOGRAPHICAL OVERVIEW OF THE EVACUATION

The basic Soviet interpretation of the evacuation and restoration of industry was set out by N. A Voznesenskii who, among other responsibilities, headed Gosplan during the war.[24] In essence, Voznesenskii served as leading commander in the wartime economic administration, although of course Stalin was Generalissimo of civilian matters as well as military affairs Voznesenskii's book established the ideological framework and provided the basic data that

. . . . .
21 Kevin R. Cox, "Redefining 'Territory'" *Political Geography Quarterly* v. 10, n. 1, 1991, pp.5–7.
22 Michael Mann, "The Autonomous Power of the State: its Origins, Mechanisms and Results," *European Journal of Sociology*, v. 25, n. 2, 1984, pp.185, 210 respectively.
23 Michael Mann, *The Sources of Social Power, Volume II: The Rise of Classes and Nation-States, 1760-1914*, (Cambridge, 1993), p.56.
24 N. Voznesenskii, *Voennaia Ekonomika SSSR v Period Otechestvennoi Voiny*, (Moscow, 1947).

would be reproduced for years to come.[25] Each chapter started and ended on an inspirational note, usually with an expression of admiration and gratitude to Stalin. Inside this frame, every chapter contained a straightforward narrative, heavily laden with statistics. Voznesenskii's appraisal of the evacuation and restoration of industry in its basic outline dominated for decades, and elements of it persist today.

> Thus, the socialist character of the Soviet economy and, arising from this, the supreme principle of the Plan, enabled the rapid military restructuring of the national economy of the USSR. The relocation of productive forces from the front-line and near-front areas to the eastern rear areas of the USSR deprived the German invaders of productive enterprises and, under the guidance of the party of Lenin and Stalin, enabled the continuous consolidation and development of the military economy of the USSR.[26]

Very little more was published concerning the evacuation for over a decade. While Stalin lived it was not a popular topic – the execution of Voznesenskii[27] was but one indication that yesterday's exploits were no longer celebrated. During the transition following Stalin's death, no one could be sure what the new general line would be. Finally, when Khrushchev was firmly in command, histories of the war began to appear again.[28] After an authoritative multi-volume history of the war was issued in 1961,[29] a stream of works on the war were published, including a number concerning the evacuation. Under Brezhnev the stream became a deluge. In the new accounts Stalin's leadership was eclipsed by 'the organizational work of the Communist Party,'[30] but the rest of the basic message remained about the same, with the addition of a new symbol of glory for the people.

. . . . .

25 There was one other article published on the evacuation at this time which provided data useful to scholars pursuing the topic, but which remained relatively obscure. See L. M. Kantor, "Perebazirovanie promyshlennosti SSSR," *Zapiski Planogo Instituta*, vyp. VI, (Leningrad), 1947, pp.57–132
26 Ibid., p.44; translation by the author.
27 Mark Harrison, *Soviet Planning in Peace and War, 1938–1945*, (Cambridge, 1985), pp. 63–102.
28 E.g., see B. S. Tel'pukhovskii, *Velikaia Otechestvennaia voina Sovetskogo Soiuza, 1941–1945 gg.*, (Moscow, 1959)
29 *Istoriia Velikoi Otechestvennoi voiny Sovetskogo Soiuza, 1941–1945*, (Moscow, 1961).
30 A. V. Mitrofanova, "Evakuatsiia Promyshlennykh Predpriiatii v Gody Velikoi Otechestvennoi Voiny (1941–1942 gg.)", *Istoriia SSSR* v. 4, n. 3, May-June, 1960, p.48.

> The successful resolution of the tasks of the evacuation demonstrated the flexibility of the socialist economic system, especially its planning organization, the organizational strength of the Communist Party, and the fortitude and bravery of Soviet man, maker and creator.[31]

The new leaders of the regime, in the wake of Khrushchev's revelations about Stalinist terror and the cultural liberalization of the 'Thaw,' were striving to bolster the legitimacy of the party. One of the main means for achieving this purpose was the creation and development of a cult of the 'Great Fatherland War.' In some respects, the new movement was a revival of cultish practices that earlier had been focused on Lenin or Stalin. However, once the 'cult of personality' had been thoroughly repudiated, the need to construct a new cult of the party, especially of its new collective leadership, could best be accomplished by glorifying the victory in World War II. Such an approach would enable the party to invoke the heroism of ordinary people, invariably seen as guided by the party, and sanctify the territory of the state as well. For example, the regime did not stop at placing memorials in thousands of sites but also came up with the innovation of designating entire 'hero cities.' It was in this spirit that the trials and tribulations of the evacuation were depicted a 'heroic epic.'[32] The cult as a whole has been interpreted at length by Nina Tumarkin, in the following vein:

> Soviet historiography of the war was fundamentally mendacious, promoting a standardized version of the experience meant to celebrate the Communist Party's wartime successes and provide an inspirational image of exemplary unity and popular heroism. That image contained truth and lies and unforgivable blank spots...[33]

There have been no full blown Russian-language revisions of the evacuation story up to the present day. With the onset of *glasnost'* and *perestroika* under Gorbachev, traditional cult themes, such as the evacuation, were elbowed off center stage by an outpouring of

---
31 A. V. Mitrofanova, G. A. Kumanev, and Iu. K. Strizhkov, "Introduction," in *Eshelony Idut na Vostok*, eds., Iu. A. Poliakov, G. A. Kumanev, N. P. Lipatov, A. V. Mitrofanova, (Moscow, 1966), p.14, translation by the author.
32 Ibid., p.5.
33 Nina Tumarkin, *The Living and the Dead: The Rise and Fall of the Cult of World War II in Russia*, (New York, 1994), p.50.

exposés. The sole exception, although an outstanding one, is G. A. Kumanev who continued to soldier on after over thirty years of work on the topic.[34] Kumanev's contribution has been especially important in the area of assessing the data and correcting long-accepted statistics. His overall perspective, however, represents a gradual evolution rather than a revision of the 'heroic epic' of the evacuation. In Kumanev's account, Stalin set the country up for a disaster, not least by preventing planning for the evacuation. But once the process was underway, in Kumanev's view, the most significant aspects were the institutional adaptations of the party/state, the successful initiatives of officials at various levels, and the sheer difficulty of accomplishing such a massive endeavor, one which he feels was 'unprecedented in the history of countries and peoples in its extent and duration.'[35]

The evacuation and restoration of industry have been mentioned most often in the literature in English by economists and economic historians.[36] Especially important in this regard is the work of Mark Harrison, which has illuminated the role of the evacuation in the wartime economy and the Soviet victory.[37] Most accessible is an article by Sanford R. Lieberman which is devoted to the evacuation and, moreover, draws attention to extraordinary administrative

- - - - -

34 G. A. Kumanev, "Sovetskie zheleznodorozhniki v pervyi period Velikoi Otechestvennoi voiny, 1941–1942," *Istoriia SSSR*, v. 3, n. 1, 1959. Also see by the same author: *Sovetskii tyl v pervyi period Velikoi Otechestvennoi voiny*, (Moscow, 1988); "V ogne tiazhelykh ispytanii (iiun' 1941 – noiabr' 1942 g.," Istoriia SSSR, v. 34, n. 2, 1991, pp.3–31.
35 G. A. Kumanev, "Sovetskaia Ekonomika i Evakuatsiia 1941 goda," *Soviet Union/ Union Soviétique* v. 18, nos. 1–3, 1991, p.151. Translation by the author.
36 Alec Nove, *An Economic History of the USSR, 1917–1991*, (Middlesex, UK, 1992), pp.273–281; Susan J. Linz, "Impact of World War II on the Soviet Economy: A Review Essay," in *The Sinews of War: Essays on the Economic History of World War II*, eds. Geofrey T. Mills and Hugh Rockoff, (Ames, Iowa, 1994), pp.83–101.
37 Mark Harrison, "The Second World War," in *The Economic Transformation of the Soviet Union, 1913–1945*, eds., R. W. Davies, Mark Harrison, and S. G. Wheatcroft, (Cambridge, 1994), pp.252–256; M. Harrison, "Fortresses of the Rear," in John Barber and Mark Harrison, *The Soviet Home Front, 1941–1945: A Social and Economic History of the USSR in World War II*, , (London, 1991), pp.123–142; M. Harrison, *Soviet Planning*, pp.63–102. In his recent analysis of the Soviet wartime economy, Harrison speculates that the redistribution of industry carried out by the evacuation in the long run contributed to the inefficiency of the Soviet economy and, thus, the country's eventual disintegration. See: M. Harrison, *Accounting for War: Soviet Production, Employment, and the Defence Burden, 1940–1945*, (Cambridge, 1996), p.168.

agencies.[38] The human dimension of the evacuation has been touched on by Sheila Fitzpatrick,[39] John Barber,[40] and William Moskoff.[41] Most importantly for the present article, a recent dissertation by Kristin Edwards focuses on the reception and resettlement of evacuees in one region.[42] However, none of the existing sources address questions of state territoriality, spatial organization, or transformation of place.

BENEATH THE MAP'S SURFACE

Some would argue that a geographical essay should always include a map, but in this case it could easily encourage misunderstanding. A realistic map of the evacuation would be too complicated a picture, and not just because of controversies concerning the data.[43] Take for example the evidently straightforward concept, 'factory.' One might picture 1500–2500 things called factories, like dots on a map, being moved to the East, set up and reactivated.[44] But in fact only a minority of plants were put back together again in forms resembling their former selves. All the plants had to be broken down into their component parts and some of these parts were loaded into the railroad

. . . . .

38 Sanford R. Lieberman, "The Evacuation of Industry in the Soviet Union During World War II," *Soviet Studies*, v. 35, no. 1, 1983, pp.90–102. Also see: Sanford R. Lieberman, "Crisis Management in the USSR: The Wartime System of Administration and Control," in *The Impact of World War II on the Soviet Union*, ed. Susan J. Linz (Totowa, NJ: 1985), pp.59–76.
39 Sheila Fitzpatrick, "*War and Society* in Soviet Context: Soviet Labor before, during, and after World War II," *International Labor and Working-Class History*, n. 35, Spring 1989, pp.37–52.
40 John Barber, "The Social Order," in Barber and Harrison, *Soviet Home Front*, pp.94–122.
41 William Moskoff, *The Bread of Affliction: The Food Supply in the USSR During World War II*, (Cambridge, 1990), pp.10–41, 161–170.
42 Kristin E. Edwards, "Fleeing to Siberia: The Wartime Relocation of Evacuees to Novosibirsk, 1941–1943," (Ph.D. diss., Stanford University, 1996).
43 For a summary of the debate concerning the data, see: ibid., pp.30–34.
44 Voznesenskii (*Voennaia Ekonomika*, p.27) and Kantor ("Perebazirovanie," p.60) claimed 1523 industrial enterprises were evacuated in 1941. This figure is still widely accepted; see: Barber and Harrison, *Soviet Home Front*, p.130; M. I. Likhomanov, L. TY. Pozina, E. I Finogenov, *Partiinoe rukovodstvo evakuatsiei v pervyi period velikoi otechestvennoi voiny, 1941–1942 gg.* (Leningrad: 1985), p.83. Kumanev supports the higher figure; see: Kumanev, *Sovetskii tyl*, 139; "V ogne," p.15.

system, where just about anything could happen. If one makes the completely unwarranted assumption that all the components for the plants could be kept track of and delivered according to plan, there remained the problem of fitting them into the socioeconomic space of the East. Suitable sites had to be found out of harm's way. Given the rudimentary development of infrastructure, usually plants had to divided up and added on to existing enterprises. Then often their product lines were altered and their input mix was changed. Also, the labor force was largely new and inexperienced, with females and adolescents playing a much larger role under as stressful conditions as workers have ever had to face. Mapping the sort of data we have would obscure such important realities. In reality, space had depth; its organization could not be transformed without affecting places.

Moreover, a dot map would not communicate much about how such a transformation of the country's economic geography was carried out. Perhaps Stalin started out with such a map. Nobody could openly resist anything that the dictator decided to change, but how could he move the necessary dots on such a scale, virtually overnight? He would have to rely on what Soviet historians used to call the 'central planning organization,' but which more accurately could be called the bimodal command system. These two modes have been described by Harrison as two distinct systems of economic management, the formal, bureaucratic planning system and the informal, personalized approach.[45]

The dual system did not just deal with economic affairs, although this of course was of vital significance, for these were the two modes of institutional administration by which the regime governed the social space of the country. Here 'social space,' that is, the whole country considered as a system of 'secondary places,' in Sack's terms, seems appropriate because the regime did indeed see everything in its territory as 're-placeable.' And not just re-placeable, because party ideology considered it necessary, proper, and even heroic to transform nature. In fact it was the regime's *raison d'être* to overcome all natural obstacles to the development of the productive forces while at the same time it transformed its human resources into socialist society.

. . . . .
45 Barber and Harrison, *Soviet Home Front*, 194–197. Lieberman also has much to say on the "personalization of power" and the "plenipotentiary system" of administration. See: Sanford R. Lieberman, "Crisis Management in the USSR: The Wartime System of Administration and Control," in *The Impact of World War II on the Soviet Union*, ed. Susan J. Linz (Totowa, NJ: 1985), pp.65–66.

Ostensibly for these purposes, and perhaps also because of the addictive allure of accumulation of power, the regime reserved the right to employ the basic technique of territorial power, the in/out loop, anytime and anyplace, at any scale from the level of the country as a whole down to individual residences. This spilled over into networks of spatial interaction, for example, by means of internal passports and residence authorizations (*propiska*) that tied citizens to particular places and barred them from entering many other types of places. The state planning system, rather than market forces, managed and transformed basic economic patterns of spatial interaction. And the party attempted to monopolize the determination of meaning, including the interpretation of the significance of place.

For all its territorial practices, including economic administration and development, the regime employed two modes, basically as described by Harrison. The formal, bureaucratic approach tended to maintain activities as they were and where they were – although incremental change could be managed. But often, and obviously in the case of the evacuation, urgent radical change was sought. However, it was not just when faced with an invasion by a mortal foe that the regime found it necessary to undermine its own administrative grid, but it did so often, whenever stagnation was perceived to be setting in. And the Communist way was not only to transgress its own bureaucracy's boundaries, but to glorify the process. Sometimes. For the activists who took part in such campaigns there was always the danger that they would be called to account for overdoing it, for becoming 'dizzy with success,' as Stalin put it when the collectivization campaign was perceived to entail disastrous consequences.

Others have thought along similar lines. Ken Jowitt reworked the Weberian framework for the classification of political regimes, combining the 'rational-legal' and 'charismatic' ideal-types, to depict Leninism as 'charismatic impersonalism.'[46] However, Jowitt did not attempt to show how this type of regime actually governed a complex conglomerate of social networks distributed over a vast space.[47] Starting with Jowitt's conception, Stephen Hanson has recently argued

---

46 Ken Jowitt, "The Leninist Phenomenon," in *New World Disorder: The Leninist Extinction*, (Berkeley, 1993), pp.1–49.
47 Rather than assuming more order than exists in reality, I follow Michael Mann's lead in considering Soviet society, like all societies, a "patterned mess," with the state the only agency that could bind all the social networks together. See Mann, *Sources of Social Power II*, p.4.

that at the heart of the Soviet experience was a dualistic conception of time, which he calls *charismatic-rational*.[48]

Hanson's highly engaging argument is primarily a study of ideas, with very selective reference to social and institutional history. His main point must be taken seriously, yet time can be considered apart from space only in a highly abstract manner. In social life, temporal relations are part of the context and order of human activities, i.e., part of place(s). What has always set Communism apart from other social systems is the degree of state control over places of all dimensions, which in other countries have been shaped by more diffusely functioning principles of social organization, like tradition, the market, or democracy. The regime attempted to manipulate time and space relations in order to transform social life. I believe the terms *bureaucracy* and *mobilization* have the broadest applicability as descriptors of the two main modes of central power,[49] not least because they can be shown to have emerged in practice. Whether or not these modes originated with Marx or earlier does not seem to be vitally significant, as Mann discusses about the general question of goals and needs.

> For a form of power may not be an original human goal at all. If it is a powerful means to other goals, it will be sought for itself. It is an *emergent* need. It emerges in the course of need satisfaction.[50]

REVOLUTIONARY STATE-MAKING

If in the USSR there was a unique 'track-laying vehicle,' in Michael Mann's re-working of a Weberian idea,[51] it was the Leninist state-building party. This innovation, however, did not spring fully formed from the leader's prominent forehead. It took shape in the desperate

. . . . .

48 Stephen E. Hanson, *Time and Revolution: Marxism and the Design of Soviet Institutions*, (Chapel Hill, 1997).
49 For a similar view, see Thomas F. Remington, *Building Socialism in Bolshevik Russia: Ideology and Industrial Organization, 1917–1921* (University of Pittsburg Press, Pittsburg 1984).
50 Michael Mann, *The Sources of Social Power, Volume I: A History of Power from the Beginning to A.D. 1760*, (Cambridge, 1987), p.6.
51 Ibid., p.28.

struggle for physical survival, as the party seized control of the state, and then the party/state asserted authority over more and more spheres of social activity. Party ideology did matter, especially its fanatical aversion to the market, but the new regime was not simply the embodiment of Lenin's reading of Marxism. In particular, the combination of bureaucracy and mobilization emerged in practice as the new state was built.

All three of the 'loops' of relationships of place were important in this process. Among the many examples of 'in/out' relations was the vilification of entire classes – the 'former people' were no longer welcome in the country, unless they served the new regime. There were intense campaigns to regulate spatial interaction, for instance, the efforts to stop the hordes of 'baggers' who attempted to haul unauthorized sacks of food to the cities.[52] As to the 'surface/depth' complexes of meaning, from 'the storming of the Winter Palace' itself, the significance of the revolution and the legitimacy of the new regime were connected with numerous specific places and to 'the land of the Soviets,' as a whole.[53]

Because of the party's organization and discipline, and the members' commitment to the cause, the party sometimes seemed to perform miracles, hence the charisma of the emergent mobilization mode. Even when results were mixed or negative, the campaign approach could inspire people with a sense of heroic struggle. But there is only limited scope for heroism in the modern world – to keep trains running on time requires routinized coordination of activities.

Better suited for such a role was the other dominant organizational form: bureaucracy. Bolsheviks hated bureaucracy and continued to hate it the whole time they were building it, but in the end most of them saw no choice. The state was supposed to be a 'dictatorship of the proletariat,' but workers could not take over all the specialized jobs in government and the management of the economy overnight, especially when they were needed at their machines or in the new Red Army. So, revolutionaries were made commissars to watch over the activities of bureaucrats and technical specialists.

---

52 Robert Argenbright, "Bolsheviks, Baggers and Railroaders: Political Power and Social Space, 1917–1922," *The Russian Review*, v. 52, n. 4, (October, 1993), pp.506–527.
53 On the image of the October Revolution and the identity of the party, see: Frederick C. Corney, "Writing October: History, Memory, Identity and the Construction of the Bolshevik Revolution, 1917–1927," (Ph.D. diss., Columbia University, 1997)

Commissars could be vigilant but they could not change bureaucracy's inherent tendency to confine social activity to set procedures and thus reproduce the existing state of affairs. Instead of revolutionizing society, the apparatus regularized it. Often when the leadership grew dissatisfied with an existing situation, or when it sought to extend the authority of the state, it launched a mobilization of political cadres to cut through red tape and break out of ossified routines. Yet these gun-waving plenipotentiaries tended to focus exclusively on their own heroic tasks, to the neglect of other goals and the systematic processes of social reproduction generally. Typically, when a campaign generated an intolerable degree of chaos the party line would shift in favor of regularization in place of mobilization.[54] Such was the alternating current of what may be called *hypercentralization*: mobilization to conquer new realms, bureaucracy to colonize them.

Maintaining a balance between bureaucracy and mobilization was one fundamental problem, while another was dealing with the limits to the whole process of hypercentralization. ommunism, as ideology, acknowledged no bounds, picturing history as a victorious campaign in which any means could be justified so long as they advanced the cause. Yet this was 'track-laying;' the longer the regime relied on hypercentralization, investing it with ideological meaning and sanctifying it with the people's sweat and blood, the more remote became the possibility of using other ways of dealing with people, their activities and places. The regime was locked into a pattern of conquering and colonizing social space, which tended to be undermined by unintended consequences that arose in all the places where policies were enacted. As a look at the evacuation will show, even one of the state's great successes appears to have been extremely costly in terms of wasted resources and damaged lives.

. . . . .
54 This is a generalization which of course obscures many significant facts. However, the alternation of the modes is apparent throughout Soviet history, e.g. in the early stages of planned industrialization. See R. W. Davies, *The Soviet Economy in Turmoil, 1929–1930*, (Cambridge, MA, 1989), pp.370–440.

EVACUATION FROM THE FRONT-LINE ZONE

Soviet historians invariably gave a great deal of credit to the centralized planning system for directing the evacuation. In fact there was no overall plan for the evacuation process as a whole, nor were there contingency plans even for major enterprises that were vulnerably located in the West. This extremely costly mistake must in the end be counted as Stalin's responsibility, part of his refusal to accept the imminence of invasion and to allow for the possible need to retreat.[55] But Stalin was outside, or above, the planning system, a fact which reminds us that the country was not run by Gosplan alone. As Harrison has convincingly argued, the bureaucracy in practice was complemented by an informal mode of administration, the direct descendent of the commissar trouble-shooters of the Civil War era.[56]

It was this informal system – really a tradition of improvisation in the face of bureaucratic impotence – that made the evacuation possible. The existing bureaucracy could never have moved quickly enough to accomplish such a complicated, unpredictable project, although many existing agencies were pressed into service.[57] But when existing organs did play important roles, they had to change their mode of operations to cope with the emergency.[58] Of course, the new ad hoc agencies were given a bureaucratic appearance when their jurisdictions and responsibilities were spelled out in decrees. Such was the case when the *Sovet po Evakuatisii* (Evacuation Council) was set up, first with Kaganovich and then Shvernik in charge, aided by Kosygin, Mikoian, and others.[59] In reality this was a very loosely structured organization that was intended to cut through existing bureaucratic boundaries and red tape. Moreover, it had to work closely with the other central agencies, most of which were entrusted to the virtual dictatorship of Stalin's chief lieutenants. Each of these

---

. . . . .
55 Kumanev, "Sovetskaia Ekonomika," pp.152–153,
56 Barber and Harrison, *Soviet Home Front*, pp.194–205. Also see: Mark Harrison, *Soviet Planning in Peace and War: 1938–1945* (Cambridge, UK: 1985), pp.63–79.
57 Edwards, "Fleeing to Siberia," p.56; Harrison & Lieberman, *Soviet Home Front*, pp.198–199; Lieberman, "Evacuation of Industry": pp.98–100.
58 A given agency could start in either mode and shift to the other in its institutional evolution. See Edwards, "Fleeing to Siberia," pp.145–146.
59 L. I. Pogrebnoi, "O deiatel'nosti Soveta po Evakuatsii," in *Eshelony idut*, pp.201–203.

potentates had his network of agents and plenipotentiaries. Matters were settled one at a time, from crisis to crisis, by means of the telegraphic correspondence between the super-commissars and their deputies, or, when the need arose, in face-to-face meetings of Stalin and his lieutenants.[60]

Thus, the coordination and direction of evacuation from above was conducted on a rather personal basis. Stalin himself was first to pick an enterprise for evacuation, the Kirov tank plant from Leningrad.[61] And it was not at all unusual for local officials to wire Stalin directly with reports concerning the evacuation, despite the formal chain of command.[62] Stalin's top lieutenants often intervened personally in situations that were not formally under their jurisdiction, doing what they thought was best, without rules or procedures effective enough to govern their actions.[63] The setting of priorities was not always a clear-cut matter because the frantic pace of events dictated their tasks. Everything was an emergency and means for coping were scarce. Therefore, given the absence of realistic norms or guidelines, it is hard to assess the efficiency or effectiveness of their work. Some activities were questionable, such as Kaganovich's personal involvement in the search for one woman's lost baggage.[64] But the other side of this scope for error was unquestioning obedience down the chain of command. Leaders like Kaganovich induced in their underlings, if not the fear of God, the realistic fear of ignoble death.[65]

There was no science, or organized body of experience to guide this work, but there was the mobilization tradition, with its Bolshevik, fighting-commissar style. The job had to be done, step-by-step in response to the movements of the enemy and under the guidance of commonsense, which of course varied among officials. Of course the central authorities sought to organize the campaign from above, to keep the process orderly at every stage, but this was not possible. The center could not keep track of what had already happened, and actually directing the whole process in detail was out of the question.

. . . . .

60 For example, see Dmitri Volkogonov, *Stalin: Triumph and Tragedy*, (New York: 1991), pp.418–419.
61 Harrison & Lieberman, *Soviet Home Front*, p.128.
62 For two examples, see: *Rossiiskii Gosudarstvennyi Arkhiv Ekonomiki* (Russian State Economic Archive, henceforth: *RGAE*), f. 1884, op. 31, d. 2996, ll. 5–6; ibid., d. 2997, ll. 4–5.
63 See the report to Beriia on evacuation along the Vinnitskaia railroad: ibid., d. 3002, ll. 1–2.
64 Ibid., d. 2997, ll. 21–22.

Orders often were issued primarily to give formal authorization to *faits accompli*. For example, in one October decree, the evacuation council changed the destinations for 76 industrial plants and large collections of resources.[66]

All the way down the chain of command, lesser officials were expected to throw their weight around to get the job done. 'Formalism' was anathema. The ideal was the Bolshevik commissar with his sleeves rolled up. But of course the Bolshevik plenipotentiary who was trying to dismantle a plant as the world disintegrated around him could not go by the 'big picture' map the bosses supposedly had in Moscow. The authorities on the spot had only insufficient scraps of information on which to base their orders. They often contradicted one another. Bombs were falling and communications ties were often severed.[67] Sometimes local officials acted in their own narrow interests, for instance by filling railroad cars with office furniture when they might have been hauling industrial equipment.[68] More often, honest mistakes were made. In the early panic especially, whole trainloads of valuable equipment and materials were sent off without protection from the elements and without guards.[69] Thus, from the start systematic spatial interaction was disrupted in the crucial railroad system.

Perhaps the most common error was to ship off valuable goods, or people, without sufficient documentation and without apprising officials along the route and at the intended destination. For instance, in early August, authorities in Gomel' without the permission of the *Sovet po Evakuatsii* sent a pedagogical institute, a medical institute, and a construction institute, all complete with staff, equipment, and materials, to Gor'kii completely without warning. Gor'kii officials also complained of carloads of prisoners arriving unannounced from NKVD (secret police) camps in Karelia without any officers or guards. Since the prisoners also had no food, money or travel passes,

---

65 For example, see the plea to Kaganovich from a railroad construction chief who had been arrested because his project fell behind schedule: ibid., d. 4233, ll. 144–145 ob.
66 Ibid., d. 3024, ll. 196–202.
67 There were many cases of enemy action disrupting the evacuation. For one example, see: *Rossiiskii Tsentr Khraneniia i Izucheniia Dokumentov Noveishei Istorii* (Russian Center for the Preservation and Study of the Documents of Contemporary History; hereafter *RTsKhIDNI*), f. 17, op. 88, d. 34, ll. 4–6.
68 GARF (Gosudarstvennyi Arkhiv Rossiiskoi Federatsii), f. 6823, op. 1, d. 1, l. 7.
69 For examples, see: RTsKhIDNI, f. 17, op. 22, d. 3681, ll. 49–51; ibid., op. 88, d. 34, ll. 4–6; RGAE, f. 1884, op. 31, d. 2997, ll. 7–8.

it was no surprise that they took to stealing in order to survive.[70] This sort of unauthorized transport caused trouble at every stage of the process, by diverting freight cars and using locomotives, occupying time/space in the railroad network, and by throwing off the plans of the local authorities at the other end who already had more than enough to deal with.

The evacuation of people presented special problems. Not everyone who wanted to leave received permission, but millions took flight anyway. And not everyone who was supposed to evacuate actually did so. In general, desperation impelled people to take initiatives that would have been unthinkable before the invasion.

Not even considering all the unauthorized self-evacuations, the state-administered process was highly disorganized. Families of party officials and military officers had priority, and their evacuation was distinct from the transfer of industry. In regard to employees and their families, individual commissariat powers unsystematically presented the Evacuation Council with requests to evacuate specified personnel.[71] Criteria for selection obviously varied widely, too widely for there to have been a firm system governing the process. In one case, bachelors were taken before workers with families in order to minimize the demand for housing in the new location.[72] But in another case, an important plant arrived in Kuibyshev without a single male among the evacuated employees.[73]

The situation in specific places was often difficult and always unpredictable. It was not unheard of for local officials to completely lose their heads. For instance, one fled in panic and caused a train wreck, which he blamed on innocent railroad workers, whom he then personally shot.[74] Beleaguered railroad officials often assigned evacuee trains destinations based on their own considerations, despite the orders of the Evacuation Council.[75] It was not uncommon even for them to send the evacuees back to the area of the front.[76]

. . . . .

70 RTsKhIDNI, f. 17, op. 88, d. 41, ll. 3–4.
71 For example, in early October, the Transportation Commissariat asked the council for permission to evacuate 100 railroader families of the Moscow-Kiev line from Kaluga Station to Chkalov; see: RGAE, f. 1884, op. 31, d. 3024, l. 175.
72 RTsKhIDNI, f. 17, op. 88, d. 63, ll. 1–2.
73 Ibid., ll. 8–8 ob.
74 Ibid., f. 111, op. 12, d. 22, ll. 53–61.
75 Edwards, "Fleeing to Siberia," p.114.
76 An evacuation official in July reported that trainloads of evacuees were being returned to the front-line zone every day. See: RGAE, f. 1884, op. 31, d. 2997, ll. 1–2 ob, 9–10.

TRANSIT BY RAILROAD

Spatial organization on the national scale in 1941 was made possible mainly by the railroad system, which therefore was crucial for evacuation.[77] Water transport was used, but it was even more unreliable and dangerous.[78] The railroads suffered greatly from the impossibility of planning, becoming the center of a vicious circle of problems, which not only affected the evacuation, but also the military effort. Every unexpected snag or unauthorized dispatch, every loss of paperwork or delay in decision-making, caused a problem in the railroad system that invariably produced other problems. A plenipotentiary or local official might score a triumph in one place, say by loading and dispatching all the components for a plant, which at the level of national spatial organization could be a detriment to evacuation movement as a whole. Any place along the way was a potential obstacle for the spatial flow.

Transportation Commissar Kaganovich tried to stay on top of the situation personally, pushing his deputies relentlessly to deal with the plethora of emergencies and keep him informed in detail. Kaganovich needed information at his fingertips when his counterparts in other agencies complained about the lack of empty freight cars for factories requiring immediate evacuation.[79] This was a problem that even the fearsome Kaganovich could not resolve. In theory, evacuation solved the return-load problem – troops to the front, machines, etc. to the rear. But cars bogged down in countless places.[80] Often there was no place to put equipment and resources even when they were transported in good order to their authorized destinations. Thousands of loaded cars awaited unloading; sometimes the backlog expanded sufficiently to clog the station's lines and impede movement of through trains.[81] For instance, the situation grew so bad on the

. . . . .

77 Holland Hunter, "Successful Spatial Management," in *The Impact of World War II on the Soviet Union*, ed. Susan J. Linz (Totowa, NJ: 1985), pp.47–58.
78 The early onset of winter stopped navigation on the upper and middle Volga; thousands of evacuees were stranded on docks until railroad cars could be provided. See: RGAE, f. 1884, op. 31, d. 2997, ll. 57, 64–65, 84–85.
79 For examples, see: ibid., ll. 12–14, 29–30, 31–35, 48. Deputies also dealt with such requests; see for example the telegram from Kosygin requesting 150 cars for the evacuation of trotters (horses): ibid., ll. 51–52. Also see Beria's request for 25 cars to move a dredge to the Amur River: RGAE, f. 1884, op. 31, d. 3002, l. 3.
80 Ibid., d. 2997, l. 101.
81 For the situation in Sverdlovsk oblast' in July, see: RTsKhIDNI, f. 17, op. 22, d. 2318, l. 64; for the even worse situation in Sverdlovsk in October, when 15,000

Southern Ural line in October that comrade Stalin himself intervened.[82]

Freight cars were also filled with evacuated people, who often endured conditions that livestock would not have survived.[83] They were supposed to be moving through space, but instead they found themselves stuck in forlorn places, such as railyards and sidings.[84] An average pace of 200–300 km. in 24 hours was not unusual, and sometimes the rate dropped to nil.[85] Group leaders often sent off desperate pleas to Stalin for aid.[86] There is no way to tell now how many people died taking part in the evacuation, but reports of fatalities from disease or the combined effects of hunger and cold were quite common.[87] Often people also suffered upon arrival, especially when the authorities had received no word of their coming.[88] Some evacuees had to remain in their freight cars for days since no better shelter was available.[89]

The confusion on the railroads severely hampered the restoration of industrial plants. Directors and party officials at receiving destinations very often complained of *nekomplektnost'*, lack of the full complement of equipment.[90] Key machines and sometimes whole shops failed to arrive.[91] All this was despite the fact that Sovnarkom

- - - - -
cars awaited unloading, see: ibid., d. 2319, ll. 188–189; for 28 cases in October when the ammunition commissariat held up freight cars, see: RGAE, f. 1884, op. 31, d. 3024, ll. 183–189; for a November complaint about enterprises holding cars too long belonging to the Kazan' and Kaganovich railroads, see ibid., ll. 5–12; on the clogging of Kuibyshev Station in November, see: RGAE, ibid., l. 275; for slow unloadings in Omsk in December, see: RTsKhIDNI, f. 17, op. 22., d. 1991, ll. 81–82.
82 Ibid., d. 3711, ll. 187 ob.-188.
83 For example, see the report on the Southern Urals line in December: ibid., d. 3712, ll. 274 ob.-275 ob; also see: Edwards, "Fleeing to Siberia, " p.119.
84 See ibid., d. 2320, ll. 141–144; RGAE, f. 1884, op. 31, d. 2997, ll. 36–38, 58–60, 66, 77, 119.
85 See: RTsKhIDNI, f. 17, op. 22., d. 1986, ll. 148–150; ibid., d. 2320, ll. 141–144; RGAE, f. 1884, op. 31, d. 2997, ll. 73–76.
86 For four such telegrams to Stalin, see: RGAE, f. 1884, op. 31, d. 2997, ll. 73-76.
87 Ibid.; see also ll. 26–27.
88 The Moscow sovet was guilty of this oversight often, see: RTsKhIDNI, f. 17, op. 88, d. 41, ll. 14–16. Also see: Edwards, "Fleeing to Siberia," p.88,
89 Ibid., d. 133, ll. 7–12.
90 For an example from Cheliabinsk, see: ibid., op. 22., d. 3711, ll. 159–159 ob.
91 To cite just one instance, 14 cars of equipment bound for Chkalov (now Orenburg) were uncoupled from their train in Gor'kii (Nizhnii Novgorod) and then added on to another heading off in different direction. Chkalov authorities later located the equipment in Sverdlovsk, but as of April, 1942, they were not sure that they would finally get possession. See: ibid., op. 88, d. 160, ll. 55–58.

on July 15 empowered Gosplan to set up unloading points for undocumented goods and to sort them out.[92] As the goods continued to pile up, Gosplan's considerable capacity for detailed record-keeping and documentation of minute matters was put to a stern test.[93] But the pace of the accumulation of cars was just too much for the agency. On July 18, Gosplan had charge of some 1200 cars full of undocumented goods. Eleven days later the total approached 40,000.[94] And many cars remained outside Gosplan's control. The context was not yet right for the systematic, bureaucratic approach of the planners.

By winter the railroad system was clogged with railroad cars full of evacuated machinery, materials, and various other things. To deal with this problem Mikoian was put in charge of a top-priority unloading committee, which succeeded the Evacuation Council. Despite the glorification of the evacuation in later years, this clearly was an ignominious end to the Council.[95] The new committee decided on a case-by-case basis what to do with the freight.[96] Sometimes it was shipped on to its original destination. Since the course of the war had shifted away from some key centers, notably Moscow, some of the freight was shipped back whence it came. Most often, the goods were unloaded wherever they happened to be, sometimes just dumped out of the way, in order to clear the way for railroad traffic. Evidently restoring circulation as a whole was considered more important than the misplaced industrial components and resources. Flow through space took precedence, so people trying to build productive places would have to improvise.

- - - - -

92 By the end of the month 33 bases were set up, 9 permanent and 24 temporary. See: RGAE, f. 4372, op. 41, d. 1759b.
93 For thousands of pages of Gosplan's decisions and correspondence concerning undocumented goods, see: ibid., d. 1760, d. 1761, d. 1762, d. 1763, d. 1764, d. 1765, d. 1769, d. 1770, d. 1771, d. 1772, d. 1773.
94 RGAE, f. 4372, op. 41, d. 1779, ll. 7, 9)
95 "During its brief existence, the Evacuation Council proved itself unable to plan and monitor the civilian evacuation program." Edwards, "Fleeing to Siberia," p.162.
96 For thousands of these decisions, see: GARF, f. 6823, op. 1, d. 1.

THE PROBLEMS OF 'RE-PLACEMENT'

The flood of evacuated plants and population was so great that no rule-governed bureaucratic system could possibly have dealt with the first phase of the resettlement process. Regular state agencies in the main took responsibility for many of the new tasks, but the work had to be conducted largely in ad hoc fashion with little central direction.[97] This 'system' or style of governance dominated the economy for some time. All sorts of problems continued to be blamed on bureaucratism and red tape.[98] In the most hectic phase, mid-1941–1942, hyper-centralized control of both sorts receded in many places in the East, as ordinary people were forced to do more for themselves.

The state continued to exercise the campaign mode, but the more systematic approach tended to come back into its own to deal with the complexities of 're-placement,' that is, not just setting up equipment, but the establishment of all the auxiliary industries with necessary infrastructure and the construction of places where people could live and work.[99] Whole cities and whole regions had to be transformed in detail. Urgency required continued reliance on the commissar approach, but the complexity of emerging needs demanded more systematic programs as well.[100]

The first job was to find places to put things. On occasion the evacuation council selected sites for major plants.[101] But most often it appears that the council, having consulted the affected commissariats, picked the region for relocation, and left it to local authorities to find specific sites.[102] However, sometimes commissariats went back to the

. . . . .

97 Edwards, "Fleeing to Siberia," pp.86–89, 128–162.
98 For instance, see: RTsKhIDNI, f. 17, op. 88, d. 91, ll. 29–32.
99 This is not to say that daunting problems did not arise just in putting a plant back together. E.g., see: Edwards, "Fleeing to Siberia," pp. 273–293.
100 Lieberman notes that regular local organizations played a greater role in the restoration phase than in evacuation, but his suggestion that this was because the rear offered "greater stability and security" is but a partial explanation, at best. See: Lieberman, "Evacuation of Industry": p.95.
101 For four examples from Kuibyshev oblast, see: RTsKhIDNI, f. 17, op. 22, d. 1558, ll. 12, 73; ibid., op. 43, d. 1059, ll. 65–67, 112–113. The last case concerns a protest of the center's decision to move various oblast' agencies from Kuibyshev to the countryside.
102 For examples from Kuibyshev oblast', see: RTsKhIDNI, f. 17, op. 22, d. 1557, ll. 93–99; ibid., d. 1558, ll. 109–110, 113–114, 187–188, 196, 216; ibid., op. 43, d. 1059, ll. 49–50, 68–71, 86–87; ibid., op. 88, d. 63, ll. 20–23; from Omsk oblast': ibid., op. 22, d. 1983, ll. 12-13; from Cheliabinsk oblast': ibid., d. 3710, l. 127; from Sverdlovsk oblast': ibid., d. 2321, l. 17.

Evacuation Council in order to overturn the local officials' decisions.[103] There were some conflicts over such 'in/out' jurisdictional changes, because they meant loss of useful space and sometimes eviction of personnel.

Generally, local officials were best able to find and sort out all potentially utilizable sites.[104] Kuibyshev officials made the logical decision to combine the Molotov Machine-tool Plant from Khar'kov with their own Machine-tool Plant #3. They also turned over the garages of the automobile administration for a ball-bearing plant and an unfinished building belonging to the city's executive committee for an aviation industry plant. They set up textile production in a culture palace, a grain mill, an unfinished *sovkhoz* school, a cardboard plant, a pedagogical school, and an agricultural institute.[105]

Local party officials, especially at first, tended to put as much responsibility as they could on the enterprises' directors and party officials for making the new productive spaces work. More often than not the enterprise leaders ran into difficulties that they could not solve on their own. Oblast' authorities typically sounded furious when they listed the errors, failures, and oversights of enterprise leaders.[106] But often the problems were such that only territorial authorities could possibly cope, so they were compelled to supervise the restoration process more closely. At the levels of the factory, the city, and the regional economy, regional self-sufficiency grew necessarily, because the center could no longer keep track of everything that needed to be done and issue the appropriate commands in a timely fashion.[107]

The problem with human evacuees was more complicated.[108] The oblast' authorities had to designate a plenipotentiary to take charge of

. . . . .

103 For an example when the Transportation Commissariat requested a site from the Council, see: RGAE, f. 1884, op. 31, d. 3024, ll. 265–266; for a similar example of a conflict between a commissariat and local officials over housing, see: ibid., ll. 220–221.
104 However, not all of them did. Tiumen' officials reportedly left it up to enterprise administrators to find their own sites as best they could: RTsKhIDNI, f. 17, op. 43, d. 1384, ll. 29–30.
105 Ibid., op. 22, d. 1558, ll. 113–114, 187–188, 196.
106 For examples from Cheliabinsk oblast': ibid., d. 3710, l. 128; ibid., d. 3712, ll. 229-230; from Sverdlovsk oblast': ibid., d. 2294, l. 74; from the Tatar obkom in Kazan', see: ibid., op. 88, d. 91, ll. 29–32.
107 Walter S. Dunn, Jr., *The Soviet Economy and the Red Army, 1930–1945*, (Westport, CN, 1995), p.36; Lieberman, "Evacuation of Industry," p.95.
108 Kristin Edwards covers the problems encountered in Novosibirsk in detail. See: "Fleeing to Siberia," pp.86–127.

caring for evacuees, whether they were arriving or en route.[109] This official was supposed to make sure that the evacuation points were functioning properly, supplying basic necessities to evacuees like boiled water, food, medical care, and, of course, enlightening agitational material.[110] The staff at the evacuation points also were supposed to see to it that evacuees went where they were supposed to go. On average 20% to 40% of an enterprise's personnel made the trip with their plant.[111] These employees were welcome in the cities. But other evacuees were not. The evacuation-point staff were supposed to prevent evacuees who were destined for rural areas from settling in the larger towns.[112] Nevertheless, many broke the in/out rule by finding ways to live in cities without authorization. Sometimes oblast or city authorities later would round up unemployed evacuees and forcibly remove them to rural areas.[113]

There were a great number of cases of inadequate care, sometimes shockingly poor care, rendered to evacuees.[114] It was hard enough to

---

. . . . .
109 Sverdlovsk oblast' officials seem to have been in the lead in trying to deal with the tide of evacuees. See: RTsKhIDNI, f. 17, op. 22, d. 2317, ll. 88–89; ibid., d. 2318, ll. 16–17. Other obkoms responded to the State Defense Committee order of November 26 and named plenipotentiaries. Examples include Omsk: ibid., d. 1984, ll. 116–117; Kuibyshev: ibid., op. 43, d. 1059, ll. 140–141; Cheliabinsk: ibid., op. 22, d. 3713, l. 120 ob.
110 For a report on the operation of the evacuation points in Omsk oblast' in August, see: ibid.,, op. 88, d. 106, ll. 18–19; in November: ibid., op. 22, d. 3712, ll. 161–162; for a report on work with evacuees on the Dzerzhinskii railroad, see: RTsKhIDNI, f. 111, op. 1, d. 11, l. 51; on shortcomings in November in Sverdlovsk oblast': RTsKhIDNI, f. 17, op. 22., d. 2320, ll. 141–144; ibid., d. 2324, ll. 67–68; on Cheliabinsk oblast's problems in December: ibid., d. 3712, ll. 274 ob.-275 ob.
111 For the 20% figure, see M. I. Likhomanov, L. TY. Pozina, E. I Finogenov, *Partiinoe rukovodstvo evakuatsiei v pervyi period velikoi otechestvennoi voiny, 1941–1942 gg.* (Leningrad: 1985), p.111. For other estimates, see: Barber and Harrison, *Soviet Home Front*, p.139.
112 For an example from Sverdlovsk, see RTsKhIDNI, f. 17, op. 22, d. 2317, ll. 142–143; from Omsk: ibid., op. 88, d. 106, ll. 18–19.
113 On such a removal from Cheliabinsk: ibid.,, op. 22, d. 3718, l. 53; in Gor'kii evacuees who lacked official permission were removed: ibid., op. 88, d. 512, l. 102 ob.
114 On inadequate care of evacuees in Omsk oblast' see: ibid., op. 22, d. 1983, ll. 24–27; ibid., d. 1986, ll. 148–150; for a complaint about treatment of evacuees in Ordzhonikidze, see: RGAE, f. 1884, op. 31, d. 2997, ll. 16–16 ob.); on poor care in Cheliabinsk oblast': RTsKhIDNI, f. 17, op. 22, d. 3710, ll. 130–131, 183–184 ob.; ibid., d. 3711, 189 ob.-190 ob.; on inadequacies in Kuibyshev oblast' see: ibid., op. 43, d. 1559, ll. 31–33; on shortcomings in Chkalov oblast': ibid., op. 88, d. 160, ll. 105–106 ob.; for Novosibirsk, see: Edwards, "Fleeing to Siberia," pp.322–332.

take care of people passing through, but many *oblasts* were flooded with new residents of various kinds, authorized and unauthorized.[115] Oblast' officials tried to get enterprises to take care of industrial personnel arriving with their plants or equipment.[116] The local officials took responsibility for children evacuated from the area of the front and people arriving with institutes, cultural facilities, and so on.[117] This was no easy task, especially since so little aid was forthcoming from the center.[118] Housing was provided usually by cramming new people into citizens' homes (*v poriadke uplotneniia*). In Kuibyshev, nearly 150,000 evacuees were squeezed into the homes of residents.[119] The local authorities, in other words, forcibly placed many evacuees *in* urban homes, while also keeping others *out* of the city. Yet in 1941 and 1942 at least, the local officials were unable to satisfactorily control the situation. People were looking out for themselves as best they could while the state was unable to perform all the functions to which it had laid claim before the war.

Evacuated families of political officials and Red Army officers received stipends, but these often were insufficient to pay their way in the villages.[120] But worse off still were the families that were evacuated pell-mell to the rural areas without the right to receive a stipend. The gap between Russian villagers and Russian outsiders was large enough.[121] But many evacuees were placed in non-Russian villages, in Tataria, Central Asia or the Caucasus.[122] Probably worst of all was the fate of Volga Germans, who were forcibly relocated en

. . . . .

115 On inadequate care for evacuees in Kuibyshev in December, see: ibid., op. 22., d. 1562, ll. 51–53.
116 Sverdlovsk officials criticised the management of one plant for failing to provide adequately for 50 families of workers. See: ibid., op. 22, d. 2317, ll. 142–143, Cheliabinsk city officials revealed poor treatment of evacuees: ibid., ll. 47-48; ibid., d. 3718, ll. 12–14.
117 On arrangements for evacuated children in Omsk oblast', see: ibid., d. 1983, l. 185.
118 Gor'kii oblast officials asked the party Central Committee, who was going to pay to support all the children's institutions and pay for the services rendered to all evacuees. See: ibid., op. 88, d. 41, l. 10.
119 Ibid., op. 88, d. 133, ll. 7–12.
120 Gor'kii oblast peasants reportedly were relatively hospitable. See: ibid., ll. 1–3.
121 On the shortcomings on collective farms in Omsk oblast', see: ibid., op. 22, d. 1985, ll. 44–45; on state farms in Cheliabinsk oblast': ibid., d. 3713, ll. 44–44 ob.
122 On reception problems in Kirgizstan, see: ibid., op. 88, d. 58, ll. 120-122; in Kabardino-Balkarskaia oblast': ibid., d. 121, ll. 1–10; in the Tatar oblast': ibid., d. 151, ll. 37–40. On the other hand the reception of evacuees in Udmurt oblast' seems to have been hospitable. See: ibid., d. 94, ll. 14–16.

masse to Siberian villages and labor camps.[123]

Housing was a problem that could not always be settled on basis of a quick initial decision by local authorities.[124] Many of the evacuees, even in the cities, lived in spaces that were scarcely habitable.[125] There were physical limits to *uplotnenie*. Some slept in their shops, not far from the machines with which they worked during the day. Some lived in corridors or stairwells of dormitories that were poorly equipped in any case.[126] Of course, the desire to contribute to the war effort helped many of the evacuees put up with such conditions. Also, at first many tolerated the wretched circumstances because they thought they would only be staying temporarily, say until the threat to Moscow was eliminated. They were in for a shock, because the government reversed its policy, informing them that their former homes would be turned over to others.[127] This decree manifested the regime's refusal to recognize any concept of place, such as 'home,' outside its direct and immediate control. The ruling naturally caused resentment, but it also prompted the evacuees to begin thinking more practically about permanent housing.[128] They began putting pressure on officials. Local authorities at first expected the evacuees to build their own housing in off-duty hours.[129] Many did what they could, but for most it proved physically impossible. Local leaders had to take more responsibility for organizing and directing housing construction. This was one of the most important areas where local leaders were compelled to begin the physical rudiments of place before the center was prepared to attend to the process.[130]

The situation with the factories was similar in this regard. By the Bolshevik-commissar method, local officials could assign a garage to

. . . . .

123 On the Germans in Krasnoiarsk Krai, see: ibid., d. 61, ll. 5–6, 20–22; in Novosibirsk oblast': ibid., d. 71, ll. 23–32.
124 For the Novosibirsk example, see Edwards, "Fleeing to Siberia," pp.293–321.
125 In Omsk, the employees of one evacuated plant were living in lean-to (shchitovye) shelters in December; see: RTsKhIDNI, f. 17, op. 22, d. 3718, ll. 12–14. In Kuibyshev some lived in huts, others in freight cars: ibid., op. 88, d. 133, ll. 7–12.
126 See the reports from Kuibyshev: ibid., op. 43, d. 1087, ll. 23–41, 158–165.
127 For reactions to the ruling in Krasnoiarsk krai, see: ibid., op. 88, d. 132, ll. 18–20; in Molotov oblast': ibid., d. 137, ll. 67–71; in Kuibyshev oblast': ibid., d. 133, ll. 7–12.
128 Sverdlovsk oblast' authorities complained that too many workers were wasting time dealing with personal matters; some had moved several times. See: ibid., d. 147, ll. 3–4.
129 See the report on the reaction to the ruling in Omsk oblast': ibid., ll. 59–63.
130 See the Sverdlovsk city authorities' directive to district authorities on the planning of housing construction: RTsKhIDNI, f. 17, op. 22, d. 2324, ll. 81–85.

be the site of a key industrial shop. But soon they found it necessary to do more than exhort the plant's leadership, if they wanted to get production going again. Almost always the buildings and other facilities required immediate modification.[131] These tasks put pressure on the local construction industry at a time when the central authorities were virtually ignoring it.[132] In Krasnoiarsk *krai*, authorities complained they had received only one-fifth of the construction workers that had been promised.[133] Labor and materials had to be found locally, and systematic plans for their exploitation had to be worked out. Central agency was a hectoring, threatening presence, but local powers had to take more responsibility for getting things done because the center was distracted by the war.

Construction was not limited just to evacuated plants. The new places had new needs, which required extension of urban and regional infrastructures.[134] Burgeoning new industrial districts had to be equipped with the whole range of amenities virtually overnight. Kuibyshev's Molotov district received 16 major defense plants; its population increased by 400% in six months.[135] The city of Krasnoiarsk nearly doubled in population in the same period, thanks to the evacuation of 25 major enterprises, 22 of them defense plants.[136] At a time when there was overwhelming pressure from above to get the defense plants going, local officials were forced to turn their attention to mundane spatial networks to supply electricity, water, and mass transit.[137] Otherwise military production would have been stunted.

131 Sometimes they were in such bad shape that the equipment could not even be unloaded. In such cases car-loads of equipment stood on the tracks, contributing to the transport crisis. For example, see: RGAE, f. 1884, op. 31, d. 3023, l. 318.
132 For examples see the reports from and Omsk oblast' on bolstering construction industry and making use of local materials: RTsKhIDNI, f. 17, op. 22., d. 1949, l. 17; ibid., d. 1986, ll. 61–62. Also see the report from Tataria: ibid., op. 88, d. 91, ll. 29–32. On the acute shortage of construction materials in Chkalov oblast', see: ibid., d. 160, ll. 55–58.
133 Ibid., d. 61, ll. 32–36.
134 See the report from Omsk oblast': ibid., op. 22., d. 1949, ll. 61–66.
135 Ibid., op. 43, d. 1085, ll. 32–33.
136 Ibid., op. 88, d. 132, ll. 1–3.
137 On the electricity shortfall in Cheliabinsk oblast', see: ibid., op. 22, d. 3711, ll. 75–76 ob.; on electricity shortage in Omsk oblast: ibid., d. 1949, l. 17; on Omsk oblast' need for water and sewage lines: ibid., d. 1985, ll. 161–164; on the urgent need for a water line in Sverdlovsk's new industrial district, see: ibid., d. 2324, ll. 45–46.

Local leaders often were dealing with apparently small details, but these details could have serious ramifications.[138] For example, if perhaps it was necessary to curtail the supply of new footwear to civilians, local leaders sometimes erred in the initial period of the evacuation by dispensing with shoe-repair facilities.[139] These had to be replaced, for people simply could not go out to work barefoot in the Russian winter.[140] This was especially the case if they had to walk several kilometers each way to and from work because the tramway routes reflected the old pattern of industrial geography before the new plants were thrown up in their ramshackle shelters. For example, evacuee workers in Kuibyshev had to walk 15 km. to work.[141]

Food was in short supply, and there were inadequate means for preparing and serving it to workers. In large part, people were left to their own devices. To survive people began doing things that the state had once been able effectively to prohibit. But now the central government's territorial grasp had weakened, especially its powers of surveillance and enforcement over obscure places in this time of flux. People once again practiced buying and selling on the black market, barter, theft of food, and illegitimate acquisition of rationing privileges.[142] As William Moskoff has concluded: 'Civilians were fed not because of the system, but in spite of it.'[143]

Local authorities had to take action, as much to maintain Soviet order as to help people. In Orsk they managed to increase the number of canteens 130%, but in the same period the number of mouths to feed rose by 320%.[144] There were in fact countless ordinarily insignificant problems which the officials found were detrimental to the production effort, as for example when there were not enough chairs or bowls in the canteens.[145] Party officials inspected new canteens only to discover workers standing in one line for bread, another line for soup, a line for the cashier, another for spoons, then

. . . .

138 For the efforts of Sverdlovsk officials, see: ibid., ll. 151–159.
139 On efforts to supply footwear in Omsk oblast', see: RTsKhIDNI, f. 17, op. 43, d. 1394, ll. 213–214.
140 See the report from Chkalov: ibid., op. 88, d. 160, ll. 105–106 ob.
141 Ibid., d. 63, ll. 1–2. In Krasnoiarsk, workers were walking 3 km. each way: ibid., d. 61, ll. 32–36.
142 Edwards, "Fleeing to Siberia," pp.123–126.
143 Moskoff, *Bread of Affliction*, p.238.
144 RTsKhIDNI, f. 17, op.43, d. 160, ll. 43–45.
145 On Krasnoiarsk's problems with stolovaias, footwear repair facilities, etc., see: ibid., d. 61, ll. 27–31.

still another for a chair.[146] Each one of these problems was difficult to solve.[147] It could take the best efforts of an energetic party commission to get hot tea to a plant's workers in the morning.[148] However much the center goaded them to produce more tanks and aircraft, local officials found they simply had to attend to the more mundane matters if production as a whole was to go forward.[149]

As the scope of these problems became clear, local and provincial officials began to deal with them in a systematic way.[150] Experiences were shared, so successful methods could be disseminated.[151] Local resources were shifted as much as possible into construction and other sectors that could support the new industry and the greatly enlarged population.[152] These support industries and services were taken into account by new economic plans, which helped revive the practice of systematic planning generally.[153] Thus, the transformation of space in the east for the purpose of radically expanding military-industrial output turned out to be a complex process of place formation which required organized, systematic programs that went beyond the Bolshevik-commissar approach.

SUMMARY

In the conclusion to her dissertation on the relocation of evacuees to Novosibirsk oblast', Kristin Edwards justifiably castigates the regime for its lack of concern for human welfare.

> [T]he civilian evacuation was carried out with too little funding and too few employees. The evacuees suffered at every turn as the direct result of the nation's foremost wartime economic

---

146 See the report from Kuibyshev oblast': ibid., d. 63, ll. 40–43.
147 Nearly every problem mentioned in the preceding four paragraphs was reported in Tataria: ibid., d. 91, ll. 42–46.
148 On tea in the morning in Tiumen': RTsKhIDNI, f. 17, op. 43, d. 1384, l. 92.
149 See: ibid., op. 22, d. 3710, ll. 183–184 ob.
150 On the efforts of Cheliabinsk oblast' officials to systematize the restoration of evacuated plants, see: ibid., d. 3712, ll. 229–230.
151 On the dissemination of successful approaches in Sverdlovsk oblast', see: ibid., op. 88, d. 147, l. 13.
152 See the plan to boost Tiumen's electricity production by 650% in 4 months, see: ibid., op. 43, d. 1393, l. 27.
153 See the discussion on the development of support industries in Omsk oblast': ibid., d. 1394, ll. 6–7.

priority: a swift and complete mobilization for military production. The single-minded emphasis on this goal stripped crucial resources from the civilian population...[O]fficials were unable to provide tolerable conditions to the vast majority of civilians en route during 1941 and 1942. Instead, evacuation point personnel seemed to be more interested in registering and controlling the evacuating population than in providing food, clothing, showers, and medical treatment... Several ad hoc agencies were created in the receiving areas...There is little evidence these agencies provided concrete aid to the evacuees; instead they too focused on counting and registering the resettled population in an effort to supply oblast authorities with demographic information on potential labor recruits. Regular state and party offices never learned how to work effectively with ad hoc agencies in the provision of evacuee services.[154]

237

People and places slipped beyond the control of the regime, not for the sake of resistance, but for survival. The state was therefore compelled to reassert control, primarily by means of resuming systematic planning, i.e., the bureaucratic mode of command. As to the main priority, Harrison has concluded that 'judged by historical and comparative criteria, the Soviet success in World War II was very striking.'[155]

In fact, mobilization was excessive; it caused a severe economic crisis in 1942, when three fifths of the national product was devoted to the war effort.[156] This intense mobilization not only caused extreme hardship for the population, but also endangered the military effort itself.[157] Local officials learned the hard way that they had to create real-world places, like workshops in factories and canteens in dormitories, before production of tanks and shells could be assured. It was the local officials who could not escape the rootedness of place, who had to take into account all the interconnected elements that make place, however much the regime might insist on raising military production statistics without delay. As the economic crisis of 1942 was materializing, local officials were already were taking steps in the direction of restoring the necessary foundation for military production

. . . .

154 Edwards, "Fleeing to Siberia," pp.332–334.
155 Harrison, *Accounting for War*, p.171.
156 Ibid., p.170.
157 On the economic crisis of 1942, see Harrison, *Soviet Planning*, pp.165–221.

in place.[158] Eventually, the center finally grasped the need to shift priorities and to restore a more systematic, planned approach to economic administration.[159]

However, this shift to more balance between mobilization and bureaucracy did not in any way signify fundamental change in the regime's nature away from hypercentralization, nor should it be taken primarily as an outpouring of concern for the population. When the war started the regime responded by shifting its regulation of social activities generally, and its territorial control practices especially, almost entirely over to the mobilization mode. The leadership in Moscow was able to look out on the whole of the country as usable space, people included.[160]

The perspective from the Kremlin was that there was nothing in the whole vast territory that was not replaceable, except for Stalin himself. Of course, there had always been a glorification of sacrifice and self-sacrifice for the sake of the revolution, but now the cause was embodied by one living man who had absolute power over the government. Just a few years before the war Stalin had shown that he considered the Red Army's top leaders replaceable by having them executed. His top lieutenants, such as Voznesenskii, also were eminently replaceable, as they well knew.[161] Similarly, no place was uniquely valuable; for Stalin almost every place was what Sack calls a *secondary place*, 'which can be re-placed without remainder by substituting the objects and interactions in its area.'[162] The one exception was Stalingrad, which Stalin refused to evacuate,[163] but its special status was derived from its name and strategic situation rather than its distinctiveness as a place.

People may be affected by a great many forces: economic scarcity, gender differences, class orientations, patriotic movements, religious revivals, fashions, and so on, ad infinitum. But to be real, to be experienced by human beings, such forces must 'take place,' i.e.,

. . . . .

158 For instance, in Kuibyshev 44 stores plus 170 canteens and other meal-service facilities had been opened by February, 1942; mass transit service was similarly improved. See: RTsKhIDNI, f. 17, op. 88, d. 133, ll. 7–12.
159 Dunn, *Soviet Economy and the Red Army*, p.35.
160 E.g., Edwards cites a typical decree which "equates the evacuee with any other industrial or agricultural commodity." See: "Fleeing to Siberia," p.213.
161 E.g., see: *Khrushchev Remembers*, tr. and ed. Strobe Talbot, (Boston, 1970), pp.227–244.
162 Sack, *Homo Geographicus*, p.32.
163 Barber and Harrison, *Soviet Home Front*, p.32.

become part of place. People must live in places not in purified abstractions. Sack urges us 'to think through how a particular event or process (such as education, work, and poverty, or categories such as meaning, nature, social relations, and the self) occurs as a series of places.'[164] Given sufficient data, it would be possible to map the journey place by place for every evacuated person, machine, or carload of resources. Yet that immense task would still provide only a very superficial depiction of this great and terrible undertaking. This chapter has attempted look beneath the map's surface at the means by which the evacuation was carried out and the consequences that ensued. However, there were incalculable ramifications in millions of human lives. How could this massive dislocation not have influenced the world views of those who survived it?

For every individual human being involved in it, the evacuation was experienced as a series of places, despite the fact that the regime remained oblivious to such mundane reality. For most people evidently, the series of places through which they passed were inhospitable and sometimes literally uninhabitable. Even when people overcame the loss of their most treasured primary place, home, and re-established themselves in a new network of places in the East, they must have been deeply affected by their geo/bio-graphical journeys.[165] To better answer the question – what difference did the evacuation make? – we will need to collect reminiscences of those journeys while they are still available.

---

164 Sack, *Homo Geographicus*, p.255.
165 For one remembrance, probably atypical, see: *Kindergarten*, written and directed by Yevgeny Yevtushenko, Filmexport, 1984, videocassette.

Delimiting National Space: the Ethnographical Principle in the Administrative Division of the RSFSR and USSR, 1918–1925

Jeremy Smith

In a country the size of Russia, regional power structures are bound to play a major role in the functions of the state. In the late 1990s, as the President and Parliament (*Duma*) in Moscow suffer from increasing political paralysis, the power of the provinces and national autonomous territories of the Russian Federation has seen a corresponding growth. A number of leading candidates for the presidential election of 2000 have built up their power bases as regional governors (or city mayors) rather than through participation in the central government and the Duma. Meanwhile, the leaders of certain autonomous republics, most notably Tatarstan and Sakha (not to mention the altogether different case of Chechenia) have been using the threat of secession to promote their effective freedom from Moscow's interference.

Indeed, it was the political elites in the Union Republics of the USSR, propelled, in some cases, by mass popular movements, which were largely responsible for the collapse of the soviet communist order in 1991. But the events of the preceding years could not have taken place in the way they did had the early Bolshevik regime not adopted a particular approach to the administrative division of the vast Soviet space: namely, the 'delimitation' of national territories, large and small, based on ethnographic principles. The term 'delimitation' is most often applied to the 1925 division of the Central Asian autonomous republics of the RSFSR, Turkestan and Kirghiziia, into five new national territories the Uzbek, Turkmen, Tadzhik, Kazakh, and Kirghiz. But one of the purposes of this chapter is to illustrate how the Central Asian delimitation was a continuation of the spatial policies which had been applied to predominantly non-Russian territories from 1918 onwards. Thus the term 'delimitation', if it is a good description of the process applied to Central Asia, should be equally applicable to the way in which national territories were constructed in the preceding years in the principle cases under examination here – Belorussia, the Tatar and Bashkir territories of the Volga region, the original Kirghiz territory, and the North Caucasus.

The way in which the Bolsheviks dealt with the administration of Soviet space addressed two problems – the vastness of the space itself, which required some sort of regionalisation of the administrative structure; and the complex multi-national character of the former Russian Empire, in which Russians formed a bare majority, which presented the possibility of consolidating and incorporating the major national groups through a federative or autonomous structure. The solution adopted to the existence of vast and multi-national space was a hierarchy of national territories organised on a quasi-federal basis. This solution was not accidental, in that specific criteria informed the exact implementation of this solution; but nor was it inevitable, as other options were discussed and made sense from a classic marxist perspective.

Bolshevik theorists had a straight forward and plausible explanation for the way in which the tsarist Russian Empire had addressed the question of the administrative division of the Russian space ever since the regime had been shaken by the Pugachev revolt in the 1770s: above all else, the regime had to be able to deal quickly and effectively with the outbursts of peasant revolt which plagued the empire from its earliest days. Failure to do so would allow one instance of rebellion to be generalised by the peasants of the adjoining areas, and lead eventually to nation-wide revolt, as had indeed happened in 1905 and 1917. The Empire was therefore divided up into a number of provinces (*gubernii* or, in Central Asia, *oblasti*) whose size and location were determined principally by this expedient. At the centre of the province would be a garrison city, which would be linked by a network of roads to the furthest borders of the province. Thus the troops stationed in the centre would be able to reach any village in the province within a certain period of time. So a revolt anywhere in the Empire could be met by a large body of troops within a period of a few days.[1]

Such considerations would not apply to the new socialist state. It was not so much that peasant risings had ceased to occur as the reorganisation of the security system. The Red militias penetrated even the more remote regions in a way that would have been impossible for a large standing army. The First World War had seen the emergence of forms of mobile warfare which the first Soviet Commissar of War, L.D. Trotsky, was keen to develop. And the new security organs, in particular the Cheka, could provide advance warning of disturbances as well as serving as an effective instrument of repression. In any case, political methods, which included legislative provisions which favoured the peasantry as well as the soviet and communist party structures which penetrated all areas of life, were preferred to armed force. So although the Red Army itself was organised spacially during the Civil War, being divided into fronts and military regions, military factors were no longer relevant to the question of civilian regional administration. At the same time, there were political reasons for deliberately abandoning the old tsarist structures and administrative divisions. As Gregory Gleason has put it:

> The retention of the existing territorial boundaries would suggest continuity with the previous political order. The Bolsheviks, intent upon overturning the nineteenth-century nation-state system, reasoned that the territorial structures would have to be changed to prevent political structures from being captured by the former privileged groups.[2]

So what were the principles under which the territorial division of Soviet space would be carried out?

In western democracies, regional and local administrative divisions tend to coincide with electoral constituencies and are therefore related to population size. A straightforward administrative division of soviet territory according to criteria of surface area or population, was neither appropriate given the geography of the territory nor did it hold any appeal to the Marxist principles of the revolutionary Bolsheviks, smacking as it did of bourgeois-democratic notions of individual

. . . .
1   M.F. Vladimirskii, 'Osnovnie polozheniia ustanovleniia granits administrativno-khoziaistvennikh rainonov', in G.M. Krzhizhanovskii (ed.), *Voprosi ekonomicheskogo raionirovaniia SSSR* (Moscow, 1959), p.58.
2   Gregory Gleason, *The Central Asian States: Discovering Independence* (Boulder and Oxford, 1997), p.49.

equality and the neutrality of the state, and conflicting with the power base of the regime in the city-dominated soviets. All the same, purely administrative criteria were at the basis of a 'Commission for the Administrative Division of Russia' set up by the all-Russian Central Executive Committee in February 1920. The work of this commission was soon merged with a plan drawn up by the State Commission for Electrifying Russia (GOELRO), which proposed initially to divide the RSFSR into eight economic districts (*raioni*). Such a plan, which put economic considerations at the heart of the regional administrative structure, was more in tune with basic Marxist principles. Interestingly, the GOELRO plan did not aim to promote a highly centralised economy as might have been expected, but instead sought a relaxation of the conditions of War Communism and a devolution of economic decision making to the regions:

> In essence, the compilation of the economic plan for the *raion* ought to be a matter for the *raion* itself, in as much as it demands a broad understanding of local conditions and the active participation of the population..."[3]

But the plan which emerged from the work of these two commissions had already been overtaken by events. The People's Commissariat of Nationality Affairs (*Narkomnats*), which had been set up soon after the October Revolution under the leadership of Iosif Stalin to oversee policies towards the non-Russians living on soviet territory, objected that the purely economic principles underpinning the plan might violate the national principle which was already in place in the administrative structure of certain territories. The principal architect of the plan, Professor I.G. Alexandrov, indicated that he was happy to accept amendments based on criteria of nationality, and in the end the entire plan was overhauled in line with Narkomnats' recommendations to ensure the integrity of national territories, and also to include the other soviet territories of Ukraine, Belorussia and Transcaucasia.[4]

By now it was clear that the main principle behind the administrative division of the Soviet space was that of nationality. So what exactly lay behind this preference for national considerations over

---

3 *Plan elektrifikatsii RSFSR – doklad VIII s'ezdu sovetov gosudarstvennoy komissii po elektrifikatsii Rossii* (2nd edn, Moscow 1955), p.185.
4 Gosuddarstvennii Arkhiv Rossiiskoi Federatsii (hereafter GARF), fond 1318, opis 1, del 6, list 82; I.G. Aleksandrov, 'Osnovi khoziaistvennogo raionirovaniia SSSR', in Krzhizhanovskii (ed.), *op. cit.* p. 222.

more practical (and more obviously Marxist) criteria of administration and economics? It has become a commonplace to regard the delimitation of soviet territory according to nationality as a deliberate attempt to break-up potential blocs of opposition to soviet rule, particularly those peoples united by the Islamic faith, into smaller, competing 'national' units.[5] But there is no evidence that the Bolsheviks had much to fear from pan-Islamism, and the ethnic criteria employed by them in the national delimitation of Soviet space were sufficiently grounded in ethnographic principles to suggest an altogether different motivation.

A common territory was, according to the Bolsheviks' chief spokesman on nationality affairs, I.V. Stalin, an essential component of nationhood:

> A nation is formed only as a result of lengthy and systematic intercourse, as a result of people living together generation after generation. But people cannot live together for lengthy periods unless they have a common territory....Thus, *a common territory* is one of the characteristic features of a nation.[6]

On this basis, Stalin argued, the Jews did not constitute a nation as they had no common territory.[7] This presented early Soviet policy makers with a choice: either to deny separate nationalities the possibility of possessing their own territory, and thereby consign them, in the long term, to oblivion as a nation; or to put nationality at the heart of any territorial-administrative system, which would ensure the survival of the multi-national character of the Soviet space.

Initially, it was not clear that the latter option would be chosen. Many Bolsheviks, drawing on the arguments of Karl Marx and the Polish socialist Rosa Luxemburg, adopted a strictly internationalist position, insisting that national particularism was a feature of capitalist class society which had no place in the socialist state. At the other extreme were nationalists who allied themselves to the Red forces in the course of the Civil War, seeing in the Bolsheviks and the soviets

---

5   For example, see Geoffrey Hosking, *A History of the Soviet Union* (London, 1985), p.112; Hélène Carrère d'Encausse, *The Great Challenge: Nationalities and the Bolshevik State, 1917–1930* (New York, 1992), pp.177–8.
6   I.V. Stalin, *Sochineniia* (Moscow, 1946ff.), vol.II, pp.293–4. Emphasis in the original.
7   Idem, p.296.

the lesser of two evils and the possibility of satisfying at least some of their national demands. Among these were the Kazan Tatar socialists, ably represented at first by Mulla Nur Vakhitov and, following the former's death at the hands of Czecho-Slovak troops, by Mirsaid Sultan-Galiev. The Tatar socialists were mostly from an intellectual background, heavily influenced by the ideas of 19th century Jadidism, and espousing elements of pan-Islam or pan-Turkism.

It was under the influence of the Tatar socialists that the first attempt to set up an autonomous territory was made – the proposed Tatar-Bashkir Republic. The original 'Proposal on a Tatar-Bashkir Republic', published in *Izvestiia VTsIK* on 24th March 1918 over the names of Stalin and three officials of the Muslim Commissariat, envisaged a large autonomous area uniting the Tatar and Bashkir peoples, comprising the Ufa and Kazan *gubernii* and portions of the Orenburg, Perm, Vyatsk, Simbirsk and Samara *gubernii*.[8] This proposal went some way to satisfying the aspirations of the Pan-Turkists who dominated in the Muslim Commissariat, rather than being based on the principles defining a national group as outlined by Stalin in 1913, or the various proclamations on national autonomy which emerged in the course of 1917 and 1918. Nevertheless the project was welcomed by Stalin, who promised in a *Pravda* article of 23rd March 1918 that the plan would meet no resistance from the Russian Central Executive Committee and Council of People's Commissars.[9] But the spread of the Civil War and the occupation of the region by White forces put paid to any immediate possibility of the realisation of the project.

But by early in 1920 the project had been dropped altogether. It is this which has led many commentators to conclude that the Bolsheviks were pursuing a tactic of divide-and-rule in the Muslim areas in particular. By splitting up the Tatar and Bashkir peoples into separate republics, the possibility of unity between the Muslims of Russia was being deliberately undermined, according to this interpretation. But no evidence has been produced to support this contention, and none is apparent in the secret archives of the Soviet government and the Russian Communist Party. In fact such an interpretation rests on the false assumption that there was a widespread movement for pan-Muslim unity in the first place. While this was certainly an objective of the mainly Tatar intelligentsia, from

---

8   *Zhizn' natsional'nostei* no.62, 8th February 1920, p.2.
9   Stalin, vol.IV, pp.49–50.

whose number many of the leading officials of the Muslim Commissariat were drawn, it was certainly not a desire shared by the majority of Bashkir people, who felt the Tatars to be their oppressors as much as, if not more than, the Russians. In fact it was the Bashkirs who were the first of the Volga peoples to receive autonomy, and in quite different circumstances from those envisaged in 1918. For most of that year, an effective Bashkir army seven regiments strong under the leadership of the nationalist Zeki Validov had been fighting on the side of Kolchak's Whites. Early in 1919 however, the Bashkirs, disillusioned by Kolchak's avowed aim of reconstituting the Russian Empire in its old form and lured by the promise of extensive autonomy from the soviets, switched sides and formed a Bashkir Revolutionary Committee (Bashrevkom) which became the government of the newly formed Bashkir Autonomous Republic with Validov at its head.[10]

The experiment in allowing Bashkir nationalists to run the Bashkir territory ended in disarray in May 1920, thanks to a series of conflicts between the Bashrevkom, the local Russian and Tatar dominated soviets, and the Red Army, which made effective government by the Bashrevkom impossible and led its disillusioned leaders to join the Basmachi revolt in Central Asia.[11] But by then the proposed Tatar-Bashkir Republic was already dead and buried. In December 1919, Bashkir delegates to the second all-Russian Congress of Peoples of the East voiced their objections to the Tatar-Bashkir proposal, arguing that it would lead to the continuing impoverishment and subordination of the Bashkir population to the 'more advanced' Tatars. This was enough to convince the Politburo of the Russian Communist Party (bolsheviks) to drop the idea and instruct Stalin to set about forming a separate Tatar republic.[12] This was not the end of the matter, however. In the pages of the journal of the People's Commissariat of Nationality Affairs, *Zhizn' Natsional'nostei*, on 1st February 1920, the Tatar communist S. Said-Galiev argued that the new republic should be named the 'Tatar-Bashkir Republic' in spite of the existence already of a separate Bashkir Republic.[13] The argument ran that the

---

10   Jonathan D. Smele, *Civil War in Siberia – the Anti-Bolshevik Government of Admiral Kolchak, 1918–1920* (Cambridge, 1997), pp.289–301.
11   Richard Pipes, 'The First Experiment in Soviet National Policy: the Bashkir Republic, 1917–1920' *Russian Review*, October 1950, vol.9, no.4, pp.311–319.
12   Rossiiskii Tsentr dlia Khraneniia i Izucheniia Dokumentov Noveishei Istorii (Hereafter RTsKhIDNI), f.17, op.3, d.58, l.5.
13   *Zhizn' natsional'nostei* no. 4 (61), 1st February 1920, p.2.

Bashkir minority in the new republic would protest against the omission of the name of their nationality from the title of the territory. A week later, however, Said-Galiev reversed his position, arguing that now the territory should be named the Tatar Soviet Socialist Republic. The pretext for this U-turn was a statement by the Bashrevkom (which was still the official representative organ of the Bashkirs at that time) which stated that, to the contrary, the Bashkir people were against the use of the term Tatar-Bashkir as it would encourage the suppression of a separate Bashkir identity and raised the suspicion that the Bashkir Republic would eventually be incorporated into a larger, Tatar-dominated republic. Another Narkomnats official, Karl Grasis, attempted to smooth over this reversal by claiming that the Tatar-Bashkir Republic had been appropriate to the international situation in 1918, but that now the priority was 'the formation of a number of republics on the territory of the former Russian Empire'.[14]

On the surface, then, it was a change in circumstances and the objections of the Bashkirs themselves which led to the abandonment of the Tatar-Bashkir project. More likely, however, is that Stalin himself ordered Said-Galiev to recant his position of 1st February and instructed Grasis to ensure that the new position prevailed. The reason for supposing this is that the separation of the Tatar and Bashkir republics was entirely consistent with what had now become the main plank of Stalin's and the Politburo's nationality policy – the creation of separate territories enjoying considerable autonomy or independence in certain areas, and under the leadership of members of the 'local' nationality, as the basis of the administrative system of the non-Russian borderlands. While the national territories were to be accorded differing statuses according to the size and 'cultural level' of the various national groups – Union Republic, Autonomous Republic, Autonomous Region, Labourers' Commune – the basis for this administrative division of a major part of the Soviet space was to be the same: as far as possible, borders were to be drawn according to the 'ethnographic principle', so that most members of each major nationality would be included in its own republic or region. The year 1920 did, indeed, witness the start of the process of 'the formation of a number of republics on the territory of the former Russian Empire'.

In practise, this was an immensely complicated process. Not only had Russian settlers been spread all over the empire, but in many areas

---

14   *Zhizn' natsional'nostei* no. 5 (62), 8th February 1920, p.2.

members of different nationalities lived side by side or in ethnically homogenous and separate villages dotted about the map in such a way as to make it impossible to draw a line separating the different nationalities. Nomads travelled from one area to the other according to the seasons in parts of Central Asia and Transcaucasia, raising the question of whether it was the summer or the winter habitats which constituted 'their' territory. The continuing predominance of tribal, as opposed to national, divisions in other areas, and the existence of several dialects, many of them without written forms, of a single base language made it a somewhat arbitrary decision as to who constituted a separate national group. The principle of the Right of Nations to Self-Determination, including a specific provision from the 7th Party Conference of April 1917 that 'the determination of boundaries of the self-governing and autonomous regions [was to be decided] by the local population itself'[15] did not provide specific guidance as to how the will of the local population was to be determined, and at how local a level the population should be divided. But this task was set about with great seriousness – commissions were formed, referenda were held, surveyors were dispatched to the field, scientific studies were made of linguistics and ethnography.[16] To illustrate the workings of this principle of the spatial division of Soviet territory, it is sufficient to look briefly at the cases of the formation of the Belorussian Soviet Republic, the Kirghiz Autonomous Republic (the first 'delimitation' of Central Asia), and a series of autonomous regions and republics in the North Caucasus.

Drawing up the borders of a Belorussian Soviet Republic based on the ethnographic principle ought to have been straightforward. Although Belorussia had never enjoyed independent statehood or a separate administrative status which might have established a historical basis for her borders, in the late nineteenth and early twentieth centuries a number of studies based mostly on linguistic criteria had established the regions of a predominantly Belorussian population: A. Rittikh in 1875, Karskii and Durnovo in 1903, and the Moscow Dialectological Committee in 1915, had each produced maps showing the spread of the Belorussian language which varied from each other only in small areas. And these studies were supported by the extensive data obtained in the all-Russian census of 1897. One of

---

15 Robert H. McNeal (ed.), *Resolutions and Decisions of the Communist Party of the Soviet Union* (Toronto, 1974), vol.I, p.226

the most active and able scholars in this field, E.F. Karskii, continued to serve the Soviet regime with distinction after 1917. But there were two major obstacles to the immediate realisation of an 'ethnographic Belorussia' based on these studies; firstly, in the course of the Revolution and Civil War, the soviets had lost territory to independent Poland in the west, and to independent Lithuania in the north, which would otherwise have been included in Belorussia. There was nothing the soviets could do about this until the occupation of these lands in the Second World War. Secondly, there turned out to be considerable resistance at a local level to the idea of inclusion in Belorussia. While the linguistic studies mentioned above were based on rural communities, the large towns of the region were dominated by Russians, Jews, and 'ethnic Belorussians' who had little or no separate identity and regarded themselves as Russians. Power in the region after the Revolution rested mainly with the urban soviets, dominated by Russians, who saw no reason to separate themselves from the stronger and richer Russian Soviet Federative Socialist Republic. It was therefore not until the authorities in Moscow had succeeded in establishing their dominance in the mid-1920s that the true ethnographic borders of Belorussia could be established to the east and to the south.

But it was clear from the beginning that the Bolshevik leadership preferred to establish the borders of Belorussia according to the ethnographic principle. The declaration of an 'Independent Socialist Republic of Belorussia' on 20th December 1918 left the question of the new republic's borders to be determined by the Belorussian Congress of Soviets which met in Minsk on 2nd February 1919.[17] In preparation for this congress, the Central Committee of the Russian Communist Party instructed its special envoy to the congress, Adolf Ioffe, to try and secure a decision including the Vitebsk, Smolensk, Minsk and Mogilev *gubernii* in the republic – that is to say, all the territory of ethnographic Belorussia which was under soviet control at that time, and as far as the old administrative division into *gubernii* allowed.[18] But Ioffe's mission was a failure. When the Belorussian Congress of Soviets convened, the delegates from Smolensk, Vitebsk and Mogilev declared their preference for remaining in the RSFSR and walked out

. . . . .

16 Shirin Akiner, 'Uzbekistan: Republic of many Tongues' in Michael Kirkwood (ed.), *Language Planning in the Soviet Union* (London, 1989), p.103.
17 *Zhizn' natsional'nostei* no. 10, 19th January 1919, p.1.
18 RTsKhIDNI, f.17, op.2, d.8, l.1.

of the congress.[19] In the end the first Belorussian Soviet Socialist Republic was restricted to a rump of a few districts of Minsk *guberniia*.

The leadership were not prepared to let the matter rest there, however. An article in *Zhizn' natsional'nostei* on 9th March 1919 complained vociferously that parts of 'ethnographic Belorussia' had not been included in the republic.[20] The advance of Polish armies into Belorussia in April 1919 rendered such debates superfluous for the time being, and the issue was not seriously addressed again until the situation had fully stabilised and Belorussia was entering into the newly formed Union of Soviet Socialist Republics in 1923. In March of that year, the 7th Congress of the Communist Party of Belorussia resolved to extend the republic's territory to include all the ethnographically Belorussian areas.[21] A series of commissions were established towards the end of the year, which resulted in a decision that included parts of Gomel, Vitebsk, Smolensk, Mogilev and Chernigov regions over the objections of local representatives.[22] The enlargement was carried out on 3rd March 1924, with further disputed territories in Gomel region being added in 1926, increasing the territory of the Belorussian Soviet Socialist Republic from 20,000 square miles to 48,500 square miles, and its population from 1.5 million to almost 5 million, over 80% of whom were Belorussian.[23] This left only those regions belonging to independent Poland and Lithuania out of the composition of ethnographic Belorussia as depicted by the linguists, ethnologists and cartographers of the late tsarist period, an omission which was unceremoniously corrected by Stalin following the annexation of those territories in the course and aftermath of World War II.

If it was a relatively straightforward task to decide on, if not to implement, the borders of ethnographic Belorussia, the same could not be said of the various nationalities and groups of Central Asia. On 6th October 1918 a Turkestan Autonomous Soviet Socialist Republic

. . . . .

19 Nicholas P. Vakar, *Bielorussia, the making of a nation* (Cambridge, Mass., 1956), p.109
20 *Zhizn' natsional'nostei* no. 8 (16), 9th March 1919, p.3.
21 *Kommunisticheskaia Partiia Belorussii v rezoliutsiiakh i resheniiakh s'ezdov i plenumov TsK, tom pervyi 1918–1927* (Minsk, 1973), p.95.
22 RTsKhIDNI f.17, op.3, d.397, l.10; f.17, op.3, d.406, l.2; *Izvestiia VTsIK* 12th January 1924, p.6. For details, see Jeremy Smith, *The Bolsheviks and the National Question, 1917–1923* (London, 1999), p.77.
23 Jan Zaprudnik, *Belarus – at a Crossroads in History* (Boulder, 1993), p.78.

had been formed as a part of the RSFSR and embracing most of the former Governor-Generalships of Turkestan and Steppe.[24] The first 'national delimitation' of the region officially occurred on the 26th August 1920 with the proclamation of a Kirghiz Autonomous Soviet Socialist Republic, popularly known as Kirghizia, and roughly corresponding to modern day Kazakhstan.[25] As well as the large-scale presence of Russian and Ukrainian settlers in the region, particularly to the north, the various Central Asian groups lived interspersed among each other, displaying tribal rather than ethnic or religious loyalties and being distinguished from each other by their methods of agriculture as much as by language or ethnic definitions. A clear Kirghiz identity did begin to crystallise, however, in the years preceding the Russian Revolution, and was consolidated on the collapse of the Russian Empire in 1917 by the formation of a national party, the Alash Orda.[26] In April 1918 the Alash Orda attempted to reach an agreement with the Bolsheviks over Kirghiz autonomy, only to be rebuffed. But it was not long before the Bolsheviks themselves took up the idea of separate Kirghiz autonomy. In May 1918 the Extraordinary Commissar for the Kirghiz Steppe, A. Dzhangil'din, proposed creating an autonomous republic from the Semipalatinsk, Turgai and Akmolinsk *oblasti* and the Bukeev *guberniia*. Preparations for the implementation of this proposal were interrupted by the Civil War, but the proposal was raised again following the expulsion of White forces in the summer of 1919.

The fact that it took over a year to implement Kirghiz autonomy indicates the complexity and ferocity of the arguments over the borders of the new republics. During the course of this year a series of commissions were formed and a number of high level meetings held, one of them chaired by Lenin himself, to sort out this question. At one

---

24 Sh. B. Batirov et al., *Pobeda sovetskoi vlasti v Srednei Azii i Kazakhstane* (Tashkent, 1967), pp.612–13.
25 Some confusion exists around the use of the terms 'Kazakh' and 'Kirghiz'. In pre-revolutionary days and for some time after both groups were known as 'Kirghiz', with the nomadic farmers of the northern steppes distinguished as 'Kazakh-Kirghiz' (sometimes Kirghiz-Kazakhs') and the more settled population to the south-east as 'Kara-Kirghiz' (or Kirghiz-Kaisak'). These groups later became commonly (and officially) known as Kazakhs and Kirghiz respectively. This distinction was formalised with the renaming of Kirghizia as Kazakhstan in the delimitation of 1925. The unclear distinction between the Kazakhs and Kirghiz explains some of the disputes over the borders of Kirghizia. For the purposes of this article 'Kirghiz' refers to the modern day Kazakhs.
26 Gleason, pp.52–3.

extreme was a proposal to create a Kirghiz republic by extending the existing Turkestan Republic into southern Siberia, thus uniting all the Turkic peoples of the region. But the most serious dispute was over the northern border, a region including several significant industrial centres and good quality agricultural land, and inhabited mostly by Russians. On the one hand, the representatives of the Kirghiz argued that it was essential to include these areas if the republic was to be economically viable, and backed up this argument with the historical claim that these lands had been taken off the Kirghiz and systematically colonised by Russians only relatively recently. On the other hand several Russian representatives, most notably the members of the Siberian Revolutionary Committee (*Sibrevkom*) pointed out that including these regions in Kirghizia would cut off a large Russian population from their brethren, and argued that in any case the Kirghiz and their leaders did not have the necessary experience and knowledge to administer the important economic installations. It is noteworthy that all that these debates were grounded mostly in economic terms, and obvious nationalist sentiments were absent – the Russian members of the Kirghiz Revolutionary Committee (*Kirrevkom*) were just as supportive of the claims and rights of the Kirghiz as were their ethnically Kirghiz colleagues. What becomes clear, then, is that regional communist officials were already in 1920 jealously defending the status of the regions over which they had responsibility, regardless of either national affiliation or Marxist internationalist doctrine.[27]

In the end, the ethnographic principle prevailed in favour of the Kirghiz, with the addition of an economic principle (specifically rejected in the case of Belorussia) in order to make the new republic viable. The principle was established that nomadic peoples had the right to include both their winter and summer habitats in their national republic[28] and sound arguments for economic efficiency were rejected in favour of providing the Kirghiz with a secure base for economic development. After all, according to Stalin, the point of national

27   GARF f.1318, op.1, d.4, ll.65–73.
28   The fact that this important principle regarding nomadic peoples was already established in 1920 is frequently overlooked when it comes to the stormy and still violent disputes over the Nagornyi Karabakh region of Transcaucasia which erupted in 1922-23. One of the usually neglected arguments for preserving the territory within the borders of Azerbaijan was that Azeri nomads still used this hilly region for their herds in the summer months, a decision which was entirely consistent with that taken earlier over Kirghizia.

autonomy was to allow the non-Russians to catch up with the Russians in economic and cultural terms,[29] and this implied an element of positive discrimination in the use of land and industry. As a result, the borders of the Kirghiz ASSR were drawn in such a way as to separate the Kirghiz from the other peoples of Central Asia as far as was practicable, while granting them additional territory to the north on the basis of historical and economic claims.

The 19 nationalities who inhabited the mountainous terrain of the North Caucasus were clearly identifiable one from the other, unlike the Kirghiz, Tatars and Bashkirs, with, in most cases, a well developed sense of national identity. On the other hand, these were much smaller groups than in the other cases, their geographical interspersal with each other was equally problematic, they lacked established literary forms or even, in some cases, any script at all, and there was no industry at all to speak of. The relationship between the local nationalities and the Russian and Cossack settlers had been even more fractious than in Central Asia throughout the 19th century.

In the delimitation of national groups in this complex region, a number of new principles emerged: above a certain level, the absolute size of the national group (in either population or area) did not necessarily matter in establishing autonomous status (though it may have influenced whether a given territory was awarded 'republic' or 'region' status); whatever the size of a national group, it ought to constitute an overall majority in its autonomous territory, or, where this was not possible, two national groups could be combined to form an overall majority; as well as needing autonomy in order to catch up with Russia economically, the more advanced nationalities could see their development retarded by being included in the same territory as 'backward' nationalities; and finally, that in addition to its positive benefits, territorial autonomy would reduce the chances of inter-ethnic conflict.

Initially, a single Gori (mountain) Autonomous Republic was established in January 1921 to administer the more mountainous western part of the North Caucasus, at the same time as a Dagestan Autonomous Republic was created in the Eastern coastal region. In the Gori Republic, each nationality was represented by a National Soviet based in the capital Vladikavkaz. The first 'delimitation' of the Gori Republic occurred on 1st September of that year, with the creation of a Kabardino-Balkar Autonomous Region, followed by the

---

29 E.g. Stalin, Vol. IV, p.75.

Karachai-Cherkess Autonomous Region in January 1922, and the Chechen Autonomous Region in November 1922. The Gori Republic was finally abolished in 1924 with the establishment of separate autonomous regions for the Ossetian and Ingush peoples.

Although it seems to have been the Kabardin people who took the initiative in establishing the first of these national regions,[30] economic principles were used to justify its existence. A detailed and turgid report was prepared by the Caucasian Bureau of the Russian Communist Party (*Kavbiuro*), showing that soil conditions and agricultural techniques meant that the local economy of the Kabardi, while still peasant and backward compared to central Russia, was significantly advance when compared with the economy of their North Caucasian neighbours. For this reason, the Kavbiuro supported their claim to autonomy.[31] The Kabardi made up 65.11% of the population of the new territory, but the other significant non-Russian nationality of the region, the Balkari (who numbered only about 27,500 but made up 15% of the population) were included in the region's title. This seems to have been something of an afterthought, as the Balkars were barely mentioned in the discussions leading up to the formation of the region. But in the case of the other dual nationality region, the Karachai-Cherkess, the reasoning is much clearer and more explicit. The 67,500 Karachai constituted one of the major groups of the region, but it was impossible to delineate a territory in which they constituted a majority of the population. In the region as finally demarcated, they were 45% of the population, so by the addition of the 37,500 Cherkess, the combined population of the two groups formed a comfortable demographic majority.[32] The report in *Zhizn natsional'nostei* which announced the formation of the new autonomous region made it clear that the reason for the dual national character was precisely to ensure such a majority for the titular nationalities.[33] And the Cherkess retained this status in spite of being the major nationality in the Adigei region slightly to the North-West, where the 91,000 Cherkess made up 70% of the population of the autonomous region formed six months later in July 1922, which had the official title 'Adigei (Cherkess) Autonomous Region'.

. . . . .

30 RTsKhIDNI, f.64, op.1, d.72, 1.10.
31 RTsKhIDNI, f.64, op.1, d.72, ll.6–9.
32 Figures from a census of 1920, given in *Zhizn natsional'nostei* book 1, 1924, p.162. [a new format for *Zhizn natsional'nostei* in 1924 explains the discrepancy in numbering].
33 *Zhizn natsional'nostei* no.130, 10th January 1922, p.4.

These last two points disprove a frequently asserted fallacy: that it was the purpose of early Soviet national policy to provide a single ethnic territory for each of the major nationalities, regardless of either the proportion of the overall population which belonged to the titular group of the territory, or the proportion of the nationality which actually lived in the territory. Along with the Cherkess, the Buriats enjoyed more than one territory. And at this time, as the Karachai-Cherkess case illustrates, it was essential that the majority population of each territory should belong to the titular group(s). The exception that proves the rule is the one region where it was impossible to engineer a demographic majority even by combining the two largest national groups, namely, Dagestan. It was for precisely this reason that the republic was given a geographical title rather than being named after one or more national groups. The other republics which had non-national names at this time, Gori and Turkestan, were exactly those which underwent national delimitation and did not survive beyond 1925. True, the principle of majority was soon flouted with the expansion of the territory of Karelia and, most significantly, the northward expansion of the Bashkir ASSR in 1922 which gave the republic a more secure economic base, but at the same time thrust the Bashkirs into a numerical minority.[34] But the sensitivity of the regime on this point is illustrated by the publication of demographic figures in 1924, in which the Bashkir and Tatar population are combined in the figures for Bashkiriia, giving an overall majority of 51.75%. This 'cheat' shows how important ethnographic principles were in the creation of autonomous territories.

Once the task of providing separate territories for the national groups of the Gori Republic had been embarked on, the last two delimitations followed as a natural consequence: the Chechens were by some way the largest group of the region, and once they had been separated out, the two remaining significant groups, the Ingush and the Ossetians, were so clearly differentiated from each other in terms of religion as well as other national determinants that they could not be held together in a single republic if there was to be any consistency at all in applying the ethnographic principle.

While there was a specific reason for each of the delimitations of the North Caucasus, an overriding principle also emerged: as early as January 1922, Sh.N. Ibragimov argued in the pages of *Zhizn*

---

34 E.H. Carr, 'Some Notes on Soviet Bashkiria' in *Soviet Studies*, January 1957, vol.8, no.3, p.222.

natsional'nostei that each and every one of the North Caucasian peoples should get a separate territory in order to solve the age-old problem of inter-ethnic violence.[35] With regard to the formation of the Chechen Autonomous Region A.I. Mikoyan, then a member of the Caucasian Bureau of the Russian Communist Party, recalled in his memoirs the widely held supposition that autonomy would bring an end to the lawlessness and violence of the region.[36] In 1923, the Georgian Bolshevik Budu Mdivani used the example of the delimitation of the North Caucasus to justify Georgia's independence of the Transcaucasian Federation, arguing that it was the threat of ethnic violence which lay behind this policy.[37]

So economic and cultural development and the interests of ethnic harmony led the early soviet regime to apply, as widely as possible, the ethnographic principle – namely, that the borders of the union republics, autonomous republics and autonomous regions which were at the centre of the administrative structure of the RSFSR and USSR should be shaped according to the national composition of the region – with some modifications based on economic principles, to the western borderlands, the northern part of Central Asia, and the North Caucasus. It was entirely consistent with these principles to carry out a further national delimitation of Central Asia. Announcing this project to a plenary meeting of the Central Committee in October 1924, I.E. Rudzutak argued quite plausibly that clearly distinct groups held together in the same republic would inevitably compete over limited resources, leading to public violence as well as political intrigue. Economic arguments, as well as the will of the local populations, also figured highly in his report.[38] There is substantial evidence that clear identities were emerging at this time and that the delimitation was carried out with the support and co-operation of the local elites, particularly among the Turkmen.[39] The delimitation, perhaps inevitably, left large numbers of each nationality in the territory of

. . . . .
35 *Zhizn natsional'nostei* no.131, 17th January 1922, p.1.
36 A.I. Mikoyan, *V nachale dvadtsatykh...*(Moscow, 1975), p.221.
37 *Dvenadtsatyi s"ezd RKP(b) 17-25 aprelia 1923 goda – stenograficheskii otchet* (Moscow, 1968), p.500.
38 RTsKhIDNI, f.17, op.2, d.153, ll.123–130.
39 Adrienne Lynn Edgar, 'Nationality Policy and National Identity: The Turkmen Soviet Socialist Republic, 1924–1929' (unpublished conference paper, March 3, 1998, based on a talk given at the Second Annual Workshop on Central Asian Studies at the University of Wisconsin, Madison in October 1997).

others in spite of several reorganisations,[40] and there were crucial and sometimes arbitrary decisions to be made about which of many available dialects should form the basis of the new national languages,[41] in addition to the border problems. But it was clear that the ethnographic principles which lay at the heart of the administrative structure of the USSR applied equally to the case of Central Asia.

The decision to base the administrative division of much of the Soviet space on national principles was not an automatic one. Indeed, the principle developed in a piece-meal, almost arbitrary manner. At the time, it was seen by many (though not Lenin or Stalin) as a temporary measure. But there was a logic behind this structure in terms of regional and cultural development and as a solution to ethnic violence. Having been established, it would have been difficult (though perhaps not impossible) to abolish. The consequences of this decision are obvious: the national fault-lines which divided up the Soviet space were reinforced and given institutional form, making it easy for the tremors of 1991 to create fissures along exactly these lines. The union republics established in the post-revolutionary years and the 1920s went their separate ways, while a further diminution of the Russian space along national lines remains a possibility.

40 Valery Tishkov, *Ethnicity, Natinalism and Conflict in and after the Soviet Union: the Mind Aflame* (London, 1997), p.34.
41 Akiner, p.104–5.

ns: 62

Crowded on the Edge of Vastness: Observations on Russian Space and Place

Richard Stites

> Through the vastness of the land ran a chain of hills and beneath them lay a long valley and through the valley flowed a deep and wide river and on the banks of the river was a cabin and in the window of the cabin sat a maiden weaving.

This is a paraphrase of the conventional opening of many Russian fairy tales. At the core of my inquiry lies the duality in Russian feelings – almost never articulated – about space, a seamless conjunction of acrophilia and claustrophilia. I employ these terms by reversing those used in Elena Hellberg's reference to Peter the Great's agoraphobia and claustrophobia – but the duality is the same.[1] Put briefly, the focus is on one of the many complexities of Russian space – in metaphor and in life – the juxtaposition in everyday life of an empty expanse with a cramped and crowded work space – shops, libraries, archives, ticket offices, hotels, and other public institutions. My essay is a strictly subjective work based on personal observations over the past thirty years rather than a rigorous scholarly treatise based on a large data-base.

Let me offer a few concrete examples before attempting to explore deeper meanings. At the St. Petersburg Railway Station in Moscow, an enormous building two blocks long, the front doors facing the square are locked. One must walk around the station along the sides

---

[1] My references to Elena Hellberg-Hirn, Timo Pirainen, and Timo Vihavainen are to their remarks at the Winter Seminars in Advanced Russian History at the Renvall Institute, 1998.

up to the train tracks and then back the entire length of the station hall to a ticket office, wait in line, and then go back to the train – six blocks instead of two blocks. The St. Petersburg Moscow Railway Station has an enormous empty hall with no benches, surrounded by tiny booths enclosed in glass with a little closed window to speak through as you bend over. The waiting room is up two floors and four staircases. If you wish to sit while waiting for your train, you must take your luggage up there to the benches. Then of course there is the railway carriage in which you must walk to the far end to get on and then walk back to your seat. The St. Petersburg Central Ticket Office on Griboedov Canal has the familiar layout: a cavernous hall ringed by tiny booths and offices fronted by glass from which are cut minuscule windowettes through which you can talk to the clerk – if you bend – who sits in her cramped space. Not a single place to sit. From the minuscule service openings stretch queues that are amoeba-shaped, never straight, showing an aversion to geometric order.

Take another kind of site: the famous research center, Pushkin House in St. Petersburg. It has big, randomly used, offices and a lot of lobby; both the Manuscript Reading Room and Library are small, the former with eleven reading tables tightly squeezed together. In Moscow, the Glinka Museum and Library has three floors with huge empty spaces in the middle, surrounded by small offices. In its library, the area is so cramped that one cannot use the card catalogue without carrying the trays to the table – of which there are a few, with chairs crammed together. Most other libraries possess enormous proportions but have tiny reading rooms with chairs jammed together and card catalogues closely aligned. Everywhere the story is the same: empty unused expanses and tiny cramped places for the workers as well as the customers, readers, clients. Why this astonishingly unbalanced use of space?

INNER SPACES

Within these tiny work-sites, three principles seem to dominate: **impregnability**, **irregularity**, and **domesticity**. The first – the bastion mentality – begins at the door, narrow single entrances usually at the wrong end of a building – that is, away from the normal route of approach. These doors seem to say 'Do not come in. Why are you here? Do not disturb. Come back tomorrow.' Very often they do speak with signs: Out to Lunch, Cleaning Day, Inventory Day, or simply

Closed – with no explanation. The doormen at empty cavernous restaurants in Soviet times turned away hopeful diners with the words 'no room.' It still happens. All these signs and habits of the workplace reflect the peculiar and specific indifference to, sometimes even an aversion to providing comfort or convenience to the public. Handiness for the multitudes is an unspoken taboo of urban Russian life.

But the very space that is fortress-like to the everyday visitor can become porous when even the flimsiest of personal relations are established. A guest can be taken into places where other employees are never permitted, can be seated in the middle of an office at someone's desk in order to work. A tiny place is cleared amid papers and books. This small intimate inner work space is collective, everybody's, nobody's. The accompaniment to this is the lack of dedication, commitment, responsibility to a task that requires long-term attention and concentration – things that are associated in Western societies with one's own desk, computer, telephone, workbooks, records and all the rest. The very social topography of an office is created by the casual – or better to say 'distanced' or 'estranged' attitude to work itself. And yet the interchangeability of stations is often accompanied by a ferocious sense of narrow specialization and absence of lateral communication. No one knows and no one wants to know anything outside the immediate range of duties. No one has the right to perform another's task: 'she's not here today; I can't help; not my job; she took the keys with her on vacation; come back in a week.'

Irregularity is a relative concept and perhaps involves a culturally biased aesthetic judgment. But here I am concerned with function: desks jammed together can impede pedestrian motion, chairs unmatched to desk size cause discomfort and fatigue, long distances between stations that require regular mutual traffic might (and do) require workers to walk through several rooms a hundred times a day to take or deliver material to another party – even though there is no particular reason for this distance. Sections, departments, work stations, and desks grow up accidentally, spontaneously, ad hoc, and at random – pretty much in the way that the ancient *prikazy* of Muscovy did – without prior planning. In a society famously based on central economic planning, one will find the most unplanned work space. Once it is there, it is there. Any suggestion to rearrange furniture or personal space in a more rational way is viewed with utmost suspicion. 'This is how we do it,' 'I don't know why,' or 'it is not important' are the usual replies to questions or suggestions. Tradition can thus be instantaneous.

By **domesticity**, I mean the workplace as home, club, and surrogate family. There is a gender element here. Most offices are staffed by women. They bring domestic and neighborhood values into the workplace, making it a home away from home. In between service to the firm or its customers (readers, clients, guests, citizens making inquiries), the day is filled with talk – to each other or on the telephone. The talk is personal, family-oriented, quotidian matters that take priority over all other matters, including and especially the business in which they are employed. Lunch is a sacred time when – besides ingesting some food – the business of life can be continued. The emotional sustenance that women and some men obtain from their Home-at-Work and their fellow employees cannot be underestimated. And the notion of transforming the workplace into a relatively cold, impersonal, site of efficient labor would require an entire cultural and psychic restructuring – a wrenching process.

As at home, audible conversations and telephone talk take place in spaces that are normally held quiet in other societies (reading rooms, for example). The boundaries within the work space are fluid. Ancient routines and procedures consume needless hours of useless work and tons of paper. Restaurants, libraries, museums, academies function as independent republics in their daily procedures. Customers are unwelcome interlopers. A common though unspoken attitude: this is our collective, this is how we do it, we are not interested in efficient service to clients or to saving them or us time. The sense of time and space is of course inseparably linked to efficiency and productivity.

OUTER SPACES

My discussion of the inner spaces of Russian urban work culture in some ways explains the non-use of available empty rooms. It seems clear that employees, if offered the option of spreading out and moving into the large halls available, would decline, preferring to remain in the intimacy of their 'family offices' or workplace clubs. Spreading out would mean individuation of work stations and distance from their colleagues. Part of the reason for such abundant empty space in Russian edifices is of course the Russian and Soviet architectural traditions of grandiosity and monumentality. Big is good, big is strong.[2] To those workers who inhabit booths and counters, the surrounding cavernous lobbies, halls, reception rooms, gallerias and the like are alien spaces, full of strangers who are there to disrupt their own private time by asking questions, ordering tickets or books or buying things.

What about front doors, grand entrances, and frontal outdoor space – so often encountered in, for example, museums and other public places. Elena Hellberg-Hirn has again highlighted a key feature of Russian spatial culture in her observations about narrow back door and side door entrances though which thousands of people are ushered.[3] Why not pass them through the front? The facades of Imperial Russian buildings contained the ceremonial or parade entrance reserved strictly for the owner's family and guests or for high officials in a government house. All others had to come through different apertures – usually at the rear. (Cf. the tradesmen's and servant's entrances in the West.) But after the Russian Revolution, the masses, especially the honored proletariat, were not tradesmen or servants but the alleged rulers of the state. And yet, the parade entrance mentality was retained; you just could not allow ordinary people in through those grand entrances. Then who would be allowed? No one, because to invite the rulers and other privileged Soviet elements would be to admit the real but inadmissible fact of privilege and inequality on a visible public scale. The same explanation probably applies to the open areas in front of some public buildings. These were organic parts of the ceremonial entry way, not to be violated by crowds. Only in the theaters, for practical reasons of ticket collecting and directing people to their seats, did the grand entrances remain open.

One of the interesting features of Russian spatial culture is the way it contradicts a fundamental self-image of the national character: *gostepriimstvo* – hospitality and welcoming generosity. But this trait – certainly rooted in social reality – had its obverse side in russian traditional practices. Stranded travelers, Holy People, friends and relatives, and the nearby *barin* were indeed given lavish welcome. But the bread and salt were not extended to any passerby; old Russian villages were plagued by bandits, horse thieves, escaped convicts (in

. . . . .
2   See Vladimir Papernyi *Kultura dva* (Chicago, 1985) and other historians of Soviet architectural style.
3   See her contribution to this volume, pp. 49–71.

the nineteenth century when it was still fairly easy to escape), unwanted beggars, or even foreign troops. The personnel in government chanceries and waiting rooms were notorious for their hostility and contempt toward petitioners. Soviet xenophobia and paranoia amplified this trait. The present-day Russian edifice continues to exude hostility and wariness to visitors. If you wander into space where you have no business, may God protect you from the verbal abuse of a *vakhtër* or *babushka* at the checkpoint. One of the greatest failures of the Soviet regime was its unwillingness or inability to induce mutual respect and *dobrota* among its people. A side result of this is the near absence of politeness and good manners among strangers in public places.

But there are still other dimensions to the spatial world. If the home is private and the workplace semiprivate, how can we characterize the surrounding urban space? In Soviet times and partly still today, this area fell into two categories which I shall call public and common – both in a sense belonging to nobody or to everybody. Public space is sacral, municipal, honorific, civic. Its squares and parks, lobbies and reception areas are maintained by the state and selectively open to the citizens. Common space is no-man's land: staircases and landings, courtyards, back-alleys, station halls, most rest rooms. Timo Pirainen has noted the visible difference between the use of this space in Western Europe and in Russia. In the latter one is struck by the stark contrast between the relative neatness and order and even comfort inside the private apartment and the utter neglect – dirt, decay – of the common areas adjacent to it.[4]

In Western European cities, this contrast is much smaller and in some places non-existent. Orderly residences are often surrounded by neat and well-kept environs; public and private space seem to flow into each other. To some observers, this is a mark of civic consciousness and even civil society. The neatness of European streets and homes has always been one of the first things Russian travelers westward have noted – from border crossings into eastern Prussia in the eighteenth century to shopping trips in Helsinki in our time. The irony of these cultural crossings resides in the fact that so many intellectuals among those Russian visitors, from the playwright Denis

---

4   Ekaterina Gerasimova "Sovetskaya kommunalnaya kvartira: istoriko-sotsiologicheskii ocherk." Paper, Renvall Institute, Helsinki, 1998. Here she describes the eternally unsuccessful efforts of laws and committees to have the inhabitants care for common space; Pirainen's remarks at the Winter Seminars – see note 1.

Von Vizen onward, have found in European spatial culture a clear sign of crabbed natures, cramped souls, and petty bourgeois sensibilities – all in contrast to the vaunted Russian need for grand spaces, the open road, and a sense of freedom.[5]

MEANING

Western office workplaces tend to be spread out, with easy lateral communication. Service areas are usually bright, welcoming, and open. Think of the physical properties of customer-clerk encounters in travel agencies, banks, libraries, and post offices: an open counter, sometimes a seat for the client, and rarely a window. The human topography is different as well. Professionalism means leaving intimacy, family, personal concerns at the door (in theory, and mostly in practice as well). One has one's own desk, personal space, responsibility, and some work privacy – allowing one to measure one's own work and achievement – and allow others to measure it as well. Interchangeable desks are uncommon as is the practice of handing over an employer's desk to a visitor or outsider. This capitalist rational environment has been the target of cultural attack and satire almost from the very beginning, its most resonant artifact being the cinema – *Modern Times* in the 1930s, *The Apartment* in the 1960s, *Brazil* in the 1980s – each probably more influential than the various anti-capitalist science fiction dystopias of our century. But one thing is clear, the capitalist workplace has separated to a significant degree the job from the home and family. How to construct the moral balance-sheet between depersonalization and productivity is a matter for some serious consideration by social scientists.

The Russian work culture that I have impressionistically – but I believe accurately – described throws some light on the fate of the petty-bourgeoisie, a topic now being explored in a very learned treatment by Timo Vihavainen. He demonstrates again and again that the concept itself was so fluid as to serve any kind of ideological

265

. . . . .
5   An Englishman in the 1830s observed that Russian towns were, per capita, three times the size of English ones: Robert Bremner, *Excursions in the Interior of Russia*, 2v. (London, 1840), Vol.II, p.164. Vast unused space for town planning seems natural in such an immense country as Russia; but that use of space did not transfer to intimate settings.

justification for social policy. Only one constant remained: an eternal aversion to petty bourgeois values, however defined at the moment. In this respect Soviet ideologists differed from the old Russian intelligentsia who zeroed in on petty bourgeois mind (*meshchanstvo*) as philistine and vulgar.[6] If the family-as-community-and-work-unit, as formulated by Proudhon, is a fairly accurate summary of the petty bourgeois outlook, then the Soviets, willy-nilly, helped or allowed it to lodge itself at the very base of its system. Not only did the Soviet family retain its own world at home as the unit of primary loyalty (even when surrounded by neighbors in a communal apartment), but it brought its ethos into the workplace as well. And in this sense, the millions of offices and stalls and counters across the land constituted a Proudhonian substructure upon which reposed a Marxist centralized planned society. This is one of the greatest ironies in the richly ironic tapestry of Russian history.

But in Russia's case, the roots of the alleged petty-bourgeois family and its work habits is the peasant village with its own notions of space, time, motion, and order. I have dealt with these in a chapter called 'Man the Machine' of a previous book.[7] There I try to describe those mentalities and practices as they contrast to the work-pace of modern industrial societies. The resulting gulf between these habits and the needs of an aspiring Soviet industrial culture of efficiency and productivity produced two startling phenomena. In the 1920s, desperate Soviet enthusiasts of time and motion – the disciples of Henry Ford and Frederick Taylor – conceived sweeping utopian devices designed to end the space-time culture of peasants and turn them into mechanized, clock-driven workers: the Scientific Organization of Labor and the League of Time. In the 1930s, under Stalin, a more manipulative and selective apparatus was put in place: shock work and the Stakhanovite movement.[8] None of these practices went deep into Soviet work styles and ethos. The regime in fact shielded the entire economy from structures of incentives and penalties that would gradually have created a modern work culture – including punctuality, alertness, lateral communication, and the rational organization of space.

. . . . .

6   Svetlana Boym, *Commonplaces: Mythologies of Everyday Life in Russia* (Cambridge, Mass., 1994).
7   Richard Stites, *Revolutionary Dreams* (New York, 1989); see also Nicholas Vakar, *The Taproot of Soviet Society* (New York, 1962).
8   Lewis Siegelbaum, *Stakhanovism and the Politics of Productivity in the USSR, 1935–1941* (New York, 1988).

And at what price? Spatial irrationality is closely linked to other aspects of the culture of work and service. All of the Russian practices mentioned above sharply diminish the level of efficiency at work. The total effect is multiplied by the impact that each act or practice has upon everyone else. In the course of a day, one potentially productive worker at any task will lose about a third or even half a day's work due to the cumulative power of other citizens' work habits. Here I offer a fictional but plausible scenario. 10:00-5:00, a good enough workday in winter time. Citizen X plans to spend two hours in the library, have a business lunch with Y at 12:00, go for rail tickets at 1:00, meet another colleague, Z, at 2:00 for a half hour, and then ride for half an hour to the university for teaching and consulting from 3:00 to 5:00. Call it a day and go home at five.

The reality we all know. The reading room, without prior announcement (nobody's business but theirs), has been taken over for a special staff meeting – even though there are seven other equally large rooms available for it. So X crosses town to another library and thus has only about 45 minutes of actual work that morning. Back to the meeting point for lunch. Y arrives forty minutes late because his plumber did not show up on time to do essential repairs. All nearby eating places are either 'full' (though nearly empty) or have long lines, so they go to a fast-food place and make it a short and not very productive stand-up business lunch. Then X gets to the railway ticket office at 2:00 instead of 1:00 and finds it closed for lunch until 3:00. Since the ticket is essential, he waits. The ticket seller returns from lunch at 3:15, but her computer is down and the repairman has not yet come to fix it. After waiting in line at another window, X has his ticket by 4:00. He has of course missed his 2:00 o'clock appointment with Z thus throwing off Z's schedule as well. He calls the university, but no one answers the phone because the receptionist has left early for the day to do the shopping and no one else in the office cares to answer it (not their job). X rushes to his class and finds that all the students have left because he is more than one hour late.

The total professional productive work time for X on that day: 45 minutes and about 15 minutes of business talk with Y. But note that Y and Z will face similar if not worse inefficiencies during the day as will practically every resident of a major Russian city. And if X, Y, and Z are relatively efficient people who want to do productive work, think of all those who are indifferent or even hostile to their jobs.

This is all too obvious and familiar to those who have lived in Russia, even for a short time. What is striking and revealing is that no Russian I have even met (inside the country) would venture to make an analysis of the real causes of an unproductive day, or week, or year. In the old Soviet days, the typical reaction of a critic – a dissident or someone indifferent to the Soviet system – would be: 'it's the fault of our system,' meaning socialism. In recent times, the comment is: 'we are in a difficult time of transition.' A more honest and cogent reply that I have often heard – though no more trenchant analytically – is: 'it's Russia.'

Though I have broadened the focus from spatial matters to the more general features of the Russian work style, space remains a key ingredient. After all, unless one has an aesthetic agenda, space – empty or full – is interesting only as it relates to the people in it or kept out of it. It seems to me that the working place defines the workers and vise-versa. In gender terms, as long as offices remain a *posidelka* for women and a village *mir* for men, productivity is not likely to increase or the work culture change. Men are more mobile through the day and certainly possess more power and get bigger wages; but it is doubtful if their collective efforts are more productive than those of women. They simply do different things in their non-work-related segments of the working day. When and if the work environment changes in a drastic way, it will bring forth a serious mental trauma and a chorus of lamentation which will, I believe, make the better-known pain of economic destitution seem mild by comparison.

To those who may have *Schadenfreude* at the prospect of such irrational people suffering for their sins, I address a few words. I cannot really apologize for the rather harsh assessment I have made of work styles and use of space in the service sector. I do not believe that hiding unpleasant truths is doing anyone a favor. On the other hand I write out of affection for those who staff those, to us, outrageously inefficient workplaces. Although still plagued by a passive attitude to the job, Russians are not by nature lazy or inefficient people. Given sufficient incentive and a supportive environment, they can perform miracles of productivity. And those grim faces that we so often encounter at service points belong to the same people who – on acquaintance – can prove to be marvelous hosts and true friends. I believe that Russians will be a lot more content in the long run in terms of comfort, convenience, and rewarding work when the old ways are abandoned and new ones adopted.

But as a historian, I am more interested in the roots of the Russian-Soviet use of working space than in speculation about the future (which interests me as a citizen). This volume addresses questions about Siberia, the broad Russian land, the symbol of boundless freedom, *volya*; and Siberia as the historic land of prisoners, of unfreedom; the broad Slavic soul and the narrow confines of daily existence; the crowded peasant *izba* and the spacious Russian steppe. After a half-dozen years of perestroika and almost a decade of political freedom and the market, I for one am persuaded that not all of the peculiarities of Russian spatial and work culture are attributable solely to Soviet socialism. Perhaps historians and literary scholars will someday uncover the deeper layers.

Robert Argenbright is Assistant Professor in the Earth Sciences Department, University of North Carolina at Wilmington. He has published articles on the historical geography of the USSR during the civil war and transition to NEP. His current projects include studies of public space in Moscow today, a NEP era show trial, civil war era agitational vehicles, and the wartime evacuations of industrial resources and population.

Chris J. Chulos is a research fellow and lectures in Russian studies at the Renvall Institute for Area and Cultural Studies at the University of Helsinki. He is the author of numerous articles about peasant religion and identity and has just completed a book entitled, *Converging Worlds: Religion, Community, and History in Modern Peasant Russia, Voronezh Province 1861-1917*. His current research concentrates on history and memory in late imperial Russia.

Jarmo Eronen is Professor of Economic Geography in the Helsinki School of Economics and Business Administration. He has published extensively on the Soviet and Russian regional economy, especially on the forestry industries, the economics of forestry, ornithology and linguistics. His current research interests include the economy of Central Asia and profitability of forest regeneration.

Paul Fryer is a Researcher at the Finnish Institute for Russian and East European Studies, Helsinki. He has published articles on ethnic revival and identities among the Finno-Ugrian peoples of Russia. After finishing his PhD in Cambridge on the Komi ethnic revival, he is currently involved in the research project "Diaspora mobilisation and identity trajectories in Russia: the case of the Eastern Mari" funded by the Academy of Finland.

Katerina Gerasimova is an Associate Researcher at the European University at St.Petersburg, and a Researcher at the Centre for Independent Sociological Research. She has published articles about Soviet housing as well as gender issues in modern Russia. She is currently working on a doctoral thesis comprising an analysis of the Soviet communal apartment from historical, anthropological and sociological perspectives.

Elena Hellberg-Hirn is a Professor and Senior Researcher of the Academy of Finland. She is author of *Soil and Soul. The Symbolic World of Russianness*, and has published extensively on Russian tradition, folklore and semiotics. Her current research projects include St Petersburg: Post-Soviet Identifications and Imperial Self and Other.

Arto Luukkanen is Docent of General Church History (University of Helsinki), and of Russian History (Univeristy of Tampere). He is presently a Senior Associate Member of St Anthony's College, Oxford. He has published two books on Soviet religious policy: *The Party of Unbelief – The Religious Policy of The Bolshevik Party, 1917–1929* and *The Religious Policy of The Stalinist State, 1929–1938*. He has recently published material on Ecumenical Relations between the Russian Orthodox Church and the Finnish Lutheran Church, and is now working on a monograph: *The Alternative Russia. The Dialogue between dissidents and Soviet power, 1953–1991*.

Sergei Medvedev is currently a professor at the George C. Marshall European Center for Security Studies in Garmisch-Partenkirchen, Germany. He publishes on issues of European security, Russian foreign policy, post-Soviet studies, political geography, social anthropology and semiotics. *Opinions expressed in this text do not reflect the views of the Marshall Center, the U.S. or the German governments.*

Christer Pursiainen is Senior Researcher at the Finnish Institute of International Affairs. He is a specialist in international relations theory, social theory, Russian political thought and politics, and Finnish foreign policy, and has published three monographs on these topics. His current research interests include civil society developments in Russia, Russia's security policy towards Northern Europe, and Finland's and the EU's policy towards Russia.

Anna Rotkirch is a Lecturer in the Department of Social Policy, University of Helsinki. She has published articles on gender issues, sexuality and activity theory. She has co-edited *Women's Voices in Russia Today* and is author of *Loves and Lives in Late 20th Century Russia*. Her current research interests include Russian women's autobiographical texts, and Russian social policy.

Jeremy Smith is Lecturer in Russian History at the Centre for Russian and East European Studies, University of Birmingham. He is author of *The Bolsheviks and the National Question, 1917–1923* and is now working on a history of nationalities in the USSR.

Richard Stites is Professor of History at Georgetown University, Washington D.C. He is the author of *The Women's Liberation Movement in Russia: Feminism, Nihilism, and Bolshevism, 1860–1930; Revolutionary Dreams: Utopian Vision and Social Experiment in the Russian Revolution* and *Russian Popular Culture: Entertainment and Society since 1900*. He is currently researching cultural history of Russia in the nineteenth century.

Pentti Stranius is a Researcher at the Karelian Institute, University of Joensuu. His research theme is the changing role and history of the Russian/Soviet Intelligentsia.

Timo Vihavainen is currently director of the Finnish Cultural Institute in St. Petersburg. His books include *Suomi neuvostolehdistössä* (Finns in the Soviet Press) and *Stalin ja suomalaiset* (Stalin and the Finns). He is currently leading a research project: "Norms, Values and Transition in Russian Society and Culture in the 1920s – 1950s".

Index

Adigei Autonomous Region 255
Aipin, Eremei 95, 106
Alexander I 57
Alexandrov, Professor I.A. 244
Alexei Mikhailovich 32
Ambartsunov, Evgeni 188
Astrakhan 51

Bakhtin, Mikhail 30
Barber, John 216
Bashkiriia 242, 247-8, 256
Baskakov, Vladimir 159-60
Basmachi 247
Belorussia/Belarus 242, 244, 249-51
Berdiaev, Nikolai 19, 72, 74-6, 90-1
Black Sea resorts 137, 140
Blok, Alexander 19
Borodin, Leonid 105, 106
Bourdieu, P. 108
Brezhnev, Leonid 155
Byzantium 15

Catherine the Great 8, 25, 57
Central Asia 203, 232, 241-2, 251-2, 257-8
Chaadaev, Pyotr 28-9, 73, 80
Chandler, Andrea 210
Checheniia 38, 256, 257
Chernobyl 34
Chernomyrdin, Viktor 37, 64
China 171-2
Clark, Katerina 167
Comintern 169
Corley, Felix 182
Cossacks 32, 54, 60, 67, 254
Council for Religious Affairs 181
Cox, Kevin 212

Dagestan 254, 256
Danilevskii, Nikolai 82,83
Derrida, Jacques 26, 43
Dostoevsky, Fedor 15, 90, 93, 99, 168, 172, 176
Duma, Russian 37
Dzhangil'din, A. 252

Edwards, Kristin 216, 236
Eisenstien, Sergei 152, 153, 156
Elias, N. 107
Engels, F. 110
Ermak, Timofeevich 8, 32
Eurasianism 83-9
Evacuation Council (*Sovet po evakuatsii*) 222, 224, 225, 228
Evangelical Lutheran Church of Finland 179, 182, 185-90
Evtushenko, Evgenii 98, 101

Feuerbach, Ludwig von 75
Fitzpatrick, Sheila 216
Fomin, Valeri 157
Foucault, Michel 71
Freudianism 28

Gagarin, Iurii 9
Galileo Galilei 71
Gal'perin, V.M. 115
Georgia 257
Gibson, James 100
Gillespie, David 105
Ginzburg, Evgenii 116
Gleason, Gregory 243
GOELRO (State Commission for Electrifying Russia) 244
Gogol, Nikolai 56-7, 92-3
Gomel' 224
Goncharov, Ivan 16
Gorbachev, Mikhail 27, 78, 79
Gordyenko, N.S. 182
Gori Autonomous Republic 254, 256
Gor'kii (city) 224
Gorky, Maxim 153
Goscilo, H. 20
Gosfilmofond (Central Film Archive) 159, 161
Goskino (State Film Committee) 154, 157, 160, 162, 164
Gosplan 228
Grasis, Karl 248
Grois, Boris 29, 91
GULAG (Main Administration of

Corrective Labour Camps) 54-5, 99-100, 204
Gumilev, L.N. 84-88
Gypsies 56

Hanson, Stephen 218-9
Harrison, Mark 215, 218, 237
Harvey, David 71
Hegel, G.W. 75, 89
Heidegger, Martin 29
Heifiz, Joseph 155
Hellberg-Hirn, Elena 19, 134, 259, 263
Helsinki 264
Hosking, Geoffrey 8,52
Huntington, Samuel 85
Husserl 43

Iadrintsev, Nikolai 104
Ibragimov, Sh. N. 256-7
Ingush 256
Ioffe, Adolf 250
Ivan III 72
Ivan IV (the Terrible) 8, 20, 51

Jadidism 246
Jowitt, Ken 218

Kabardino-Balkaria 254-5
Kaganovich, Lazar 222, 223, 226
Kagansky, Vladimir 16
Karachai-Cherkessiia 255-6
Karelia 224, 256
Karskii, E.F. 249-50
Kazakhstan 252
Kazan 51
Kekkonen, Urho 187
Khomikov, A.S. 74
Khrushchev, Nikita 78, 154, 180-1
Kiev 50-51
Kirghiziia 241, 242, 252-4
Kirrevkom (Kirghiz Revolutionary Committee) 253
Klyuchevsky, Vassily 31
Kolchak, Admiral Aleksandr 247
Komsomol'sk-na-Amure 101
Kordonsky, Simon 43
Kortunov, Sergei 91-2
Kosygin, Aleksei 222
Kotkin, Stephen 121
Krasnoiarsk *krai* 234

Kryanev, Y.V. 182
Kuibyshev (city) 225, 230, 232, 234, 235
Kumanev, G.A. 215
Kurile Islands 60
Kuznetsk Basin 101

Le Goff, Jacques 191
Lenin, V.I. 9, 30, 68, 76, 77, 91, 152, 179, 199, 202, 220, 252
Lewin, Moshe 125
Lieberman, Sanford R. 215
Lotman, Yuri 41, 169, 171
Luxemburg, Rosa 245

Magnitogorsk 121
Mann, Michael 212, 219
Marx, Karl; Marxism 29, 71, 75, 77, 78, 79, 219, 220, 245
Matrioshka 64-6
Mdivani, Budu 257
Mendeleev, D.I. 44
Mikhalkov, Nikita 163
Mikoian, A.I. 222, 228, 257
Mir space station 9, 52
Mongols 83-4, 86
Moscow 17, 34, 36, 40, 50-1, 52, 259
Moskoff, William 216, 235

Nabokov, Vladimir 25, 93
Napoleon 20
Narkomnats (People's Commissariat of Nationality Affairs) 244
Narkomzdrav (People's Commissariat for Health) 111
Narodniks 158
Nicholas I 57
Nietszsche, Friedrich 29, 43
Nihilism 75
Nikodim (Metropolitan) 185
Nikitin, Ivan 61
NKVD (People's Commissariat of Internal Affairs) 24
North Caucasus 242, 254-7

Orlov, Count A.F. 57
Orsk 235
Ossetians 256

Palace of the Soviets 40
Panarin, A.S. 88-9

275

Paperny, Vladimir 33
Pasternak, Boris 102
Peirce, C.S. 135
Peter I (the Great) 8, 32, 42, 62-3, 259
Peter III 57
Pirainen, Timo 264
Pirinen, professor 188
Plahov, Andrei 163
Platonov, Andrei 32
Plekhanov, G.V. 75
Pogodin, Mikhail P. 7
"Potemkin Villages" 25
Proudhon, P.J. 266
Pugachev Revolt 242
Pushkin, Alexander 56, 57, 99

Rasputin, Valentin 98, 102-3, 105, 106
Red Pens 157, 159, 161, 165
Refuseniks 173
Riasanovsky, Nicholas 7, 208
Rittikh, A. 249
Romanov, Alexei 159
Romanov, Panteleimon 125
Rousseau, Jean-Jacques 170
Rudzutak, I.E.
Russian Federation 7, 50, 241
Russian Orthodox Church 179, 180, 182, 185-90
Rybakov, Anatolii 99, 100
Rytkheu, Iurii 95

Sack, Robert David 207, 208-12, 217, 238-9
Said-Galiev, S. 247-8
Sakharov, Andrei 173
Salo, Simo, S. 185
Salomies (Archbishop) 185
Savitskii 83
Schopenhauer, A. 29
Shalamov, Varlam 100
Shalin, Dmitrii 178
Shvernik 222
Siberia 32, 50, 51, 53-5, 95-106, 201, 202, 203-4, 232-3
Sibrevkom (Siberian Revolutionary Committee) 253
Simmel, George 59
Simojoki, Martti 185, 188
Sinyavsky, Andrei 170

Slavophiles and Panslavists 73-4, 82-3, 168, 172
Smirnyagin, Leonid 16
Soloviev, Vladimir 30, 89-91
Solzhenitsyn, Aleksandr 99, 100, 103, 155, 162, 173, 177
St. Petersburg/Leningrad 32, 39, 50-1, 58, 62-3, 68, 109, 117, 120, 122, 123-9, 260
Stakhanovites 115, 266
Stalin, Iosif 25, 30, 40, 42, 77, 91, 153-4, 217, 218, 222-3, 227, 238, 244, 245, 246, 247, 248, 253-4
Stalingrad 238
Steinberg, Mark 199
Stites, Richard 199
Stolypin, Peter 32
Suslov, Mikhail 159

Tatar-Bashkir Republic 246-8
Tatariia/Tatarstan 232, 242
Thompson, John M. 208
Transcaucasia 244
Turkestan 241, 242, 251-2, 256
Turkmen 257
Turksib railroad 211

Ukraine 56, 244
Uvarov, Count 30

Vakhitov, Mulla Nur 246
Validov, Zeki 247
Vernadsky, George 208
Vihavainen, Timo 265
Vikström (Archbishop) 186, 189
Von Vizen, Denis 264-5
Voznesenskii, N.A. 212-3, 238

Weber, Max 107, 204-5, 218, 219
Writers' Union 153, 156

Yakutia/Sakha 38
Yeltsin, Boris 34-6, 38
Yurenev, Rostislav 159-60
Yutkevich, 159-60

Zapadnichestvo 73, 74-6, 77, 79-82, 89-93